Chinese Bondage
in
PERU

A History of the Chinese Coolie in Peru,
1849-1874

BY

WATT STEWART

GREENWOOD PRESS, PUBLISHERS
WESTPORT, CONNECTICUT

CHINESE BONDAGE
IN PERU

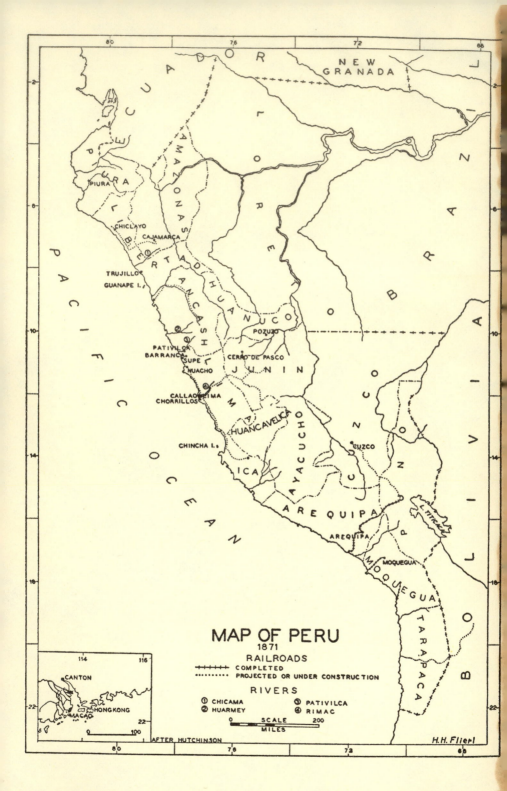

MAP OF PERU
1871

RAILROADS
┼┼┼┼┼ COMPLETED
∙∙∙∙∙∙ PROJECTED OR UNDER CONSTRUCTION

RIVERS
① CHICAMA   ③ PATIVILCA
② HUARMEY   ④ RIMAC

SCALE
0 — 200
MILES

AFTER HUTCHINSON

H. H. Flierl

To

JORGE BASADRE
Historian
Scholar
Friend

FOREWORD

THE CENTURY just passed has witnessed a great movement of the sons of China from their huge country to other portions of the globe. Hundreds of thousands have fanned out southwestward, southward, and southeastward into various parts of the Pacific world. Many thousands have moved eastward to Hawaii and beyond to the mainland of North and South America. Other thousands have been borne to Panama and to Cuba. The movement was in part forced, or at least semi-forced.

This movement was the consequence of, and it likewise entailed, many problems of a social and economic nature, with added political aspects and implications. It was a movement of human beings which, while it has had superficial notice in various works, has not yet been adequately investigated. It is important enough to merit a full historical record, particularly as we are now in an era when international understanding is of such extreme moment. The peoples of the world will better understand one another if the antecedents of present conditions are thoroughly and widely known.

The present study has particular reference to the transference of Chinese to Peru and to their experiences in that country. As such it can make no claim to being exhaustive of the general subject. However, the author hopes that this work may become a definitive chapter of the greater story. If others co-operate, eventually some scholar will be able to make a synthesis of the whole. It will be an absorbing story when finished, one with many overtones of personal tragedy and with its unadmirable elements of personal greed and inhumanity.

The research on which this study is based was done mainly in Peru, to which the author made three visits in the course of the thirteen years which the project has covered. The greater part of the work was done in 1936-1937 in the course of a sabbatical year most of which was spent in Lima. It was continued in the summer of 1941, thanks to a grant-in-aid provided by the Social Science Research Council, and was completed for that area in the spring of 1947, when another sabbatical provided opportunity for travel and study. Valuable materials for the study were also located in Washington, in the National Archives and in the Library of Congress.

My thanks for aid are due to a considerable number of persons and institutions. Foremost among the institutions is the National Social Science Research Council for the grant-in-aid mentioned above. I am deeply in debt to the National Library of Peru. I might use the term "libraries" since I was cordially welcomed in both the lamented library which was almost totally destroyed by fire in the spring of 1943 and also in the re-created library which is now operating in its splendid new locale thanks to the modern miracle of reconstruction which has been performed under the inspired leadership of its director, Dr. Jorge Basadre. The Archives of the Peruvian Ministry of Foreign Relations and the Peruvian Library of Congress were freely opened to me, as were the National Archives and the Library of Congress in Washington.

Numerous individuals have aided me with advice and criticism. The chief of these was Dr. Basadre. When I first met him thirteen years ago in the role of librarian and professor of the Greater University of San Marcos, he assisted me in making contacts and in organizing my work in Lima. In March and April of 1947, as director of the new National Library, he gave me further invaluable aid. Though the collections in his care were not at the time open to the general public since the new library edifice was not yet completed, he permitted me to make use of them and gave hours of his own time as well as of a number of his subordinates to assist me. Moreover, Dr. Basadre read the preliminary draft of my manuscript and made valuable criticisms. The Peruvian Minister of Foreign Relations, Dr. Enrique García Sayán, whose grandfather appears prominently in the following pages, and the director of the archives of the Ministry, Dr. Jorge Bailey Lembecke, were also most generous in lending aid.

The late Percy Alvin Martin, of Leland Stanford University, and Dr. James Ferguson King, former editor of the *Hispanic American Historical Review*, gave me friendly encouragement. Professor J. Fred Rippy, of the University of Chicago, specialist in the field of Latin American history and, in a sense, my intellectual godfather, not only encouraged me but also was so generous as to devote many hours to reading the manuscript in a late form and to criticizing it, thus greatly improving it. Professor Frank D. Reeve, of the University of New Mexico and editor of the *New Mexico Historical Review*— my genial host for six months in Albuquerque during which time the greater part of the initial work of composition was done—also read and criticized portions of the manuscript. Professor Theodore G. Standing, sociologist and colleague at the New York State College for Teachers, Albany, likewise read the manuscript and commented helpfully. Miss Helen Fraser, of Albany, loyal and sometimes patient friend, who declares she has been waiting for this book ever since her mother talked to her in her childhood of the Chinese whom she has seen working in Peru, gave me much helpful criticism, as did an old friend and former colleague, Dr. Edward F. Willis. For the map of Peru, I am indebted to my friend and colleague, Mr. H. H. Flierl, geographer.

To these generous institutions and helpful friends, I am indeed happy to extend my deepest appreciation of their aid. One of the greatest rewards which the scholar gains from such work as this study has entailed is derived from the contacts which he makes with such interested and generous individuals.

WATT STEWART.

Albany, New York,
December 1, 1950

CONTENTS

CHINESE BONDAGE
IN PERU

I

SETTING—EARLY PERIOD

ONE WHO has even the most casual interest in matters sociological, if he strolls along the two blocks
of Lima's Calle Capón, near the Central Market, will
observe many interesting human types. A large proportion of them, on close observation, will reveal traits of
both the Indian and the Chinese. These people are in
most cases of spare build and less than medium height
with high cheek bones, slant eyes, and a color that mingles
the bronze of the native Indian with the yellow of the
Oriental. They are a consequence of the entry into Peru
in the third quarter of the nineteenth century of some tens
of thousands of Chinese coolies.

Few of the social and economic problems that the
Peruvian Republic has faced during its century and a
quarter of existence have been more serious than that of
the Asiatic immigrant. Primarily because of a labor shortage, due in part to a labor system that did not enlist the
co-operation of the native laborer, these coolies were
brought to Peru. Their presence gave rise, in the course
of time, to domestic problems of extreme gravity and,
ultimately, was the cause of an international crisis. Their
history presents another case of the exploitation of one
group of human beings by another, while it is at the same
time a chapter of interest and importance in the history of
the relations of the Chinese with the Westerner.

Peru's need for labor arose from a complex of causes.

After the war for independence ended successfully in
1825, economic progress, while interrupted frequently by
internal and external wars until the mid-forties, was fairly
steady. The numerous fertile river valleys of the coastal
strip were occupied by cochineal, sugar, and cotton plantations, the demand for the products of which increased with
the passage of time. By 1840 the many guano (bird
manure) beds of the coastal headlands and offshore islands
were being worked profitably, the foreign market was
growing steadily, and the fertilizer's value to the nation
was increasingly evident. Throughout the three hundred
years of the colonial period, mining had been important,
and mining activity was continuing and growing. About
1850 Peruvian economists and capitalists began agitating
for internal improvements—canals for irrigation, tele-
graphs, harbors, and, especially, railroads.[1] All of these
activities demanded labor and more labor. Eventually it
became evident that the population of the country, under
existing conditions, could not in itself supply the need.[2]

The inhabitants of Peru by a count made in 1862
numbered only 2,487,916.[3] The census of 1876 disclosed
a population of 2,699,945.[4] If the rate of increase in
previous years was comparable, the population in 1850
must have been somewhat more than 2,000,000. This is
not a large figure for a country of some half a million
square miles. Moreover, the composition and character
of the population rendered it less than normally efficient.

[1] See Manuel Pardo, *Estudios sobre la Provincia de Jauja* (Lima, 1862),
for an argument on the need for railroads.
[2] For further details on economic developments in the lines mentioned,
see César Antonio Ugarte, *Bosquejo de la historia económica del Perú*
(Lima, 1926), pp. 54-60.
[3] Jorge Basadre, *Historia de la República del Perú* (2d ed. rev. and
aug.; Lima, 1940), p. 385.
[4] *Resumen del censo general de habitantes del Perú hecho en 1876*
(Lima, 1878), general summary between pp. 846 and 847.

In the period of this study, probably 70 per cent of Peru's people were Indian, either pure or mixed blood, the former predominating. The larger part of the Indians lived in the sierras, where the individual cultivated his farm, sometimes communal, and cared for his animals. The inhabitant of the sierra, the serrano, did not like labor in the mines or on the coast. It often meant separation from his family; and the humid, often hot, coastal climate was not to his liking. A Peruvian writer declared, "The *serrano* makes a hasty visit to the lowlands in winter time, returning to his mountain home as soon as he has got together ten or twenty dollars."[5] In the colonial period the Indian had been very badly misused in the mines as well as on the plantations. After independence the dominant whites continued to exploit him; living conditions were poor and wages low. If he became a tenant farmer, the terms of contract were strongly favorable to the owner. Moreover, as the capitalist system was unknown in communal Peru in pre-Spanish times, the Indian did not well understand it. It is not strange that in such circumstances the native Indian should have worked only as it pleased him or as it was necessary.

There was a Negro element among the laboring class, though it was not particularly numerous. When emancipation was decreed, there were but 17,000 slaves.[6] The number of Negroes already free was probably not much greater. Use of Negro slaves, especially in the coastal region, had been common while Peru was a colony of Spain. While it was decreed at the beginning of the nation's existence that children born of slaves in Peru should be free, it was not until thirty years after independence

[5] *Callao and Lima Gazette* (Callao), Aug. 15, 1871.
[6] Mario E. del Río, *La inmigración y su desarrollo en el Perú* (Lima, 1929), p. 38.

was won that the slaves were emancipated, with compensation to the owners. And at one point there was even a resumption of free introduction of Negro slaves from abroad. Late in 1854 President Castilla issued the emancipation decree.[7] A period of disorganization for the Negroes followed, as after the Civil War in the United States, before they became adjusted to their freedom. Even so, they were not very industrious. The Peruvian commentator quoted above on the Indian says, "The Negro will not work at all." It will be seen later, however, that in time he became of some importance on the coastal haciendas, or plantations.

The white proletarian, as a laborer, also had his serious limitations, aside from his lack of numbers. From Spain the early colonists brought the conviction that work with the hands was not honorable. That feeling had not, and has not yet, entirely been eliminated in Peru. The white Peruvian, when it was at all possible, much preferred the professions, a government position, or some other sort of white-collar occupation.

Many Peruvians, writing on social and economic subjects, have lamented the indisposition of their countrymen to labor industriously. Days of fiesta abounded—and still abound. Perhaps the Peruvian who wrote these lines was unduly pessimistic, but his observations have meaning:

As to hours of labor, we believe we are not mistaken in our computation that the Peruvian laborer refrains from working three months in the year; either because of religious functions, civic festivals, or the customs and incidents of domestic life. And in the nine remaining months, his ordinary labor is, on the average, 6 hours, and in some cases 7 and 8 hours.[8]

[7] Basadre, *op. cit.*, pp. 309-311.
[8] *El Trabajo* (Lima), Aug. 29, 1874.

Another statement on this point from a Peruvian source runs:

It is an astounding fact that not less than one third of the people of Peru, as a mass, perform little or no labor at all— nothing at all by which the nation is enriched, and they themselves made better, more intelligent, more enlightened. It cannot have escaped the notice of observant men, native and foreign, much less of those who form the hiring class among us, what a vast number of the population idle away their time.[9]

When the immigration of foreigners was under fire and seemed likely to be interrupted, an editorial writer, observing that the government was eager to promote immigration, declared, "If the people were industrious, four times the labor now secured from them would be obtained; but they are not."[10]

Considering the economic developments of the time, noting the very extensive program of railway building that the nation undertook in the late 1860's and the early 1870's,[11] and bearing in mind the character of the laboring class, one readily sees that Peru's own labor resources were inadequate for supplying the nation's needs.

This lack of labor was the subject of much discussion. An astute and brilliant Peruvian, Juan de Arona (pseudonym of Juan Pedro Paz Soldán y Unánue), made the assertion that the most absolute of Peruvian axioms was "the lack of hands." He continued:

What Peru had been searching for in all the corners of the earth, precipitating diplomatic questions, international conflicts, and even a war [with Spain in 1866], has been hands rather than immigrants. That *dying* and *moribund* agriculture of which

[9] *Callao and Lima Gazette*, Nov. 30, 1871.

[10] *South Pacific Times* (Lima), Oct. 30, 1873. This periodical was the successor to the *Callao and Lima Gazette.*

[11] For detailed information concerning this matter of the railroads, see Watt Stewart, *Henry Meiggs: Yankee Pizarro* (Durham, N. C., 1946).

the Peruvian press has been speaking from the first day of independence until today [1891], has always been like the Venus
de Milo, without arms, according to the graceful comparison of
a French writer.[12]

In these circumstances it was necessary to look abroad
for the fulfilment of labor needs.

During the whole of the colonial period Spanish
America, legally speaking, was strictly closed to immigration except for Spaniards; and even on them there
were severe restrictions.   However, since independence
the Peruvians have been uniformly favorable to the entry
of Europeans into their country, particularly those of the
laboring class.   Numerous laws have been passed to create
conditions favorable to such immigration.   Commissions,
public and private, have been formed from time to time
to encourage their coming.   But, while considerable numbers of foreigners from widely distributed areas have gone
to Peru for business or professional purposes, the country
has been unsuccessful in its efforts to attract an appreciable
number of European laborers.   The reasons for this failure
are not obscure.

In this era of Peru's history the great landowners were,
aside from the Church, perhaps, the strongest power in
the country.   It was very difficult for any government to
refuse to listen to their demands.   This fact, more than
any other, explains the failure to attract the European
immigrant.   The great sugar or cotton planter did not
want the land settled by the modest husbandman, the gen-
uine colonizer.   He merely wanted hands to work his
broad acres, and at a good profit—which meant cheap
labor.   This point and an additional one of some interest

[12] *La inmigración en el Perú* (Lima, 1891), p. 36. For a sketch of
the life of Juan de Arona and a critique of his literary work, see Luis
Fabio Xammar, *Juan de Arona, Romántico del Perú* (Lima, 1943).

are made by Juan de Arona in his inimitable style (which, unfortunately, loses much in translation) in these phrases:

> Immigration in Peru, in its infinite attempts, has always failed: Why? First, because men have been brought as goods are brought, men not being goods, but human beings who are to be appreciated only in their entirety; and second, because it has been hoped to plant immigration scientifically; and in Peru, a country essentially, perhaps exclusively, "hit or miss," nothing goes well unless it is undertaken in a practical and empirical manner, which plays the game in conformity with the general condition. The only Peruvian agriculturist who never became rich was one who proceeded scientifically; and that one of our politicians who never falls is that one who never opens a book; we could say the same about lawyers, doctors, literary people, etc. Our society is constituted thus, and to wish to change it is almost sacrilegious.[13]

The European laborer, if he came to Peru, wanted eventually to become independent, to possess, if he were a farmer, his own land. But the scale of wages was low; hence opportunities for saving and securing one's own small business or farm were decidedly limited. Furthermore, the farmer would find it next to impossible to secure desirable land. Most of the arable coastal land was already in the hands of large landholders. Extensive rural holdings had been a tradition of colonial days and the tradition was—and is—a continuing one. Not only was the possessor of river valley acres unwilling to relinquish any of them to the small farmer—native or foreign—but he was busily engaged in securing the tracts in his vicinity still owned by the modest farmer. The system of plantation labor approached peonage, when not actually that, and such labor was not attractive to Europeans.

There was, of course, much public land in the sierras and in the hot, humid jungle country beyond, particularly

---

[13] *Op. cit.*, p. 111.

in the latter. But in general the high altitudes of the sierras repelled the European and the extreme isolation of the trans-Andean region, almost without communications at the time, made life there undesirable from his viewpoint.

Enough Europeans for a few experiments were induced to come, but the results were not encouraging, either to the Peruvian government and people or to the colonists. A group of some 300 Germans established themselves in 1857 at Pozuzo in the transmountain country. By 1879 the colony numbered but 360, the population had deteriorated, and, as an English commentator put it, "Their progress had not been very brilliant."[14] Another group was composed of some 200 Spaniards who in 1860 were induced to become contract laborers on the plantation of Talambo in Chiclayo Department.[15] Differences between them and the master of the hacienda became the pretext, if not the cause, of the war with Spain to which Arona referred in the quotation above.

Another reason for the nonsuccess of efforts to attract European laborers, in addition to the scarcity of good available land and the unattractive conditions of labor, is presented in these words of a Peruvian:

> The evil lies in the fact that we have not made ourselves known in Europe, and there perhaps the sole idea, the only data that the majority possess concerning our social condition is that we are always involved in fratricidal wars and that, because of these struggles, insecurity of persons and property, the ruin of agriculture, and hatred of the foreigner, have come to be the normal state of the country.[16]

While the writer implies that the impression was a

[14] A. J. Duffield, *Peru in the Guano Age* (London, 1877), p. 40.
[15] For further details concerning this group, see Basadre, *op. cit.*, p. 408.
[16] Félix Cirpriano C. Zegarra, *La condición jurídica de los estranjeros en el Perú* (Santiago de Chile, 1872), pp. 114-115.

mistaken one, there was considerable basis for it in fact, as still another Peruvian admitted:

> Why is it that . . . Germans, and the Irish with them, prefer the almost polar uninhabited sections of the States of the West in the republic of Washington, in preference to the soft climates and the splendid and hospitable natural conditions of South America? Because in general, here we are not able to give them what the North Americans present them with full hands: security and country. A country, above all, in the elevated and moral sense of that word.[17]

In foreign lands the impression was, in fact, widespread that Peru did not offer conditions of security, and that impression militated against the migration of Europeans to Peru. Zegarra presents this summation of the reasons for failure to attract the European emigrant:

> Whatever, then, be the motives that have conspired to kill the immigration, they are to be sought in the little judgment of governments, in the absence of skill in selecting colonists, in the entire lack of study of their customs, religious beliefs, assimilative capacities or moral and social state; indeed one may discover these faults in the inadequate measures which are to be observed for leading the emigrant to forsake his own country, and in the absolute ignorance of the economic laws which have presided over his introduction into this country.[18]

Since the combination of circumstances sketched above prevented the introduction of a sufficient number of Europeans to meet Peru's need, where should the country turn? Only the Pacific and the Far East remained, and attention, consequently, was directed to that extensive and densely populated portion of the globe.

Actually, an eye had been cast toward the Pacific some time before the Germans and Spaniards mentioned above

[17] *La Patria* (Lima), April 30, 1873.
[18] *Op. cit.*, p. 112.

came to Peru. It had early become pretty clear that the European field would not yield an abundant harvest of workers. César Antonio Ugarte, a Peruvian economist, states that toward the year 1850 the optimistic belief of the founders of independent Peru that the superabundance of the population of Europe was going to overflow to Peruvian shores and cover them with laborers was begining to be modified. He quotes José Gregorio Paz Soldán as saying in 1846, "For twenty-three years we have futilely expected them, and even now the first is yet to appear."[19]

Manuel E. de la Torre, member of the Chamber of Deputies, presented to the chamber in 1847 a bill for the encouragement of immigration. It would authorize the executive to make contracts for ten years with capitalists and landowners who wished to introduce foreigners. The persons bringing colonists would be given a premium of four tons of guano for each colonist. The individuals so brought would be free of taxes, and when their period of labor was finished, each one who wished to remain in the country would be granted twenty-five acres of land and given a small sum of money. The bill failed of approval, but its discussion aroused interest in the problem. The following year the government circulated a questionnaire to prefects of departments and to the Agricultural Society of Lima with a view to obtaining exact data on which to formulate a plan of action.

On the basis of the information thus secured, and influenced greatly by Domingo Elías, a prominent capitalist and owner of much land,[20] the congress passed a general

[19] *Op. cit.,* pp. 60-61.

[20] Elías was one of the richest men of Peru. He possessed vast properties, in the main devoted to the production of grapes and cotton. It was he who began in Peru the production of cotton on a grand scale. He participated in national politics and was at one time Minister of the Treasury

immigration law on November 17, 1849. Since its principal object was to make possible the introduction of Chinese, Paz Soldán, a stubborn opponent, dubbed it the "Chinese Law," and as such it became popularly known. With modifications, it became the basis of the movement of Chinese into Peru.

The law conceded to every person who should introduce foreign colonists of either sex to the number of not less than fifty and of the ages of ten to forty years, 30 pesos for each person. The law further conceded to Domingo Elías and Juan Rodríguez the exclusive privilege, for the term of four years, of introducing Chinese into the Departments of Lima and La Libertad.[21]

Proponents of the measure advanced various considerations, in addition to the poor prospect of securing laborers elsewhere, to justify this importation of Chinese. In China, they asserted, life was so hard that fathers often cast their children into a river or left them on the public highway; people so situated would welcome the opportunity to migrate to a country "to which Providence with a liberal hand had conceded all its gifts."[22] Moreover, as the Chinese had long been accustomed to a low scale of living, their labor would be cheap. The immigration of Chinese, they thought, would present fewer possibilities of diplomatic involvements with foreign nations. Peru at that time had no relations whatsoever with China, and Britain's

---

and at another time Peruvian minister to France. With the Spaniard Nicolás Rodrigo, he founded in 1841 the high school of Our Lady of Guadalupe, now Peru's largest public high school. He died in 1867 at the age of 62 years (*Enciclopedia Universal Ilustrada*, XIX, 761-762).

[21] Ugarte, *op. cit.*, pp. 61-62; Basadre, *op. cit.*, p. 258.

[22] Representation of Elías and Rodríguez to the Senate in 1851, quoted in a pamphlet, *Inmigración de Chinos: Ventajas que proporcionan al país.* (Una representación de la Empresa a la H. Cámara de Senadores: "Colonos Chinos.") (Lima, 1851), p. 2. The "Empresa" is the company of Elías and Rodríguez.

efforts in defense of human freedom were thought to
be concerned chiefly with the African slave trade.[23]
They believed further that conditions of labor on the
plantations of Peru would not be objectionable to the
Chinese, since those conditions would be, in all probability,
as good as those to which they had been accustomed in
their own country. Voices were raised in question and
criticism when the law was under consideration, but the
interests of the agriculturist prevailed, and it was passed.

With the passage of the "Chinese Law" the stage was
set for the introduction into the country of the Chinese
laborer, or coolie, frequently, though incorrectly, referred
to as a "colonist." His history in Peru—for the purpose
of this study—falls into two rather definite periods, the
first (to be treated briefly, since it was much the less important) from 1849 to 1856, the second from 1861 to
1875.

Every human migratory movement is due, of course,
not only to the attractions, real or supposed, in the country of destination, but also to the propulsive forces in the
country of origin. In China—in the southern region in
particular—strong motives for an outward movement of
population existed in the middle years of the nineteenth
century. The multiplied millions of the Chinese have for
centuries pressed upon the resources of their land. Let
the normal pressure be but slightly increased or the normal
condition of society be but a little disturbed, and the im-
pulse toward migration is great. The conditions of life in
South China at the time mentioned were decidedly abnormal. The chief cause of this abnormality was the
Taiping Rebellion, a civil war of great magnitude which
began in 1849 and was not ended until 1864. Historians
have described it as the most devastating civil war in all

[23] Zegarra, *op. cit.*, p. 106.

history, since they estimate that it caused the death of twenty million persons. Its cause may in part be attributed to Western influences, for its leader, a religious fanatic, claimed to base his movement upon the principles of Christianity.[24] The southern and southwestern provinces of China were especially affected. A constant series of petty feuds and local insurrections occurred from 1848 in Kwangtung and Kwangsi. Armed bands of men wandered from village to village, plundering private houses and robbing public granaries.[25] Under these conditions hundreds of thousands of the laboring class found themselves in extreme misery and sought a place—any place—where a living might be gained.

An American, S. Wells Williams, who resided in China many years from 1833 and merits the title of an authority on matters Chinese,[26] stated that all Chinese emigrants to other lands were furnished by six departments lying along the coasts of the two provinces of Kwangtung and Fukien, the population center of the region being Canton. As compared with the northern

[24] John W. Foster, *American Diplomacy in the Orient* (Boston and New York, 1903), p. 208. See also Harley Farnsworth MacNair, *Modern Chinese History; Selected Readings* (Shanghai, 1923), pp. 328-376, and Holger Cahill, *A Yankee Adventurer: The Story of Ward and the Taiping Rebellion* (New York, 1930).

[25] Lindsay Brine, *The Taiping Rebellion in China* (London, 1862), p. 97.

[26] On his twenty-first birthday, in 1833, Williams was en route to Canton. For almost twenty years he was active as a missionary in the region of Canton, and he resided and labored for some time on the island of Macao. In 1855 Dr. Williams was appointed secretary and interpreter of the American Legation in China, and for almost two decades he was associated with it in one capacity or another, frequently discharging the duties of *chargé* in the absence of the minister. In 1848 he published a two-volume work on China, *The Middle Kingdom,* an authoritative treatment of Chinese history and society. Late in life he returned to his country and ended a highly useful existence as professor of Chinese and Chinese history at Yale College. See Frederick Williams, *The Life and Letters of Samuel Wells Williams, LL.D., Missionary, Diplomatist, Sinologue* (New York, 1889).

Chinese, said Dr. Williams, the men of this region are "smaller and more swarthy, have more commercial enterprise, are better educated, and exhibit higher mechanical skill."[27] He estimated that the total number of Chinese coolies carried away in the years 1850-1875 was "over 300,000."[28] Dr. Williams made a distinction between the free Chinese worker such as went to California and Australia in those years and the coolie[29] contract laborer such as was taken to Peru, Cuba, Panama, Brazil, or other sections of the Americas. He asserted that the ignorance of Chinese laborers concerning foreign countries "led them readily to infer that when once out of China they would at last reach the Gold Hills," as California was called in China.[30]

Repelled by home conditions, attracted by tales of wealth to be gained abroad, many thousands of these Chinese came to the west coast of the United States, where at first they were heartily welcomed, since the new land needed laborers, a need soon to be heightened by the construction of the Pacific Railway. Other tens of thousands found employment on the sugar plantations of Cuba and Brazil, on the Panama Railway then under construction, and in various work elsewhere. The first recorded shipment of contract laborers to the American continent was

[27] *Chinese Immigration* (New York, 1879), pp. 6-7.
[28] *Ibid.*, p. 10.
[29] Dr. Williams' explanation of the origin of the word "coolie" is as follows: It is Bengalee and was originally the name of a hill tribe in India who were wont to go down to the plains in harvest time. Their name was gradually extended to all transient laborers, and in 1835 such people were hired at Calcutta under contract to go to Mauritius, where laborers were needed. Application of the term to Chinese contract labor was easy, says Dr. Williams, for it was already in use among foreigners in China for lower house servants and day laborers. He says the Chinese supposed it to be an English word and that probably, not knowing much English, they called themselves coolies in San Francisco (*Chinese Immigration*, p. 9).
[30] *Ibid.*, p. 8.

made from Amoy in 1847. In that year some 800 "nom-
inally free" laborers were sent to Cuba, where, it was reported, they had "thriven and realized the expectation
formed of their labor."[31]

Another branch of this stream of migrants was welcomed to Peru under the terms of the "Chinese Law."
In the quarter century 1849-1874, these humble workers
in numbers variously estimated at from eighty to one
hundred thousand arrived on the shores of the land of
Pizarro.

In October, 1849, Elías and Rodríguez had brought
to the country seventy-five Chinese "colonists." The government, despite the fact that the "Chinese Law" was
not passed until a month later, paid them the bounty
provided by that law.[32] It was not long before the
monopolists were introducing these men in considerable
numbers. According to the official report of Peru's Minister of Government in mid-1853, between the dates of
February 25, 1850, and July 5, 1853, 3,932 colonists were
brought, of whom 2,516 were Chinese.[33] From another
Peruvian source is derived the statement that in the years
1850-1859 the Chinese introduced numbered 13,000.[34]
Some were embarked in Amoy or other Chinese ports, but
the greater number probably passed through the Portuguese colony of Macao, located very conveniently on an
island near Canton, center of one of China's most thickly
populated regions.

The law of 1849 had been passed under pressure and

[31] Hosea Ballou Morse, *The International Relations of the Chinese
Empire* (3 vols., London and New York, 1910, 1918), II, 165.
[32] Basadre, *op. cit.*, p. 258.
[33] Ugarte, *op. cit.*, p. 62. The others—520 Irish, 1906 Germans—
were taken to the mountains (*ibid.*).
[34] César Borja, *La inmigración china* (Lima, 1877), quoted by Arona,
op. cit., p. 56.

to satisfy the demands of the planters. Considered as an immigration law, it suffered from many defects. The importers of Chinese laborers were businessmen, and they were in the business for profit. They gave little attention to the physical aptitude of the Chinese for the work he was to perform, nor did they worry about his customs and characteristics. Neither was his comfort on the long voyage given much consideration. The ships that conveyed the coolies became known as "floating hells," and for very good reasons. While an English regulation published in 1853 to govern the movement of Chinese through Hongkong allowed twelve square feet (two feet by six) for each man, it could be enforced only at Hongkong, and in general only eight square feet were allotted, and overcrowding of the ships was the rule. To appreciate the seriousness of this fact, it is only necessary to observe that the voyage of some nine thousand miles from Macao to Callao, Peru's seaport, required in many cases 120 days of navigation. The mortality rate was extreme. In 1850, of 740 emigrants embarked on two ships for Callao, 247 died on the voyage, more than 33 per cent.[35] The ship *Empresa* of 446 tons, which made the voyage from Amoy to Callao in 114 days, took aboard 323 Chinese, but when it reached Callao on November 7, 1852, it carried but 246. The other 77—or almost 24 per cent—had died at sea.[36] In 1854, of 325 emigrants in one ship to Callao, 47 died, or 1 in 7.[37] Such brutal disregard of the lives of the coolies could not fail to challenge a reaction, the nature of which may be judged from the experience of three ships. In 1850 the coolies bound for Peru on the French ship *Albert* mutinied—"the captain cut their tails; they

[35] Morse, *op. cit.*, II, 172.
[36] Arona, *op. cit.*, p. 71 n.
[37] Morse, *op. cit.*, II, 172.

killed him and landed in China." In 1851 the emigrants to Peru in the British ship *Victory* "rose and killed the captain and landed in the China sea." In 1852 those on the Peruvian ship *Rosa Elías* (with an English master) "rose and killed the captain and landed near Singapore."[38]

The British Passenger Act of 1855, which contained regulations respecting seaworthiness and equipment of vessels as well as securities for the passengers respecting their contracts, had the effect of closing Hongkong to the coolie trade and driving to Macao those who wished to continue practicing it.[39]

When the coolie reached Peru, after his trying voyage, all was far from well. On the plantation or in the guano beds he was too often considered as merely a tool for laboring. The Peruvian natives were hostile and some bloody incidents occurred on the haciendas where the Chinese were employed.[40]

The early contract under which Elías and Rodríguez brought coolies provided that the Chinese should serve his *patrón*, or master, for a period of five years from the date of the contract, not counting the time of illnesses; that he should perform whatever labor the *patrón* should order; that he should not move from the place of his labor without written permission; that he should clothe himself; and that he should repay at the rate of one peso per month the advance paid him in China. In return, the *patrón* agreed to pay him four pesos per month, furnish his food, and cure his illnesses, provided the illness did not result from the coolie's own bad conduct.[41]

[38] *Ibid.*

[39] See Thornton, British Minister, to Hamilton Fish, Secretary of State, Washington, Jan. 23, 1874, *United States Foreign Relations, 1874*, p. 549; also Harley Farnsworth MacNair, *The Chinese Abroad, Their Position and Protection: A Study in International Law and Relations* (Shanghai, 1924), pp. 211-212.

[40] Ugarte, *op. cit.*, p. 63.   [41] *Inmigración de Chinos.*

Most of the Chinese brought in this early period were employed by the owners of haciendas on the coast in the north-central province of Libertad, the capital of which is Trujillo, and in the region around Lima. It was in these districts, it is to be remembered, that Elías and Rodríguez held their monopoly. Considerable numbers, however, were used as house servants, cooks, bakers, mill hands, gardeners, porters, workers in printing shops, and handymen about mercantile establishments.[42] The Elías-Rodríguez partnership, in an effort to forestall a threatened abrogation of the "Chinese Law," requested a hundred persons who had taken one or more Chinese to make a statement regarding their efficiency, and the replies were published in a pamphlet. In the main they were favorable to the Chinese. Along with the reply of one Dr. Gallagher, it was stated that "Doctor Gallagher, who as everybody knows, brought from Europe several Irish families, has thought it advisable to take Chinese: the said Dr. Gallagher has dismissed his European colonists, seeing that it was impossible to make them contented in spite of giving them in food twice the value of what the Asiatics and workers of the country consume."[43]

A counselor of state, Dr. José Gregorio Paz Soldán, was asked to make a statement concerning 100 Chinese that were being used in the sugar factories in Cañete. He stated that the masters of the haciendas of Casa Blanca, La Quebrada, Unánue, and Montalván had assured him that the Chinese did well in the operations of the factory, but that for field labor they were weak and lacking in intelli-

[42] *Ibid.* In the pamphlet are printed statements from almost a hundred employers of Chinese who had been asked by the Empresa to make a statement regarding the coolies as workers. The compilers state that letters were not written to those employers who were known to be satisfied with the Chinese. It is possible from this list to gain a knowledge of the occupations and the distribution of the men.

[43] *Ibid.*, p. 41.

gence; that they did their tasks with exactitude and arose very early; that on finishing their work they bathed; and that they supplied very well the lack of workers. Dr. Paz Soldán said he had been assured that those Chinese who were working in the guano beds of the Chincha Islands and in other places were inclined to "ontanismo y pescado rufado," because of which they were becoming ill and destroying themselves. He added, "The Empresa ought to consider remedying this evil, and of not separating husbands from their women, nor forcing them into crime by depriving them of the satisfactions of the family."[44] The state of the Chinese in the guano beds was particularly bad, as is attested by many witnesses whose evidence will later receive further attention.

The multiple abuses associated with the introduction of the Orientals and the sharp criticism to which they gave rise forced the government at last to take some action to ameliorate them. The monopoly of Elías and Rodríguez was promptly declared at an end when the four years of its term expired on November 17, 1853. Dr. José G. Paz Soldán, a consistent critic of the importation of coolies, as minister countersigned the decree, which read succinctly: "Considering: that the immigration permitted under the law of November 17, 1849, has not fulfilled the desires of the nation, it is abrogated."[45]

Decrees designed to improve the condition of the coolies were issued on March 3, 1853, and July 9, 1854.[46] They had little effect, and the government finally decided to abrogate the "Chinese Law" and to prohibit the traffic in Asiatics. The decree of abrogation bears date of March 6, 1856, and certain of its phrases are so significant as to

[44] *Ibid.*, pp. 27-28.
[45] del Río, *op. cit.*, p. 46.
[46] Alberto Ulloa Sotomayor, *La organización social y legal del trabajo en el Perú* (Lima, 1916), p. 44.

deserve quotation. They are remarkably frank for such a document. One may think, as was very possibly the case, that through them the government was "laying the rod" on some of its political opponents. Here is the decree almost in its entirety:

Considering:

1. That the introduction of Asiatic colonists, in addition to the fact that it does not suit the country because of its being a degraded race, is degenerating into a kind of Negro slave trade, . . .

.   .   .   .

3. That the excessive number of men embarked in small boats, and the scarcity and bad quality of the food, have occasioned the death of at least a third part of the colonists; and the arrival at the port of the remainder with dangerous diseases;

4. That sometimes the severity employed on the boats, as a means consequent to the deception and violence with which these criminal speculations are made, has occasioned repeated catastrophes which it is necessary to avoid;

5. That the Government ought not authorize an abuse as repugnant as it is offensive to morals and to right, from which only those concerned in the traffic realize benefit;

It is Resolved:

Art. 1. That four months from the date, the introduction of Asiatic colonists by means of contracts and in the cruel and violent manner in which it has been practiced up to now, shall be prohibited. . . .[47]

The traffic did not cease completely with the publication of this decree. On October 1 of the same year, shortly before the decree was to become effective, the government made a contract with an English company for the construction of a short railway linking Lima with Chorrillos, a coastal residential town, and inserted a clause which permitted the introduction of 700 Chinese under the

[47] *El Peruano; Periódico Oficial* (Lima), March 8, 1856.

former system of contracts.[48] Later, special licenses were
granted on the plea of absolute necessity for introducing
fixed numbers of coolies under direct contract with the
recipients of the licenses, most of them issued to planters.
Alluding to these special licenses in a veto message in
1861, the president, Grand Marshal Ramón Castilla, declared, "But, as it is so easy to elude, outside the territory
of the Republic, the dispositions of the Government,
abuses continued to be committed against its will."[49] It
thus appears that considerable numbers of Chinese continued to be brought in, though much fewer than prior to
the abrogation of 1856. It seems possible, however, to
consider the year 1856 as marking the termination, more
or less, of this early period in the history of Chinese immigration to Peru.

The seven-year experiment with the new immigrant,
while it provided a certain amount of labor for needy
hacendados, the exploiters of guano, and various other
employers, could not be considered a success. The law
under which the Chinese coolies were brought had been
carelessly drawn, and the importer took full advantage of
its imperfections. The conditions surrounding the movement were in almost every sense bad from the humanitarian viewpoint. The Chinese, when they reached
Peru after the long and cruelly crowded crossing, were in
many cases weak and unable to endure the conditions of
life and labor to which they were subjected. Furthermore,
they were not liked by Peru's laboring class. Certainly
there were wholly adequate reasons for repealing the
"Chinese Law." But the needs of the great landowners

[48] Federico Costa y Laurent, *Reseña histórica de los ferrocarriles del Perú* (Lima, 1908), pp. 45-46.
[49] *El Peruano; Periódico Oficial,* March 23, 1861.

were still exigent, and their clamors continued, as the granting of special licenses attests. Perhaps no government less strong than that of Grand Marshal Castilla (who had but recently abolished Negro slavery) would have, or could have, dared to disregard those clamors; and, as the sequel will show, his daring effected little more than a recess in the movement.

II

THE "COOLIE TRADE" AT MACAO

PERU'S PLANTER CLASS bitterly opposed, and were never reconciled to, the abrogation of the "Chinese Law." Early in 1861 their continued insistence, combined with other motives, forced a reopening of the country to the importation of coolies. One of the additional motives arose from the fact that the Civil War in the United States was clearly approaching, and the prospective disruption of the trade in cotton of the Southern States offered the Peruvian cotton growers a wonderful opportunity for gain. An American who spent the years 1863-1865 in Peru in a diplomatic post wrote on this point:

> During the American Civil War, when cotton commanded its highest price, the people of Peru rushed its cultivation as if the price of the staple would never fall. Cochineal and sugar plantations were ploughed up and put into cotton. Lands augmented in value; and in the vicinity of Arica the people, unable to obtain lands capable of irrigation from the few running streams, sunk wells near the sea, where fresh water from the mountains, having leached through the sands to the sea-level, was found in abundance.[1]

[1] Ephraim George Squier, *Incidents of Travel and Exploration in the Land of the Incas* (New York, 1877), pp. 219-220. See also *Memoria del Ministro de Hacienda y Comercio, 1864*, p. 35: "Las plantaciones de algodón que se propagan con rapidez asombrosa y que dan copiosas cosechas son otro manantial fecundo de riqueza social y de capitales." It would be helpful if specific data respecting production and export of cotton and sugar in these years could be given, but they cannot, for such figures simply do not exist. The Peruvian Minister of the Treasury and Commerce, in his report to Congress in 1868 (p. 39), reminded that body that the preceding

The preamble to the new "Chinese Law," which was
first passed on January 15, 1861, lists four reasons for its
passage: the leading industry of the country was agriculture, "without which no society could exist"; the farming sections were deserted as a consequence of the manu-
mission of slaves; the lack of a code to regulate rural
labor made it necessary to adopt measures for meeting
existing difficulties; and, lastly, "if Congress should remain indifferent or refuse to abrogate the decree of March
5 [6], 1856, very soon articles of consumption and of first
necessity for life, would rise in price so greatly that it
could not be met by what was gained in the work or industry to which the citizenry was devoting itself." Followed
then the four articles of the law:

Art. 1. It is permitted to introduce Asiatic colonists intended
for the cultivation of rural lands on the coasts of Peru, for the useful arts, and for domestic service, on condition that they be contracted directly by the masters who are to use them, or by their
representatives, in the ports from which they come, or in Peru on
their arrival.

Art. 2. The boats which bring Asiatics will not take on board
a number of colonists greater than one for each ton of registry,
under pain of a fine of five hundred *pesos* for each one in excess.

Art. 3. The contracts which are made abroad will have effect
in so far as they are not contrary to the laws of the Republic,

administration had suppressed the Statistical Section of his ministry. "From
this," he continued, "arises the absolute lack of data to give even an
approximate idea of the mercantile operations which have taken place
during the last biennium." In October, 1862, an American consul in
Peru wrote to the Secretary of State, "I find it very difficult to arrive at
any exact conclusions as to the state of trade and commerce in this Consular District, owing to the want of any complete Record of the Imports
and Exports" (John E. Lovejoy to Seward, Callao, Oct. 1, Consular
Despatches, Callao 4; this despatch, as are all consular and diplomatic
despatches cited hereinafter, is to be found in the Archives of the State
Department in the National Archives). A careful search of the archives
reveals no reliable or helpful figures for the commodities mentioned.

and the transfer of said contracts without the consent of the contracting colonist is forbidden.

Art. 4. The decree of March 5, 1856, concerning the immigration of Asiatic colonists, in so far as it is opposed to the present
law, is abrogated.[2]

Since he did not approve of the law, Marshal Castilla
on January 24 sent it back to Congress with a veto and a
number of critical observations. They were to the effect
that (1) societies *had* existed without agriculture, (2) the
abolition of slavery could not be said to have had the effect
stated, and (3) the lack of a law for regulating farm labor
would not be supplied by the law in question but rather
by the drawing of a rural code. Developing these points,
the president admitted that hands were needed for agriculture but declared that they ought not be those of men
"weak, sickly, degraded and corrupted as were the Asiatics." Experience had shown that those men either died
with great frequency at their hard tasks or, mocking their
obligations, abandoned them to engage in other occupations or gave themselves over to pillage in the villages
and cities. Calling attention to other grave evils associated with the coolie immigration, he reminded the legis-
lators:

The avidity of the speculators in the introduction of Chinese renewed all the evils of the reprehensible slave traffic. Taking advantage of the ignorance and the misery of the unfortunate Asiatics, they snatched them from their country with seductive and
deceiving promises, and, drawing up a contract which the Asiatic
did not understand, they considered themselves authorized to bring
them to Peru. Then in growing numbers they brought them
crowded into constricted boats, deprived of ventilation and even
of the most essential food, and subjected during the voyage, to a
barbarous treatment. Well known are the frightful scenes which

[2] *El Peruano; Periódico Oficial*, March 23, 1861.

the desperation of the Asiatics, caused by these cruelties, produced repeatedly on board those boats. When these dealers in men reached Callao with the victims of their cupidity, they sold them to the highest bidder.[3]

The president also made the point that it was impossible for the coolie to know to what he was obligating himself when he signed the contract, and, consequently, there being ignorance on the part of one of its parties, "the contract suffered from nullity." However, despite the president's opposition and his strong veto message, the Congress repassed the law, and he was obliged to accept it. He promulgated it on March 14, 1861.[4]

The bar to further introduction of Asiatics thus removed, recourse was first had to the Hawaiian Islands for securing the laborers that were needed. One J. C. Byrne was granted the right to transport to Peru for the period of five years for agricultural and domestic service, colonists of both sexes from "the islands of the southwest of the Pacific." The Hawaiians brought in under this arrangement were ill adapted to the conditions of work in Peru. Said Duffield, "They all died like flies that had been poisoned."[5] Various decrees were issued in an effort to correct abuses, but without effect.[6] The Hawaiian *chargé* protested, as did also the French.[7]

Juan Antonio Ribeyro, an influential Peruvian, writing to the chief minister on April 27, 1863, respecting this immigration, declared that it had produced no advantageous effects and that the statistics of mortality of the unfortunate islanders had "mounted to a figure that causes as much compassion as astonishment."[8] On the following

[3] *Ibid.*   [4] *Ibid.*
[5] *Peru in the Guano Age*, p. 42.
[6] *El Peruano; Periódico Oficial*, Jan. 3 and Feb. 20, 1863.
[7] Arona, *La inmigración en el Peru*, pp. 36-38.
[8] *El Peruano; Periódico Oficial*, May 2, 1863, p. 199.

day appeared an executive decree on the subject. Reference was made to grave excesses which could not be stopped, then followed these words: "the Government suspends absolutely the concession of licenses for the introduction of Polynesian colonists." The licenses already issued were to be used with great care.[9] An editorial which appeared in *El Peruano,* the official periodical, simultaneously with the published decree, stated that the Hawaiians were even less well adapted to the needs of the Peruvian fields than were the Chinese. It asserted that, born where Nature permitted them to breathe in idleness, they lacked "sufficient morale to devote themselves to labor, for they have not learned that this is the fatal law of man in society and that without labor, there is no society, there are no virtues, there is no religion."

Statistics concerning the number of Hawaiians brought to Peru are quite scarce. A Peruian writer of a later date, citing no authority, says that "of 750 Polynesians who entered the country the greater part died."[10] In any event, the number could hardly have been large. The government repatriated a considerable group of those yet alive when the traffic was discontinued, paying the planters S/50.00 (soles) as indemnity for each Hawaiian.[11]

In the early 1860's, then, Peru resumed the importation of Chinese coolies. The experiences of the earlier period had not been forgotten, but the planters were clamoring for laborers, and those citizens who saw in such importation a social evil were not strong enough, or sufficiently numerous, to make their opposition effective. With the close of the Civil War in the United States came the

[9] *Ibid.,* p. 200.
[10] del Río, *La inmigración y su desarrollo en el Perú,* pp. 50-51.
[11] Arona, *op. cit.,* pp. 36-38. The Peruvian sol (sun) during the greater part of the period of this study was valued at about ninety-six cents, U. S.

period of difficulty with Spain, already referred to. A
civil war followed the trouble with the former mother
country. But by 1868 these matters had been adjusted,
and peace again reigned in Peru. In that year, at the
conclusion of the civil war, a government came into power
which was highly enthusiastic about public works; the
president, Colonel José Balta, may be said to have had a
mania for them. These works took the form, in great
part, of railroads. The building of railroads also required
hands, consequently the planter was joined by the public
works proponent and the industrialist in the cry for more
laborers. This augmented need accounts for the much
greater number of coolies brought to Peru in the years
between 1861 and 1875 than in the earlier period of importation. It is to the detailed study of this later period
that attention is now turned. While the succeeding chap-
ters are written with particular reference to the conditions
and developments of the later period, it is to be understood
that in general, as far as conditions of securing, transporting, distributing, and managing the Chinese are concerned,
there is a great deal of similarity in the two periods.

The center of the traffic in Chinese coolies—destined
for Cuba and certain other parts of the Americas as well
as for Peru—was the Portuguese colony of Macao. The
Island of Macao, held by Portugal for some three hundred
years, is located at the southwest side of the great estuary
in southeast China which is known as the Canton River.
Canton, largest city of southern China and the focus of one
of the most densely populated regions of that country,
lies some one hundred miles up the river. Hongkong,
the British colony, is situated a somewhat shorter distance
across the estuary to the east. Macao is sufficiently near
the mainland for the channel to be bridged, as it was in the
period with which this story is concerned. The British

regulations already mentioned[12] had driven the coolie trade from Hongkong, and the Chinese Empire had been for centuries officially opposed to the emigration of its subjects.[13] Moreover, the Portuguese officials at Macao appear to have been somewhat "liberal," to say the least, in the exercise of their functions in so far as they related to emigration. All of these factors combined to make of Macao the logical center of the coolie trade. (See map.)

It should be understood that Portugal's possession of Macao had never been recognized by China and was not so recognized until 1887.[14] Previous to that date the claim of the Portuguese was "stoutly denied." An American minister wrote to his Secretary of State in 1872, "The Government feels keenly the wrong and injustice of having a portion of its territory taken possession of by a foreign Government and made a depot for smuggling operations and a slave mart for the forcible and fraudulent sale of its own subjects."[15] China could doubtless have ejected the Portuguese if other nations had practiced a "hands-off" policy, but that was not the case, since they feared the effect which such an action might have on foreign interests generally.[16] In these circumstances the Chinese Empire was constrained to watch its subject funneled into Macao and sent abroad as contract laborers and for years was reduced to making impotent decrees designed to prevent their going to Macao, decrees which, generally, were disregarded by subordinate authorities and by those engaged in the coolie traffic.[17]

[12] See p. 19.
[13] MacNair, *Modern Chinese History*, p. 409; Morse, *The International Relations of the Chinese Empire*, II, 164.
[14] Morse, *op. cit.*, III, 181.
[15] F. F. Low, Peking, June 26, 1872, Diplomatic Despatches, China 32.
[16] *Ibid.*
[17] S. Wells Williams to Secretary of State, Peking, Nov. 6, 1873 (No. 8), Diplomatic Despatches, China 35.

Not without interest is a contemporary statement regarding the three chief sources from which these coolies were secured:

... prisoners taken in clan fights ... of the province of Kwangtung, and who are sold by their captors to Chinese or Portuguese man-buyers upon the interior waters; villagers or fishermen forcibly kidnapped along the coast ... ; and thirdly, individuals who are tempted by prowling agents to gamble [in Macao] ... and who on losing ... surrender their persons in payment according to the peculiar Chinese notions of liability in this respect.[18]

During the period of practical suspension of the traffic by Peru (1856-1861), operations continued in China, for there was no cessation of the movement to Cuba. The activities of Chinese agents became exceedingly dangerous to the Chinese laboring man in this southern region—so much so indeed that some Chinese gentry of Amoy, inspired in part, it may well be, by fear of a possible labor shortage there, issued a proclamation warning the lower classes against the false promises of kidnapers and seducers. A portion of it ran:

They [the kidnaped ones] might implore Heaven, and their tears wet the earth, but their complaints are uttered in vain. When carried to the barbarian regions, day and night they are impelled to labor, without intervals even for sleep. Death is their sole relief. ... Alas, those who living were denizens of the central flowery country, dead, their ghosts wander in strange lands. O, azure Heaven above! in this way are destroyed our righteous people.[19]

About 1859 acts of fraud and violence associated with the coolie traffic reached such a pitch that there was general alarm among the people. It was not safe to go abroad

---

[18] W. F. Mayers, N. B. Denny, and Chas. King, *The Ports of China*, p. 229, quoted by MacNair, *The Chinese Abroad*, pp. 210-211.
[19] Foster, *American Diplomacy in the Orient*, p. 277.

even by day lest one fall prey to a kidnaper. The people became aroused to their peril and took the law into their own hands, several kidnapers being killed by the mob "with vindictive cruelty."[20]   Macao, however, was beyond the reach of the Chinese authorities, and the trade went ahead—at a greatly accelerated pace in the later 1860's and early 1870's when conditions in Peru reached the state described above.

Let it be supposed that a ship of Peruvian registry, capable of supplying passage for three hundred Chinese, has arrived at Macao with the design of transporting that number of coolies to Callao. The ship has already, in all probability, spent some days at Hongkong taking on supplies and getting everything in readiness for its "cargo" and its voyage. It is scheduled, let us say, to depart for Peru in eight days. The process of securing its quota of coolies would go something like this:

The captain, or perhaps an agent of the Peruvian "dealer" (who, of course, represents the Peruvian, or Peruvians, in whose names the contracts are to be drawn) gets in touch with a local labor agent. This agent may be a Chinese, or he may be of some other nationality. It is agreed that this local agent, on stated terms, shall furnish the three hundred coolies. If the local agent does not have the required number on hand on the island awaiting disposal, he sends out his subagents—called variously "runners" or "crimps"—into the near-by territory to secure them. These "crimps" are always Chinese. They make contact with individuals who may wish to emigrate for any of the reasons already mentioned, or, failing to find those who have a positive desire to go, they induce men in some manner to go to Macao. There the contract

---

[20] Consul Alcock, Canton; quoted by MacNair, *Modern Chinese History*, pp. 409-410.

is drawn.   It is presumably entered into freely and is
signed by the laborer and the representative of his future
Peruvian master.   It is witnessed by various officials, including a Portuguese and a Peruvian consul.   Eventually
the requisite number of coolies is secured, they are taken
aboard, and, all formalities being duly observed, the captain sets sail for Callao.   On the surface, the entire procedure amounts to a voluntary meeting of minds between
the man in Peru who needs a laborer and the coolie who
needs labor.   It is all quite legal—on the surface.   However, attention that was later given the matter, the investigations made of the "trade," and the exposures to which
it was subjected—by Peruvians, let it be noted, as well as
by non-Peruvians—drew the lines of a somewhat different
picture.   It is a picture which demands further study and
analysis.

Since emigration of Chinese was illegal, the Chinese
"runners," when not actively engaged in their vocation,
lived in Macao, where they were not subject to the Chinese
authorities.   As it was contrary to the wish of those authorities that Chinese workers be persuaded to leave the
country, and as the runners' gain depended on getting
men, it may quite readily be supposed, as was frequently
charged, that these local agents were not too conscientious
regarding the manner in which they performed their task.
One who called himself "An Eye Witness" described their
operations thus:

Their plan is to seek out a part of the country, where the people
are, as is often the case, suffering from want and hunger, and
where the poor people are constrained to listen to the proposals
made to them.   The agent gives a dollar or two to the families in
need, and he is at once considered a friend.   The bargain is soon
finished.   He contracts at four to five dollars per head a month—
not in Peru, or any country outside of Peru—but in the Portu-

guese territory of Macao, well known to every man in the country.[21]

In case the agent who made the arrangement with the
ship's captain or the representative of the future Peruvian
master should fail to secure the requisite number of men
by the day agreed upon, the latter was in a position to
make claims on the agent for return of advances made and
for damages sustained by reason of delay. In such case
the agent might have recourse to his runners to indemnify himself. Reclamations on the runner might even
force him to dispose of all his property or even to sell his
wife and children.[22] The report of a group of influential
Chinese from which these points are taken continues:

It is readily understood that such a prospect of ruin makes the
subordinate [the runner] somewhat unscrupulous in the means
which he employs to induce the coolies to emigrate. Thus it is
that, sometimes deception is used, narcotics are resorted to, and,
as a final measure, recourse is had to violence. If it happens that
the runner takes a man of some intelligence, who understands and
writes his own and the foreign language, once kidnapped, he is
thrown into an isolated prison, deprived absolutely of communication with the outside. When he is taken to Macao, he is confined on the island and they seek a third man to go to the contracting office and to make the contract in the kidnapper's place
and name, then the kidnapped man is taken on board. As it is
natural that this man, when he has had a chance to communicate
with others, should tell them of the violence to which he has been
subjected, the contractor makes up a story of this sort: "This
man has taken my money under false pretences; various times he
was asked before the authorities if he wished to emigrate and he
said 'yes,' and now that he has spent the advances made to him,

[21] *South Pacific Times*, May 25, 1872. The letter is dated May 23.
[22] "Faithful Account of the Manner of Embarking and Contracting
Chinese," a report presented to the governor of Hongkong by a deputa-
tion of influential citizens of that place (*La Patria*, Lima, Oct. 8, 1873, re-
produced from the New York *Evening Post*, published originally in the
Pall Mall Gazette).

he refuses to leave." Those friendly to the contractor repeat the fable and those placed in these circumstances do not know what to do.

The ignorant rustics are embarked with much more ease. They are induced by deceit to sign the contract, rejoiced at the idea of gaining a few dollars; they are made to believe that a year in foreign countries equals six months in China, and that a dollar in those countries in worth as much as two in this. When these men of the fields, led by the hand, arrive at the place of meeting and understand the deception of which they have been the victims, they want to go back; but they are immediately confined and made to suffer the most cruel punishments of the whip, etc., being taken before a suborned inspector, they are obliged to declare their willingness to emigrate; if they do not do so, they are punished under the pretext of having received money for such and such purpose; if they get away from there the runner follows them pursuing his objective; thus, if the said officer does not sentence them to more cruel punishments, taking them to other places where they are made to suffer new penalties and are submitted to more barbarous penalties, insisting on them until they are obliged to declare their willingness to emigrate. After which the runner takes them to a real foreign inspector of contracts, before whom they are questioned.

These abuses are accomplished with the support of inspectors suborned to that end. And if it should happen that an inspector decides to protect the abused one, it happens frequently that he cannot do justice to his complaints, owing to the diversity of dialects of these people, it being difficult to find an interpreter who knows and understands.[23]

Reference must be made in this and other connections to the findings of a Chinese commission which, in 1874, made an extensive examination of the condition of the tens of thousands of Chinese coolies who were at that time in Cuba and of the means used to get them there. The governments of China and Spain were at the time engaged

[23] *Ibid.*

in a heated controversy over a treaty which was designed
to control relations between the two nations. Prominent
in the controversy was the Chinese government's complaint of harsh treatment of the coolies in Cuba. The
Spanish minister denied accusations that they were being
cruelly mistreated. Dr. S. Wells Williams suggested
that the best means of learning the true condition of those
Chinese was to send a commission to investigate.[24] Such
a commission was formed, and by March 17, 1874, it was
in Cuba prepared to begin its work. Its three members
remained in the island until May 8, visiting many places
where coolies were employed, questioning them, taking
their depositions, and receiving their petitions. More than
2,500 Chinese told their stories to the commissioners.[25]
Exact statistics on the point are contained in the sentence,
"1,176 depositions have been collected, and 85 petitions,
supported by 1,655 signatures have been received."[26]
While the specific findings of the commission regarding
distribution and treatment relate to Cuba, the fact that
the major part of the Cuban coolies sailed from Macao,
whence most of those for Peru departed, justifies accepting their depositions—in so far as they touch on conditions
of their enlistment and treatment at Macao and on the

[24] Williams to the Chinese Foreign Office, Aug. 1, 1873 (enclosure No.
4 with Despatch No. 8), Diplomatic Despatches, China 35.
[25] *Chinese Emigration; Report of the Commission Sent by China to
Ascertain the Condition of Chinese Coolies in Cuba* (Shanghai, 1874), pp.
3-4. (To be cited in future as *Report of Cuba Commission.*) Copies of
this report are not easy to find. That which was used for this study is in
State Department National Archives; Legation Archives, Miscellany,
LXXVII (No. 247), 329-733. The commission consisted of Chan Lan-
pin, at the time of his appointment in the United States in charge of pupils
sent abroad (Prince Kung, Secretary of State for Foreign Affairs, to Williams, Tungchi, Sept. 24, 1873, copy enclosed with Williams' No. 8,
Despatches, China 35), A. Macpherson, commissioner of customs at Han-
kow, and A. Huber, commissioner of customs at Tientsin. The last two
made the English translation of the report.
[26] *Ibid.*, p. 4.

sea—as representing also the experiences of the coolies who were taken to Peru.

"All investigations of Chinese," the commission's report declares, "were conducted verbally and in person by ourselves. The depositions and petitions show that 8/10ths of the entire number declared that they had been kidnapped or decoyed."[27] It is a remarkable coincidence that a Peruvian newspaper, *La Patria,* which bears the date March 17, 1874—the very day on which the Chinese commissioners assembled in Havana, and before they had made their investigations or could have formed any definite conclusions—published an editorial in which occurs this paragraph:

The greater part, at least 80%, of the Asiatics who arrive at Paita [a port in Northern Peru] and Callao, have been victims of the most cruel deception. Some are made drunk by the speculators themselves who are engaged in providing the boats of transport for this sort of merchandise, or others are deceived with the idea that they are contracting to go to Japan or some other nearby country of that part of the Oriental Hemisphere.

As a means of striking a balance by eliminating the possible prejudice in these last two statements, one may note the opinion of Dr. S. Wells Williams, the contemporary American authority on Chinese matters. His judgment is contained in a dispatch to the Secretary of State and runs in part as follows:

The history of the coolie traffic since 1849, when the Peruvians came to Canton to get laborers to dig guano in the Chinchas Is., is a sad result of the foreign intercourse which has been forced upon China and its people. In carrying it on, the most flagitious acts have been committed by the natives upon each other, under the stimulus of rewards offered by foreigners to bring them coolies; while the character of all foreigners has been covered with

[27] *Ibid.,* p. 3.

infamy among the inhabitants of Canton province, especially in the rural districts. The cruel treatment suffered by many of these deceived people in the barracoons to force them to sign contracts and embark, is too well authenticated to be doubted. . . .

The records of this Legation contain so many statements going to prove these remarks, that I need not enlarge. . . .

Poverty and ignorance underlie the whole business, and are worked upon by crafty agents to fill their own pockets. Yet I think it altogether probable that the largest proportion of the coolies go willingly, though stupidly ignorant where they are going and what they are to do.[28]

These several witnesses are thus unanimous in their assertions respecting the use of force and deception by the runners. Almost all of the available evidence, and there is much more than has been presented, supports them. When it is recalled that the term "shanghai" was widely used in that period to describe the forcible enlistment of a ship's complement of sailors, it is not difficult to regard these statements as true.

The crimp's fee at the outset was $3.00. There was no possible check on malpractices, and it appears that he also often appropriated to himself the $8.00 which was usually advanced to the emigrant.[29] The crimp's fee eventually became more or less stabilized at $7.00 to $10.00, paid on delivery of the coolie at the collecting depots, or barracoons, in Macao.[30] The crimp's responsibility ended at the door of the barracoon. The worth of a man at Macao—that is, the sum paid by the Peruvian agent to the local agent—ranged usually from $60.00 to $80.00.[31]

Arrived at the barracoon, the coolie was under the con-

[28] Peking, April 3, 1866 (No. 27), Legation Archives, Williams, 1865-1866, XXXIII, 471-477.
[29] Morse, *op. cit.*, II, 167.
[30] MacNair, *The Chinese Abroad*, p. 211.
[31] *Callao and Lima Gazette*, July 25, 1871.

trol of the contracting agent. The barracoon was at the outset a lodging place maintained by an agent collecting emigrants for one ship sailing to one destination. Eventually, independent depots were established for the assembling and retention of coolies until an opportunity should arrive for disposing of them "in batches to speculators loading vessels."[32] By various devices the emigrant shortly was made indebted to the agent, and he was not free from the moment he entered the barracoon.[33] The barracoons at Macao were barnlike structures of considerable size. They were provided with stands where numerous articles could be obtained for a price, opium, by many reports, being one of them. There the idle men could while away their time and use the small advances of money made them in such games as fan-tan. The masters of the barracoons were usually either Chinese or Portuguese. When the man was taken into the barracoon, it was presumed that he was qualified for emigration. As indicated above, this place was also the scene of cruel punishments or "persuasions."

When the occasion for providing a ship with coolies arrived, the superintendent of emigration was requested to proceed with the formal processing and contracting of the emigrants. The contracts—at least when the regulations were observed—were made in a hall maintained for the purpose by the Portuguese government. In it the coolie candidate for emigration appeared before a commission consisting of the agent, the ship's captain, a representative of the governor of the colony, an interpreter, and two doctors, one representing the government, the other the agent. The purpose of the examination was to determine the age of the applicant (to be qualified he must

[32] Morse, *op. cit.*, II, 168.
[33] *Ibid.*

have reached at least twenty), his physical fitness for the long voyage, and his willingness to make a contract.[34] Any member of the board had a right to reject any man who appeared before it. A Peruvian merchant ship's captain, Guillermo García y García, who had experience in the coolie traffic and is the authority for the immediately preceding statements, declares that always more than half the men who appeared were rejected. After this examination, those chosen for emigration were placed in a government barracoon, where they remained three days. It was during these days that the contract was drawn and signed, according to García y García. The coolie was asked if he wished to emigrate, was told the number of days the voyage would require, and was instructed that he ought not believe any of the statements the runner may have made to him to induce him to emigrate, that the only certain facts were those specified in the contract. The contract was then read to him, and, if he signified his desire to emigrate, he passed to a near-by table and signed it, or made his mark, or "chop." At any moment, declares our authority, the coolie was free to leave Macao and return to his home if he desired to do so.[35]

[34] Guillermo García y García, "Informe que contiene importantes detalles sobre la conducta con los emigrantes chinos y otros datos relativos a esta emigración," *Documentos Parlamentarios, 1874,* "Documentos—Memoria del Ministro de Relaciones Exteriores al Congreso Ordinario de 1874," I, 195-196. This document will in future be referred to as "Guillermo García y García Report." It was written in London under date of July 14, 1873, at the request of Pedro Gálvez, Minister of Peru to Great Britain, and was incorporated in a memorial which Gálvez presented to the British government soon afterward. García y García had himself commanded a number of ships on the coolie voyage from Macao to Peru and was, it is to be presumed, thoroughly conversant with the procedure of securing the coolies, as well as transporting them. At the same time, considering the use to which the report was to be put—which the author doubtless knew when he was writing it—it is certain that he would have minimized the shady side of the operation.

[35] *Ibid.,* p. 196.

Though it is a bit long, it appears necessary because of its importance to quote one of these contracts. It purports to be the actual contract of Chie Lom, though the spaces for the date, ship, and contractor are left blank, and is typical of contracts made from about 1868:

No.....

Contract celebrated at Macao, China, this the ...... day of ....in the year of our Lord ...., between Don .... acting on behalf of Don .... of Lima on the one part, and Chie Lom a native of the district of Hiempen in China, aged 21 occupation coolie.

IT IS SOLEMNLY DECLARED in the present contract that I Chie Lom, have freely and spontaneously agreed with Don ..... to embark on board the Italian bark .... with the object of going to Peru—and I bind myself, as soon as I arrive, to place myself at the orders of the before mentioned gentleman: with which object I will serve as agricultural laborer, gardener, shepherd, house servant, or general workman, for the term of eight years, to count from the day on which I begin to serve, during which period I will plough the fields, clear the ground of bush, take care of cattle, work in the garden; or in a word I will do any other kind [of] work that may be demanded of me, making use of any knowledge as a mechanic or artizan [*sic*] that I may possess. But not in the work of extracting Guano in the Islands. It is agreed, that I am quite willing that the before mentioned term of eight years shall commence to count from the day on which I begin to serve, as has been stated, and I am fully aware, that the word *month* means, and is intended to mean a calendar month and that the word *year* means and is intended to mean twelve of such months.

IT IS AGREED that when the period of eight years has expired I shall be able to dispose freely of my labour nor can any debt which I have contracted serve as a pretext to prolong the period of my engagement, and that such debt must be sued for before the tribunals of the country.

IT IS AGREED that I am to avail myself of any benefits the laws of the country may concede me.

IT IS AGREED that during the said period of eight years I will not work for myself or any other person, save for Don . . . . or the person to whom he may make this contract over—and that I will not absent myself from his house without a written permission.

IT IS AGREED, and I am satisfied, that there shall be deducted from the salary which has been stipulated in return for my services, one sol monthly until the total of the sum of eight dollars is paid back. The said eight dollars I confess to having received from Don . . . . . . as an advance of wages.

IT IS AGREED that I shall have an hour daily for each of my two meals, and that the hours and duration of my work shall be those which are customary in the place or town to which I may be sent.

IT IS AGREED, finally, to avoid mistake, I bind myself to observe all and every one of the above clauses, not only with Don . . . . his heirs, assigns, and agents, but also with each person to whom the present contract may be transferred, according to the decree dated Jan. 7th, 1859 [1869?]—to effect which I authorize them from now, entirely and completely; nor after having done so, shall they have contracted any responsibility regarding me.

IT IS ALSO AGREED ON OUR PART, that I, the undersigned Don . . . . bind myself that as soon as possible after the arrival of the before mentioned ship, the said Don . . . . will pay the coolie, monthly, four soles, and will, besides, furnish him with lodging, as well as sufficient and wholesome food.

IT IS AGREED that during sickness, I shall be supplied in the sick quarters with the attendance my malady requires; as well as the medical help and assistance which may be necessary for my recovery, however long my illness may last. And that my wages shall still go on, except my state should have been brought about by my own fault. I am also to receive two suits of clothing— one flannel shirt, and a blanket yearly, as well as three changes to be given me on embarkation.

IT IS AGREED that my passage and maintenance from here to Peru will be paid for by Don ...., as well as any expenses which may be occasioned in the transit.

IT IS AGREED that I shall have three days, at the beginning of each new year to celebrate my religious rites.

AND IN TESTIMONY OF THE ABOVE: both parties declare that, before attaching our respective signature, we have read for the last time in a loud voice, and slowly, each and every one of the obligations to which we have mutually bound ourselves; so that at no time, nor under any circumstances, can ignorance be adduced, nor shall there be any claims made, except in case either party should fail to comply with the above stipulations, with regard to each and every one of which we are perfectly agreed.

IN PROOF of which we have today signed this solemn contract with our own hands.

Signature of CONTRACTOR.
Signature of PROCURADOR.
Signature of EMIGRATION SUPT.

The reverse page of the contract bears the signature of the Registrar; then comes the contract in Chinese and the chop of Chie Lom—the interpreter finally certifying that all is correct.[36]

Discussion of the extent to which the terms of this contract were observed in actual practice in Peru is reserved for a later chapter. Here it is necessary only to note the difficulty of securing an actual meeting of minds of the parties—a difficulty so great, it will be recalled, that a president of Peru branded such a contract as null.[37] The great majority of the Chinese laborers were illiterate. The estimate of one commentator that at least two thirds of those who went to Peru could neither read nor write[38] may well have been an understatement. Furthermore,

[36] "Trefoil," in *South Pacific Times*, June 19, 1873.
[37] See p. 28.
[38] Editorial, *La Patria*, March 17, 1874.

because of the many dialects spoken in China it was sometimes difficult, no doubt, to find an interpreter who could make a clear translation for the coolie. None of the coolies knew Spanish, the version of the contract which would be operative in Peru. It is clear that a worker might easily misunderstand the statement of obligations to which he put his mark or his name.

It is also to be noted that a contract was not always actually signed by the parties. A Peruvian source declared that "most of the so-called contracts, in spite of their bearing the certification and seal aforementioned [i.e., of the Peruvian consul], have been fulfilled and cancelled without bearing either the signature of the parties, or the date on which it was presumed by the aforementioned consul the contract was made."[39]

Respecting the contract and its making, the statement of the Cuban Commission, referring to the coolies in Cuba transported from Macao, should be noted carefully:

. . . the great majority . . . either received no contracts, or were entrapped into accepting them, or constrained by force to sign them, or induced to affix their names as if doing so merely on behalf of others; whilst the documents themselves were in some instances delivered in the barracoons and in others on board ship. None of the indicated officers [i.e., representatives of Spain and Portugal] were present when contracts were signed, and none of the specified authorizations were produced, so that provisions prescribed by both China and Spain were violated.[40]

It is well also to recall at this point the charges made of the employment of threats by crimps or in the barracoons for the purpose of persuading the coolie to testify to his willingness to emigrate. In such cases, even if the process was always conducted in the manner described by

[39] "Some Friends of Justice," *El Comercio* (Lima), Sept. 15, 1870.
[40] *Report of Cuba Commission*, p. 9.

Guillermo García y García, the use of force is not ruled
out. On this point also the Cuban Commission reported:

The petition of Yeh Fu-chün and 52 others states, "after entering
[the barracoon], the gates were closed by a foreigner, and as all
exit was prevented we perceived how we had been betrayed, but
there was no remedy; in the same chambers were more than 100
others, most of whom passed their days and nights in tears, whilst
some were dripping with blood,—the result of chastisements inflicted on account of a suspected intention of escape, or of a
declaration of their unwillingness, when interrogated by the
Portuguese inspector. The barracoon was of great depth, and,
at the time of punishment, as an additional precaution to prevent
the cries being overheard, gongs were beaten, and fireworks dis-
charged, so that death even might have ensued without detection;
and witnessing this violence, there was no course open to us but
assent, receiving at the embarkation a document, which we were
told was a contract for eight years.[41]

If all the charges made respecting fraud and deception employed in the drawing of the contract be true, a
picture of the blackest hues is seen. At least some of them
must have been true, for measures (to be discussed later)
were taken by both Peruvian and Portuguese governments
to effect changes in the situations where abuses were
charged.

Certain other features of the superintendency of the
Portuguese authorities over emigration of the coolie should
be mentioned. Each man, before embarkation, must be
furnished (at the Peruvian contractor's expense, as the
contract proves) three new suits of clothes, a small chest
about as large as a tea chest, a blanket, and a bamboo pil-
low. The suits consisted of a jumper and a wide pair of
trousers of coarse calico.[42] That they should be of the
cheapest quality was to be expected. They were also pro-

[41] *Ibid.*
[42] "Trefoil," *loc. cit.*, July 12, 1873.

vided with the necessary equipment for eating, sometimes too with cooking utensils. One witness states that when, in the course of the voyage, the ship approached a cold climate, winter clothing was issued. When the port of destination was neared, each man was issued a new suit[43] in order that he might present his best appearance for the distributive process.

The governmental authorities at Macao issued definite regulations concerning the ship itself. They must be met, presumably, before the ship was permitted to sail. The between-decks space must be at least six feet; no vessel could take more than twenty Chinese passengers without having medical stores; none could take Chinese without interpreters approved by the Chinese agency; the deck space allotted to each passenger must be at least two and a half meters. No emigrants should be received on board until the ship had been thoroughly disinfected with chloride of lime, the mixture for which was prescribed; emigrant quarters must be swept out regularly both in port and at sea and disinfected at least twice daily.[44] The regulations contained other features, but as they were designed to govern procedures while the ship was at sea, mention of them is postponed. Some idea of the extent to which they were observed in practice will be gained when the subject of the Pacific passage is treated in the succeeding chapter.

A change of administration was made at Macao in 1868 when Antonio Sergio de Sousa became governor. De Sousa made an effort to improve conditions of the coolie trade.[45] In that year wide publicity was given a story regarding the alleged branding of forty-eight coolies in

[43] Guillermo García y García Report, p. 197.
[44] *South Pacific Times*, June 14, 1873, quoting New York *World*.
[45] J. Ross Browne, U. S. Minister, to Secretary of State, Peking, June 3, 1868, Legation Archives, Browne (China), 1868, XLVII, 937-938.

Peru. The matter, along with some severe comments on
the treatment of the Chinese, was related to de Sousa by
the consul-general of Portugal in Peru. This scandal
evoked a temporary suspension of the trade at Macao,[46]
but a suspension which did not for long endure.

The abuses associated with this trade in human goods
became more notorious after 1870 when the affair of the
Nouvelle Penelope was published to the world. This
ship, of French registry, sailed from Macao on September
30, 1870, bound for Callao with 310 coolies aboard.
Some days out of port, the coolies took possession of the
ship, killing in the process the captain and eight members
of the crew.[47] They then turned the ship back to China.
Some of the passengers suceeded in escaping, but not all.
The French consul at Canton asked for and obtained the
execution of sixteen of the coolies who had been apprehended. "A Chinese gunboat brought them down from
Canton, and, landing them on a Chinese island within
sight of the windows of houses in Macao, there these sixteen men were, on the 7th of February last [1871], with
the pomp and circumstance of a grand ceremony, as on a
gala day in the presence of hundreds of spectators, be-
headed by Chinese headsmen."[48] This was not the end
of the matter, since one of the coolies, Kwok-a-sing, man-
aged to escape to the British colony of Hongkong. The
Chinese viceroy at Canton, under pressure, requested in-
formally of the English governor the rendition of the
man. Friends of Kwok-a-sing employed an attorney, a
Mr. Francis, to defend him. Application was made for a
writ of habeas corpus. A protracted process followed in a

[46] See copy of decree of suspension and of the consul-general's note as
reprinted in *El Comercio*, Feb. 27, 1869.
[47] "Judicial Opinion on the Coolie Trade to Peru," *Callao and Lima
Gazette*, July 25, 1871.
[48] *Ibid.*

British court in the course of which the history of the *Nouvelle Penelope* was pretty thoroughly investigated with regard to the recruitment and treatment of the 310 coolies which it had taken aboard.

It was established that some 180 of the coolies had been for several days awaiting a boat in the barracoons and that the remainder had been brought in on the day preceding the ship's departure. They had been taken aboard in small boats of some thirty to the boat, each load accompanied by Portuguese soldiers armed with muskets and fixed bayonets. This assertion respecting the armed soldiers was supported by statements of Portuguese authorities, crewmen of the ship, and coolies. According to the Portuguese officials the soldiers were there for the protection of the Chinese against anyone who might wish to abuse them.[49] But, according to the Chinese, the object of the soldiers was to see that none of them escaped en route to the ship.[50] In the trial it developed that at least one hundred of the coolies had not wished to emigrate to Peru but had been deceived or kidnaped. The coolie Won Ahee declared he had consented to emigrate for fear of the runner Chea Ahfook. He continued:

I indicated to the authorities my willingness to emigrate to Peru; but in the depth of my soul I never desired any such thing, although it seemed so and I said so because I was afraid of being sent to Canton and having my head cut off there, with which Chea Ahfook always threatened me. . . . I was mad at Chea Ahfook who had deceived me. I never thought of going to Peru; but I saw myself obliged by force to go aboard the ship. I was taken by two or three foreigners who followed me and some men of the "barracoon." Along with me a party of some thirty

[49] *El Comercio*, Feb. 20, 1872, quoting a statement of the Portuguese Secretary of State for Naval Matters of Aug. 9, 1871.
[50] See editorial, *ibid.*, July 22, 1871.

coolies were taken to the ship: some seemed to go with a good spirit, others with bad, crying that they had been kidnaped.[51]

The arrangements made on the boat for the passage were adduced in the trial as an indication that force was used with the coolies and that it was anticipated that they would resent the treatment to be accorded them.

There was a barrier across the deck, abaft the mainmast, constructed of strong wood four inches square and seven or eight feet high. There were two open barred doors opening aft in the barrier, and there was a cannon at each door with the muzzle pointed forward. The coolies were not allowed to pass aft the barrier, where during the day a sentry stood on duty. At night they were confined to the hold of the ship, one of the crew keeping watch at the hatchway. Aft of the barrier slept the captain and the crew, who, in addition to the two cannon mentioned above had twelve muskets and bayonets, some swords and revolvers. The ship, moreover, carried a quantity of gunpowder and grapeshot.[52]

García y García declared in his report that such arrangements as those described were "a precaution taken against cases of uprising."[53]

The evidence also brought out the facts that many of the coolies cried as they were taken aboard; that one was recaptured—and punished—when he leaped overboard intending to swim ashore; and that, after the ship reached the open sea, another sprang overboard and committed suicide.[54]

Kwok-a-sing's counsel contended that the captain of

[51] *Ibid.*

[52] *Callao and Lima Gazette*, July 25, 1871. Translation of a direct quotation by *El Comercio* of July 22, 1871, which in turn took its account from the *Hongkong Daily Press*, which had given a full account of the trial and of the sentence pronounced by the judge on March 26, 1871.

[53] *Loc. cit.*, p. 198.

[54] *El Comercio*, July 22, 1871, summarizing report of trial in *Hongkong Daily Press*.

the *Nouvelle Penelope* was engaged in a commerce notorious for its crimes, especially for that of man-stealing, that he was prima facie responsible before the law for these crimes and for the preparation of the boat for the detention of the coolies on board. It was asserted that even if slight proof could be brought to show that the captain knew that *force majeure* was used against the emigrants, under English law, assuming he were still alive, he would be punished as a pirate.

After the evidence was in, the magistrate released Kwok-a-sing. The judgment that sustained his action made these points: (1) that the commerce in coolies was a true slave trade; (2) that, consequently, one who was being forced to emigrate was in full exercise of his rights if he had recourse to violence against his oppressors in order to recover his liberty.[55]

Friends of the coolie traffic condemned the English judgment, of course, as being a product, not of a humanitarian spirit or of justice, but of a desire to favor England's own commerce in human beings.[56] However, the moral atmosphere of the West at that time was not one to condone traffic in human beings, even though the object were only "John Chinaman," still largely misunderstood and unappreciated in this part of the world. The Civil War in the United States had ended not long since with its accompanying emancipation of more than three million Negroes. Brazil was proceeding by degrees toward the abolition of slavery—the Rio Branco law was passed in the year following that in which the *Nouvelle Penelope* incident occurred.[57] And, perhaps more decisive for the fate of the Macao trade, Great Britain, for centuries an ally

[55] *Ibid.*, and July 24, 1871.
[56] See *El Comercio*, Aug. 4, 1871.
[57] That law decreed that all children of slaves were born free.

of Portugal and pretty much dominant in that country's foreign policy, was strongly set against the traffic.

The immediate response of Peru and Portugal to the condemnation of the Macao trade was a face-saving— perhaps—gesture which took the form of a consular convention, made on February 24, 1872. It confirmed for both parties the right to make in the territory of the other contracts for services or maritime transport.[58] Peru also decided about this time to appoint a minister plenipotentiary to the king of Portugal in order that measures respecting the crisis at Macao might better be attended to.[59]

In the years following the *Nouvelle Penelope* affair, foreign governments—China, England, the United States —brought pressure to bear on the Portuguese government,[60] and publicity on a wide scale continued to attack the coolie traffic at Macao. As a consequence, the trade declined considerably, as is testified by a statement from a Peruvian newspaper, quoting a mail dispatch from Hongkong:

The Fray Bentos, Peruvian ship, has been officially inspected at Macao and declared capable of taking 379 coolies. The barracoons are almost empty, and arrivals have been very scanty, seventy per cent of those examined refusing to emigrate. Trade, therefore, is very discouraging, and will be more so if the rice harvest turns out a good one. The San Juan, Luisa Canevaro, Emigrante, Manco-Capac, Rosalia, Providencia, and Fray Bentos,

[58] Peru, *Documentos Parlamentarios, 1872*, "Documentos," with Memoria del Ministro de Relaciones Exteriores al Congreso de 1872, I, 8-9. On p. vii appears the statement that this convention superseded one made in 1853.

[59] *Ibid.*, p. vii. Pedro Gálvez, minister to England and France, was appointed to the post.

[60] Pedro Gálvez to Peruvian Minister of Foreign Relations, Lisbon, April 22, 1874. *Documentos Parlamentarios, 1874*, "Documentos— Memoria del Ministro de Relaciones Exteriores al Congreso Ordinario de 1874," I, 241.

all Peruvian ships, aggregating a total of 6,676 tons, are on the berth waiting.[61]

These various pressures at length produced a closure of Macao to the coolie trade. The governor of the colony issued a decree to the effect that from March 27, 1874, no more coolies would be permitted to embark. Further, the decree embodied a provision declaring that the runners previously engaged in recruiting coolies, when they were unable to give proof of other means of subsistence, should be considered vagrants, arrested as such, and within three days shipped to their native countries.[62]

This decree virtually extinguished the trade, since the port of Macao had been for some years the only one from which vessels could clear with coolies, and was the only place where they could be forcibly detained while awaiting shipment. The governments of Peru and China were at the moment in process of negotiating a treaty which was to affect this matter importantly—a subject which will be given extended treatment in a later chapter.

From the material presented, it is quite evident that the human conscience had little place in the coolie trade.

[61] *South Pacific Times*, July 19, 1873.
[62] *Ibid.*, March 26, 1874. S. Wells Williams, consistent friend of the Chinese and critic of the coolie traffic, reporting to his government on the closure, quoted a correspondent of a Hongkong paper as announcing that the remaining vestiges of the trade were being effaced. Said the correspondent, "That large army of crimps and their satellites have disappeared; and the few Macaistas who derived their income from the traffic, have once more directed their energies and labor to other sources. Some of the late barracoons are still closed, and others have already been opened and occupied by native tradesmen; but in every one of them traces of barricades, strong iron bolts and gratings fastened by Chubb's locks are disappearing, and the floors—once dampened with tears of thousands of entrapped wretches—have been washed and oiled, so that the visitor will be able now to trace out the old Aceldama. The inhabitants now live more peacefully, and the misery and famine predicted by the disappointed coolie-catchers, still remain a vision of ill-will. . . . The coolie trade is dead forever!" (To Secretary of State, July 25, 1874 [No. 49], Diplomatic Despatches, China 36).

Those who engaged in it, whether of Portuguese, Peruvian, Chinese, or other nationality, were in it for financial gain.   While there is no doubt that some of the coolies departed for Peru, or other foreign countries, voluntarily, a great proportion of them—in all probability more than a majority—went because they were deceived or taken by force.   It is a chapter of modern history in which no one today can take pride.

III

THE PACIFIC PASSAGE

FOREIGNERS, and Peruvians as well, frequently characterized the traffic in coolies as another "African slave trade." The degree of justice contained in this description can be determined in part by a consideration of the handling of the Chinese in the 9,000-mile passage across the broadest stretch of the Pacific Ocean. Those who know something of the horrors of the "middle passage" from Africa to America in the heyday of the trade in Negroes will recall the packed holds where many suffocated; the chains with which they were loaded, the whips with which they were lashed; the instances when, to avoid capture, and perhaps hanging, the captain of the vessel ordered all of the "passengers" thrown overboard in their chains, to be sunk without trace. It will be well to bear these matters in mind when giving attention to the Pacific passage of the coolies.

The boats engaged in the trade were of several nationalities. Some evidence on this point—not a controversial one—is contained in a statement of the English governor of Hongkong, who was certainly in a position to have information regarding it. The governor, according to a Peruvian source,

says that the Italian flag was most active in it [the coolie trade] at one time, then the Peruvian and others of various nations of Central America. From the 1st of January to the 19th of October of 1872, the following boats have set sail from Hong-Kong to Macao, the greater part of which were employed in the coolie traffic: 15 Peruvian—10 French—9 Spanish—3 Dutch—1 Austrian—total: 38. Two British, two German, and two American [ships] have been sold and are now found in the service of said traffic.[1]

It has been shown that a British law of 1855 ended the participation of English vessels in the coolie trade.[2] For a time a number of vessels of the United States were active in it. But missionaries in China were strongly opposed to the traffic and exerted their influence against it,[3] and with the outbreak of the Civil War—fought, at least in part, for the purpose of freeing Negro slaves—it became very illogical that American vessels should be permitted to continue such activity. Consequently, Congress in 1862 passed an act which, while it forbade the importation of coolie contract labor into the United States, also drove American vessels from the trade.[4]

Analysis of two available lists of ships engaged in this trade will afford a somewhat more accurate idea of the nationality of the participants. One was compiled from Peruvian periodicals and covers arrivals at Callao during the period April, 1871, to late July, 1874. The list is not complete but may be considered a pretty fair sampling. The other is from Peruvian official sources and covers the nine-month period from January to October, 1872. In the latter list only arrivals at Callao are included; almost all the arrivals from Macao did, however, anchor at Callao. The table which follows presents a summary of both lists. Figures in parentheses indicate the number of different ships, additional arrivals of the same ship being eliminated:

[1] *La Patria*, Oct. 8, 1873.
[2] See p. 19.
[3] Foster, *American Diplomacy in the Orient*, p. 28.
[4] *United States Statutes-at-Large*, 1859-1863 (Boston, 1863), pp. 340-341.

	Periodicals April, 1871-July, 1874	Government Jan. 1-Oct. 3, 1872[5]
Peruvian	28 (20)	18 (14)
French	4 (4)	4 (4)
Russian	1 (1)	0
Austrian	1 (1)	0
Portuguese	3 (2)	2 (2)
Dutch	2 (1)	2 (2)
	39 (29)	26 (22)

Scattered statements from other sources agree in indicating that, in the later years at any rate, the participation of ships other than Peruvian was not heavy. With the passage of years Peruvian ships tended to take over, though the French and Portuguese persisted somewhat. To such an extent did the ships of foreign registry drop out that for the last few months of the trade—January to July, 1874—the periodicals from which the above list was compiled noted the arrival at Callao of not a single coolie ship other than Peruvian.

When the trade was begun, the ships engaged in it were not especially adapted to it, being old passenger vessels or, in some cases perhaps, converted cargo ships. All were, and for the most part continued to be, sailing vessels. As time passed and the Portuguese and Peruvian governments imposed minimum regulations regarding accommodations, the ships in general were somewhat better adapted to the activity. However, at best they were far from being well fitted for carrying large numbers of human beings long distances in a civilized manner.

The clearest description of the sleeping arrangements of one of these ships that has been encountered is that of an American scientist, J. B. Steere.[6] In 1873 he made the

[5] Figures furnished by Captain of the Port, Juan A. Moore, to Thomas J. Hutchinson, printed in *Two Years in Peru with Explorations of Its Antiquities* (London, 1873), I, 246-247.

[6] Steere was sent out by the University of Michigan to make collections in natural history. Steere himself said that he entered Peru from the

voyage from Callao to China on one of the coolie ships which was returning to China for a cargo.   He wrote:

The ship on which I made the voyage from Callao to China was of 1,300 tons burden, and her hold was fitted up with bunks for eight hundred Chinese.   [Note the overloading; on the two-ton ratio, then presumably in effect, it should have carried but 650.] There were two tiers of platforms, one above the other, running entirely around the vessel, and upon them were numbered, in Chinese and Arabic, the space allotted to each man, which was something less than two feet in width and five in length.   There was also a double tier of the same running down the center of the ship, leaving a narrow passage on each side between bunks.[7]

Sir Clements Markham, an English historian and a great friend of Peru, made an effort to defend the Peruvians when criticism of the traffic became very bitter.   All he said of the ships is contained in this passage:

The ships taking coolies from Macao to Callao may be divided into two classes—first, those belonging to the emigration companies established at Lima, and second, those which are hired.   The first class consist of large, well-found vessels, with 6½ feet between decks, and sufficient space for each emigrant.   These ships are well ventilated, and there is provision for medical attendance.   The Isabel, America, Camilo Cavour, Fray Bentos, and Rosalia are good for their class; and Messrs. Samuda have recently built a steamer on purpose for this traffic, in which hygiene and ventilation have been especially studied.[8]

Markham's statements are not detailed.   His vagueness may well have been owing to a desire to put the

Amazon, crossing to the Pacific near Trujillo.   He visited the northern part of Peru, the region about Lima, and the Andean heights north and east of Lima (Bailey to Davis, Hongkong, Sept. 12, 1873, and enclosure 3 [Steere's letter], *United States Foreign Relations*, 1873, pp. 207-208).
    [7] *Ibid.*
    [8] "From China to Peru—The Emigration Question," published originally in the *Geographical Magazine*, reprinted in *South Pacific Times*, Jan. 21, 1875.

matter in a good light for Peru.   In fact, two of the boats which he mentioned by name, the *América* and the *Rosalia*, will later be found listed with ships on which had occurred a very high death rate on the passage.

Guillermo García y García, in his "Report," also touches very lightly on the arrangement of these ships which were used previous to 1874 but goes into great detail in describing the excellent features of the Samuda boat—referred to by Markham—which was shortly to be launched![9] This boat may have been the *Florencia*. From another source we learn that this vessel, probably put into the trade late in 1873, was fitted up "in a costly manner" with several improvements. They included between-decks ventilation, separate quarters for the sick, an "admirable" means of cooking, a distilling apparatus to be used in case the 50,000 gallons of water of the storage tanks should be exhausted, and security from fire—provided by iron decks covered with cement below and with wood on upper decks and a large complement of lifeboats. "It will thus be seen that one of the various efforts which have been made to deprive the coolie-emigration of one of its most objectionable features [misery on the passage] . . . is in a fair way of being carried out."[10]   Actually, when the *Florencia* was launched, it was already too late to be of much use before the trade was ended.   So much would scarcely have been made of these new items of equipment if they had been standard on the ships formerly in use.   The fact that the two Peruvian apologists had so little to say of the older ships may be considered significant.

The better captains at the commencement of the voyage effected an efficient organization for the daily regime of the boat, i.e., for handling the Chinese.   Guillermo

[9] *Loc. cit.*, pp. 194-195.
[10] *South Pacific Times*, Jan. 6, 1874.

García y García may be considered one such captain if, as it may be presumed was the case, he put into effect the organization which he described as customary:

All the colonists are organized on board on a military footing. The mass of them is divided into platoons of fifty men each, and each platoon into squads of ten. For each platoon a sergeant is named who is paid four pesos at the departure from Macao and four pesos on arrival in Peru, and a barber with three pesos on departure and three pesos on arrival. For each squad is named a corporal charged with caring for the food and cleaning the utensils, a laundryman and a tailor (*costurero*). To command the entire expedition, a superior chief is named, to whom is lent every class of aid and considerations. Ten or a dozen men are appointed as cooks with three pesos each, ten or fifteen as stewards with two pesos each, and thirty or forty as sailors, who aid the crew in good weather and only in work on deck. With the expedition thus organized, the interior policing of the boat is executed with the precision of a warship and thus, personal cleanliness, the cleanliness of the ship, and marching exercises are daily and obligatory. Everyone is always uniformed and every three days clothing is changed, and the soiled washed and dried well. Baths are always required when the weather and the health of the individual permit them. In the between-decks in different places are posted the regulations for interior police, written in Chinese.[11]

Part of the procedure thus detailed was in compliance with the Portuguese regulations for cleanliness and hygiene en route. It was required by those regulations to disinfect the boat regularly; to inspect the emigrants each day to see that they kept themselves, their bedding, and their garments properly clean. Smoking of tobacco in quarters was strictly forbidden, but a section of the ship was reserved for smoking—tobacco, and opium in small quantities—at prescribed times. Once a week the emi-

[11] Report, p. 198.

grants must open their chests and air their clothing on deck, and once a week their change of clothing must be washed in boiling water with bleaching powder.[12] Too, the men were to be given daily an opportunity to take the air and the sun on deck. García y García stated that for the entertainment of the colonists Chinese musical instruments—violins, flutes, tambourines, drums, and others— were distributed, and that they were encouraged to present comic skits and other entertainment that suited their taste.[13]

The regulations read well. However, no government inspector traveled on the vessels and, judged by results, they must often have been honored merely in the breach. For example, in the case of one vessel, the *Luisa Canevaro*, of Peruvian registry, where a very high death rate had been experienced on the voyage, the fact was explained as due to the misfortune of continued storms and high winds which lasted a month and necessitated the battening down of the hatches for that period. In all that time, presumably, the men were not brought on deck, nor would they have been able to do much in the way of washing garments and bedding. Neither could their quarters have been disinfected while they were occupied.[14] The appearance of dysentery—stated as the cause of the deaths— would not, in such circumstances, be surprising. Nor would it be astonishing if some smothered for lack of air. At any rate, of the 739 coolies embarked (in a vessel of only 1,043 tons—an overload of 50 per cent), 192 died before the ship reached Callao—about 26 per cent.

Already we have seen that the mortality in the 1850's was often very high.[15] A case in point not previously

[12] *South Pacific Times*, June 14, 1873.
[13] Report, p. 199.
[14] *South Pacific Times*, May 23, 1872.
[15] See p. 18 for the cases of the *Empresa* and another boat.

noted is that of the Peruvian boat *Cora*. It lost on the crossing 117 of a passenger total of 292—about 40 per cent—presumably from the bad quality of the water consumed.[16] Such losses as these help to account for the abolition of the commerce in coolies in 1856.

After the trade was resumed in 1861, it shortly became evident that comprehensive regulations must be imposed if such tragic results were not to be repeated. If the available figures can be trusted—and we believe they merit that tribute—for the years 1860-1863 the annual mortality percentages were, respectively, 29.59, 22.58, 41.55, and 29.13. The total of embarkations in these four years was 7,884, of deaths 2,400—mortality for the four years 30.44 per cent.[17] What a ghastly sacrifice of human life for monetary gain! No wonder the government of Peru decided that a regulatory decree was in order. It appeared under date of October 9, 1864. The minister who published it, Gómez Sánchez, wrote this revealing introduction:

By data which I have and communications that have been brought to my attention, I am informed that the immigration of Asiatics is taking place under such bad conditions that their mortality ascends to the fourth part and even the third part of those that each boat brings. This calamity results from the excessive number of colonists embarked in cramped and badly equipped boats, from the food of scant quantity and bad quality, from careless and even cruel treatment, and from lack of observance, in short, of all the rules of hygiene with which they ought to be transported.

The minister then, in the name of the president, went on to state the dispositions which must in future be observed on all coolie-carrying boats that sailed for Peru.

[16] Arona, *La inmigración en el Perú*, p. 71 n.
[17] Hutchinson, *op. cit.*, I, 246.

The Peruvian consul in China, i.e., in Macao, was directed to see that they were enforced. They ran:

1st. That no boat shall embark more than one colonist for each registered ton, according to the requirements of the law of March 14, 1861.

2nd. That the food shall be healthful and in quantity more than sufficient for the number embarked.

3rd. That the clothing for the use of each immigrant shall be appropriate to the waters navigated and each shall be furnished the necessary shelter.

4th. That the bed assigned for the lodgment of the colonists shall be spacious, clean, and sufficiently ventilated.

5th. That each boat shall have a doctor and the medicines necessary for the healing of emigrants, and

6th. That the Consul shall comply with all of the dispositions contained in the cited law, and remit the certificate which accredits the boat coming with having fulfilled the requirements.

Furthermore, a copy of the decree was sent to the Prefect of the Province of Callao with instructions to examine each boat arriving to ascertain whether or not the conditions had been fulfilled. He was also directed to report to the minister the measures of punishment taken in cases of violation.[18] The thoughtful reader will observe that the decree was indefinite in its terms and decidedly lacking in "teeth." For instance, how much space is "spacious"?

By an additional decree, issued in 1868, the English rule respecting number of passengers each boat might carry was put into effect—that no boat might carry coolies to a number greater than one to each two tons of registry.[19]

[18] Zegarra, *La condición jurídica de los estranjeros en el Perú*, "Apéndice," pp. 34-35.
[19] Aurelio García y García to Peruvian Minister of Foreign Relations, Tientsin, Nov. 26, 1873. *Documentos Parlamentarios, 1874,* "Documentos, etc.," I, 226.

This regulation—when observed—meant a cutting in half of the legitimate number of passengers possible under the decree of 1864.

The minimum food requirements were not stated in the Peruvian decree of 1864. The Portuguese regulation cited previously was, however, quite specific. The daily food ration was prescribed in these terms:

Rice, 1 1/2 lbs.
Salt pork, or 2/3 salt pork and 1/3 fish, or 1/3 pork, 1/3 beef, and 1/3 fish, 1/2 lb.
Vegetables, 1/2 lb.
Tea, 1/3 oz.
Fire wood for cooking, 20 oz.

Seven gallons of water a week must be provided each Chinese. The ship must carry provisions for one hundred days, if a sailing vessel bound for California or western America north of the equator, between October and March, and for seventy-five days on a voyage between April and September. South of the equator, the passage from Macao to America must be calculated at one hundred and twenty days the year around.[20]

While the daily ration of two and one-half pounds of meat, rice, and vegetables, with one-third ounce of tea, may be considered adequate under the circumstances, as far as quantity was concerned, it did not afford much opportunity for variety. On a voyage of one hundred days, more or less, it must have become very monotonous, if not actually repulsive. No doubt the outbreaks of scurvy which were sometimes experienced could be traced to dietary deficiencies. Moreover, verification at Macao that required quantities for this diet were on board when the boat sailed was, in itself, no guarantee that those quantities

[20] *South Pacific Times*, June 14, 1873, quoting New York *World*.

were issued to the men during the voyage. Facts later to be noted suggest that in many instances ships' captains or contractors issued rations much below the Portuguese requirements. The fact that the coolies had to prepare their own meals and that the quantity of water provided was but one gallon per capita per day, gave much latitude for unhygienic handling of food and cooking utensils. It is perhaps not surprising that neither the shipping men of the time ,nor the humble Chinese were very cleanliness-conscious.

Guillermo García y García declared that the imputation that food on board these boats was insufficient was "calumnious and absurd." He went on to say: "Without fear of equivocation I can give assurance that the greater part of the colonists have not in their lives had better food than during the time of their stay on board." To the items of food already indicated, he added as being provided, "preserved vegetables, fresh cereals, tea and *aguardiente* or wine." He further declared that the ships always arrived at Callao with a bountiful surplus of various articles of food (which might be given a meaning quite contrary to that which he intended). According to him, for 450 men "six head of cattle and 20 live hogs were always embarked."[21] The worthy captain cannot be criticized, perhaps, for "putting his best foot forward" when he wrote for British eyes his report on the traffic in which he himself had played a role, but the history of the matter scarcely bears out his declarations.

The terrible mortality rate en route in the years 1860-1863 has already been remarked. The subject merits further attention. The same table from which the rates previously mentioned were calculated presents figures up to and including the year 1870. In those additional seven

[21] Report, p. 199.

years, 35,417 coolies were embarked at Macao for Peru; 2,253 died at sea. This represents a mortality rate of 6.6 per cent.[22] There was, then, a remarkable drop in deaths on the crossing in the latter part of the decad 1860-1870, a drop which had begun even prior to the publication of the decree of October, 1864. Perhaps fore-knowledge of the coming decree was influential in pro-ducing it—or it may be that so many deaths reduc⁓ ' profits unbearably. If the eleven years included in the two sets of figures be considered together, the mortality rate obtained is 10.74 per cent.

Another set of specific, official figures on this point covers the period January 1-October 3, 1872. In that period of nine months the coolies embarked for Peru numbered 11,933. Deaths on the voyage were 956—a rate of 8 per cent.[23] One additional set of figures: In the five years 1870-1874 (to the end of July only, since the trade was ended in July), 41,190 coolies were taken aboard at Macao; 3,047 died en route—a mortality of 6.5 per cent.[24] After the decree of 1864 went into effect, the annual death rate on the passage wavered between 6 and 9 per cent. In the 1870's, after the one-coolie-to-two-tons-of-registry decree, the rate was at times considerably less.

Even after 1868, however, there were not a few individual voyages on which the rate was tragically higher. The following table includes a list of such cases, probably most of them, for they excited attention. The relative data are included. A remarkable fact to be noted is the frequency with which the name of Canevaro & Company, as consignee, appears in these cases of unusually high death rates:

[22] Hutchinson, *op. cit.*, I, 246.
[23] *Ibid.*, I, 247.
[24] Arona, *op. cit.*, p. 55.

FLOGGING COOLIES

From *Harper's New Monthly Magazine*, XXIX (June, 1864), 5.

CASES OF EXCEPTIONAL MORTALITY

Ship	Registry	Arr. Callao	Coolies Embkd.	Died en Route	Per Cent Deaths	Consignee
Enrique IV	French	12/20/1868	458	'142	31.00[25]	?
Luisa Canevaro	Peruv.	5/11/1872	739	192	25.90	Canevaro & Co.[26]
Emigrante	Portug.	6/11/1872	499	107	21.84	Canevaro & Co.[27]
Rosalia	Peruv.	6/12/1872	457	64	14.00	Dim. Filgueira [28]
América	Peruv.	6/13/1872	690	105	15.20	Cía. Marítima[29]
Antares	French	6/30/1872	263	82	31.10	Canevaro & Co.[30]
Hong Kong	Peruv.	9/12/1872	314	37	11.80	Canevaro & Co.[31]
Onrust	Dutch	9/28/1872	453	45	9.89	Canevaro & Co.[32]
Bengolar	French	12/17/1872	341	38	11.00	?[33]
Colombia	Austr.	3/26/1873	300(?)	100+	c. 33.00	?[34]
San Juan	Peruv.	9/ 9/1873	866	168	19.40	Juan Ugarte[35]
Emigrante	Portug.	9/ ?/1873	502	75	14.90	Canevaro & Co.[36]
Guillermo	Peruv.	1/ ?/1874	224	32	14.30	?[37]
Totals (13 voyages)			6,106	1,187	19.44	

Information respecting the specific causes of death has proved impossible to obtain with clarity and exactness. In one case, after the number of deaths was chronicled, the cause was given as "of different diseases, plus one who threw himself into the water."[38] The loss on the notorious passage of the *Luisa Canevaro* was attributed officially to dysentery. In the *Colombia* case, scurvy was given as the cause.[39] Respecting the *San Juan's* deaths, no expla-

[25] *El Mercurio* (Santiago de Chile), Dec. 23, 1868, quoting Callao's *El Porvenir*.
[26] *South Pacific Times*, May 23, 1872.
[27] *South Pacific Times*, June 13, 1872; Hutchinson, *op. cit.*, I, 247.
[28] *Hutchinson*, ibid.
[29] *Ibid.*
[30] *Ibid.*
[31] *Ibid.*
[32] *South Pacific Times*, Oct. 1, 1872.
[33] *Ibid.*, Dec. 19, 1872.
[34] *Ibid.*, March 27, 1873. The data are not exact, the paper merely reporting, "The frigate *Colombia* and the bark *Cecilia* arrived recently from Macao with more than 600 coolies," and adding that the first had had a bad passage, losing more than 100 of the emigrants aboard.
[35] *Ibid.*, Sept. 4 and 11, 1873.
[36] *Ibid.*, Sept. 25, 1873.
[37] *Ibid.*, Jan. 13, 1874. Exact date of arrival not noted.
[38] *El Porvenir*, March 13, 1871.
[39] *South Pacific Times*, March 27, 1873.

nation is ventured, but the newspaper declared that it was
thought that the captain had acted in good faith, whatever
that may mean.[40]

But if there is a dearth of adequate official statements
of causes of death, there is no lack of unofficial explanations. Among them are mentioned overcrowding, bad
food, insufficient food, lack of proper ventilation, bad hygienic conditions, carelessness of captain and, over and
over, a desire for gain so strong that it leads to carelessness
regarding the coolie's life. A specimen indictment runs:

> The lack of hygiene is the sole cause of the frightful mortality
> which the manifest of the captains discloses. Without light, with-
> out ventilation, mixed together in a confused heap (*revueltos en
> confuso acinamiento*), subjected to miserable food, they are
> thrown into a veritable pigsty and they perish under the influence
> of such causes combined.[41]

Perhaps most, if not all, of the factors mentioned are
needed to explain the death rate. Even the annual average of 6 to 9 per cent of the later years can scarcely be
called low except by comparison with the fearfully high
rates of an earlier time. There had to be something badly
wrong to occasion so many deaths. There were even some
who believed that the numbers of the dead were not correctly reported, that sometimes the true figures were two
or three times those announced to the public.[42] Many
critics of the trade dwell upon the emaciated and woebe-
gone appearance of the coolies when they were taken from
the boats at Callao. It may well be that physical inspection at Macao did not eliminate many who were unfit
for the voyage. At any rate, one conclusion readily arrived
at is that the trade must have paid very well indeed if such

[40] *Ibid.*, Sept. 11, 1873.
[41] *La Patria*, July 9, 1872.
[42] See editorial in *El Comercio*, July 24, 1871.

losses could be sustained and the dealer yet be able to remain in the business.

Competition between the carriers has been advanced as one of the causes of overcrowding. For the passage from Macao to Peru the sum usually paid was $70.00. Competition took the form of overloading and not of reducing the charge for passage.[43] This type of competition was, of course, practiced in direct contravention of both Peruvian and Portuguese regulations.

Given the conditions that surrounded the movement of the coolie from his home through Macao and to the decks of the boat, and the hard situation in which he found himself on the ocean voyage, it can be understood that the captain and crew of the ship should have been concerned about their personal safety. The strong barrier on the deck which divided the section reserved for the coolies from that of the captain and crew, the cannon, and the closed hatches with their armed guards—mentioned when the case of the *Nouvelle Penelope* was being investigated —become highly logical matters. They are also very revealing. Such equipment is not needed when men are moving of their own will and when they are receiving decent treatment. Its presence leads to some damning conclusions.

These conclusions are not weakened by what we know of the efforts frequently made by the coolies to protect themselves by use of force. Public opinion believed such efforts to be numerous. Said an editorial writer in one of Peru's leading newspapers:

... it can be established in an almost absolute manner, and without possibility of denial, but for one or another very rare exception, that there is not a boat that arrives in Callao with Chinese

[43] Morse, *The International Relations of the Chinese Empire*, II, 170.

immigrants, on which there has not been one or more uprisings, or threats of uprisings, at least, during the voyage.[44]

The Englishman Duffield relates an incident that is worth repeating. He says that in Peru it was once his lot to be seated in a very small room, filled for the most part with guano men, when he was compelled to listen to the tale of an Italian who had served as chief mate on a ship freighted with Chinese. The Italian declared that once he thought his life was in danger.

"And what did you do under the circumstances?" enquired someone.

"I shot two of them down, *sacramento*," answered the villain-ous-looking wretch; on which there was a burst of laughter that did not seem to me to be very appropriate.

"And what was done with *you?*" I enquired in no sym-pathising tone.

"Senor," replied the assassin, "the captain, Senor Venturini, accommodated me with a passage in his gig to the shore, where I remained to make an extensive acquaintance with the Celestial Empire."

The cold insolence of this criminal suggested to me that I had just as well keep my troublesome tongue as still as possible.[45]

Dr. Williams reported from Peking on a number of cases where, early in 1866, the Chinese took matters into their own hands. The *Napoleon Canevaro*, when bound for Havana from Macao, was set on fire not far from the coast. From members of the crew that were picked up, it was learned that "symptoms of insubordination appear-ing among the coolies, the captain drove them below and battened down the hatches; flames soon appeared, which the captain vainly endeavored to extinguish, and left the ship in the boats, without even taking off the hatches." A

[44] *El Comercio*, July 24, 1871. See also *La Patria*, March 17, 1874.
[45] *Peru in the Guano Age*, p. 44.

few weeks earlier, a British ship, *Pride of the Ganges*, bound for Guiana with some three to four hundred emigrants, had been captured by the passengers who rose up against the captain and crew and compelled the first mate to land them on Hainan Island. A third ship, the French boat *Hongkong*, bound for Havana with more than three hundred Chinese, was taken over by a score of them "who had armed themselves at Whampoa." Aided by the rest, they took what treasure there was and nearly all escaped to land, "where they in turn were plundered by the fishermen."[46]

The coolies, in not a few cases, were so determined to avoid going to Peru that they set fire to their ship. *El Comercio*, in an editorial of the issue of July 25, 1871, declared that "in recent times" boats with more than three thouand coolies aboard had been scuttled, burned, or in other manners destroyed, or taken possession of by coolies, with great loss of life. The assertion was made apropos of a discussion of the case of the *Nouvelle Penelope*. The same editorial mentioned the burning of the coolie ship *Dolores Ugarte*. Another case in which the passengers made great efforts to escape was that of the *Maria Luz*. This incident, probably the most notorious of the sort, is reserved for later treatment in some detail.

The uprisings on shipboard were explained by some as being due, not to scarcity or badness of food, but rather to the fact that so many of the Chinese had been deceived or kidnaped to get them aboard.[47]

A proper finale for this subject of the treatment of the coolies on board ship is a paragraph from the report of the Cuba Commission. It is deeply pathetic and highly revealing:

[46] To Secretary of State, Peking, April 3, 1866 (No. 78 ½). Legation Archives, Williams, 1865-1866, XXXIII, 477-478.
[47] *La Patria*, March 17, 1874.

The petition of Chao-ch'un and 165 others states, "when, quitting Macao, we proceeded to sea, we were confined in the hold below; some were even shut up in bamboo cages, or chained to iron posts, and a few were indiscriminately selected and flogged as a means of intimidating all others; whilst we cannot estimate the deaths that, in all, took place, from sickness, blows, hunger, thirst, or from suicide or by leaping into the sea." The petition of Ch'iu Pi-shan and 35 others states, "If the master be a good man the sufferings are only those produced by grave maladies, but if his disposition be cruel there is no limit to the ill-usage, and there have been cases when more than half the number on board have died. Ten thousand hardships have to be endured during the voyage of several months." ... The petition of Yeh Fu-chün and 52 others states, "the winds and waves on the ocean were great, and three months have passed away, but we had not arrived; as there was no water issued it had to be bought, and for a single cup a dollar was paid. The hatchway only allowed one man at a time to go down or up, and the stench below from the crowd of men was most offensive, and the deaths thence produced were without number."[48]

How many coolies were introduced into Peru? This is a question to which it is not possible to give an absolute answer since Peruvian statistics of the time, whether of entering coolies or many other matters, are lacking or incomplete. It is to be recalled that there was trouble with Spain in the years 1864-1866 and that a civil war followed in 1867. Even if a good system of records had been in operation earlier, it would have been very hard to keep it operating perfectly in those circumstances. The difficulties respecting arriving at exact numbers of coolies are clearly stated in these words of a highly placed Peruvian official in a statement of 1870:

As much for lack of statistical data as because of the irregu-

[48] Pp. 12-13. Of the more than 140,000 coolies who sailed for Cuba, more than 16,000 died en route, a percentage of some 11.4 (*ibid.*).

larity and confusion in which the Chinese immigration finds itself in consequence of the disorder which has reigned relative to the number of shiploads introduced, the transference of their contracts, the permanence or not of the colonists on the farms to which they have been sent, and those who have terminated their contracts, it is in every respect difficult to designate the number of those who have been introduced into the Republic, although the most judicious calculations are approximated at forty to fifty thousand, actually residing in the territory.[49]

Juan de Arona quoted a Peruvian writer to the effect that in the decade 1850-1859 the Chinese that arrived in Peru numbered 13,000.[50] This convenient round number may well be an approximation. The British consul-general to Peru in the early 1870's, Thomas J. Hutchinson, who was in a position to secure his figures from an official source, and so credited them, gives in his book a table of arrivals for the eleven years 1860-1870. His total for the period is 38,648.[51] Arona states that in the lustrum 1870-1874 the number of entries totaled 43,-143.[52] If the figures for the overlapping year 1870, as Hutchinson gives them, be deducted, we have for the four years 1871-1874 the number 35,599. The following total for the period 1850-1874 is, therefore, obtained:

CHINESE ARRIVALS 1850-1874

1850-1859	13,000
1860-1870	38,648
1871-1874	35,599[53]
Total	87,247

[49] *Memoria que presenta el Ministro de Estado en el despacho de Gobierno, Policía y Obras Públicas al Congreso de 1870* (Lima, 1870), pp. 56-57 (a pamphlet).
[50] *Op. cit.*, p. 56, quoting Borja, *La inmigración china.*
[51] *Op. cit.*, p. 246.   [52] *Op. cit.*, p. 55.
[53] "The last cargo of Chinese contracted to the number of 369 entered Callao on July 2, 1874, in the Peruvian frigate *Lola* of 904 tons, proceeding from Macao in 95 days and consigned to Juan de Ugarte" (Arona, *op. cit.*, p. 55).

Richard Gibbs, minister of the United States to Peru, arrives at a slightly different total. Attributing his statistics to "trustworthy sources," he reported to his government at the end of 1874, when the trade had ended, that the Chinese taken to Peru in the years 1860-1874 numbered 86,692. If the 13,000 taken in the 1850's be added, the total is 99,692.[54] A German traveler's total (no authority cited), is 87,952.[55] The Peruvian del Río gives the number for the entire twenty-five years as 87,393.[56] Except for Gibbs's figures, there is very close agreement. It may be that his total was actually meant to include the decade of the fifties. The Peruvian Envoy Extraordinary and Minister Plenipotentiary to China, Naval Captain Aurelio García y García, made to a high Chinese official the statement that the total of Chinese immigration to Peru reached nearly one hundred thousand.[57] The figures already presented are not far from the generalization of the minister. It is quite possible, of course, that the statistics presented are incomplete in some respects, e.g., no account has been taken anywhere of the coolies who were brought in 1849—they could hardly have been more than a few hundred. It seems reasonable, from the evidence, to take the round number 90,000 as representing approximately the Chinese "immigration" to Peru in the quarter century 1849-1874.

For its probable interest to the reader and because it gives the basis for some significant conclusions and, in some sense, summarizes a part of the material presented

[54] To Secretary of State, Lima, Nov. 13, 1874 (No. 107), Diplomatic Despatches, Peru 28.
[55] E. W. Middendorf, *Peru: Beobachten und Studien über das Land und Seiner Bewohner während eines 25 Jährigen Aufenthalts. I Band Lima* (Berlin, 1893), p. 241.
[56] *La inmigración y su desarrollo en el Perú*, p. 46.
[57] To Peruvian Minister of Foreign Relations, Tientsin, Oct. 31, 1873, *Documentos Parlamentarios, 1874*, "Documentos, etc.," I, 210.

above, the Hutchinson table several times cited is presented herewith. The mortality percentages are not in the original but are calculated from Hutchinson's figures:

ARRIVALS OF CHINESE IN CALLAO 1860-1870

Year	Arrived	Sailed from Macao	Deaths on Passage	Percentage deaths on passage
1860	1,413	2,007	594	29.59
1861	1,440	1,860	420	22.58
1862	1,003	1,716	713	41.55
1863	1,628	2,301	673	29.13
1864	6,410	7,010	600	8.56
1865	4,540[58]	4,794	254	5.30
1866	5,929	6,543	614	9.38
1867	2,184[59]	2,400	216	9.00
1868	4,266	4,387	121	2.79
1869	2,291[60]	2,366	75	3.21
1870	7,544	7,917	373	4.71
	38,648	43,301	4,653[61]	10.74

It will be observed from this table and from the totals cited for the period 1871-1874 that, despite the miseries of the passage, the deaths en route, and the severe criticism leveled at the trade by Peruvian and foreigner, there was a gradual increase in importations, the great immigration taking place during the last half dozen years. Business was booming in Peru in those years. Cotton, because of continued disorganization in the cotton-producing section of the United States, was selling at a high price. Agricultural products of other types, because of the Franco-Prussian War, had a better market than formerly. Moreover, Henry Meiggs was building railroads, or projecting them, all over the Andes. They required a great increase in the labor forces of the country, and part of the requirement, as will be seen more clearly later, was supplied by

[58] Drop caused by the war with Spain.
[59] Drop caused by the civil war.
[60] Drop due to temporary suspension of coolie trade at Macao.
[61] *Op. cit.*, I, 246.

the coolie trade. Certain types of small industry also were making use of the coolie.

With every effort to be fair, it must be admitted that the coolie trade did, in many respects, resemble the African slave trade. In the force used in securing many of the "passengers" for the coolie boats; in the disregard at sea of the well-being of the Chinese so frequently proved by the tragic death rate; in the extreme distrust of each other of coolies and ships' captains and crews which sometimes led to insurrections and the burning of ships; in the interest in profits to the exclusion of humane treatment of "cargo"—in all of this is evident a disregard of the Chinese coolie as a human being. And from it all rises a stench as from the hold of a slave ship. The procurement and the passage do not, of course, tell the whole story. There still remains to be examined the treatment accorded the coolie when he became a laborer and was subject to a Peruvian master.

IV

RECEPTION AT CALLAO; DISTRIBUTION

AS THE COOLIE SHIP approached the Peruvian port, crew and coolies enacted a bustling scene of cleansing activity. The coolies washed their garments and got their scanty equipment in as good order as possible, very probably with much emphatic encouragement from captain and crew members. Each "passenger," says Guillermo García y García, received "a new summer suit, a hat, and a pair of shoes."[1] Decks were scrubbed, and immigrant quarters were cleaned and fumigated. Everything possible was done to get the sick on their feet. The ship must pass official inspection, and the "cargo" must be disposed of.

While procedure at Callao probably varied somewhat in different periods of the trade and with the decrees and laws promulgated for its regulation, there was always some type of official inspection, however cursory it may have been. In the 1870's, at the height of the trade, it went in the manner to be described. Our description is derived from the defenders of the trade, hence it may be presumed that everything was put in the best possible light and that shortcomings, when they existed, were ignored or glossed over.

On arrival, the ship was held incommunicado until it had received the visit of the port health authorities and undergone an inspection to verify its freedom from communicable diseases. It was then visited by the captain of

[1] Report, p. 197.

the port. This official examined the ship's documents, received those which were his due, and was given information of any accidents that may have occurred in the course of the voyage.[2] Then followed inspection by a group headed by the prefect of the Department of Callao, highest ranking representative of the national government. The prefect was accompanied by the captain of the port, a member of the Municipality of Callao, and an interpreter. This group were under obligation to inspect the food, note the cleanliness (or the contrary) of the boat, its general hygienic arrangements, and the state of health of the coolies. The interpreter was present to enable the inspectors to determine whether or not the Chinese had entered into their contracts voluntarily as well as to enable them to make complaints of their treatment during the voyage.[3] It will be recalled that the decree of October, 1864, had placed on the prefect the obligation of punishing captains for any infractions of the decree and reporting to the executive the nature of punishments inflicted.[4]

The governor of Macao, late in the 1860's, had recommended particularly to the Portuguese consul-general in Peru that he visit on its arrival in Peru every boat laden with coolies from Macao and report to the governor the treatment which the Chinese had received on the passage.[5] If this injunction was observed—and García y García declared that it was[6]—then the Portuguese official must also have visited the ship, very probably.in company with the Peruvian officials above mentioned.

Critics of the trade spoke often of the ill effects of the

[2] *Ibid.*, p. 200.   [3] Contributor to *El Comercio*, Aug. 8, 1871.
[4] See p. 63.
[5] Narciso Velarde, Portuguese consul-general, to Juan M. Polar, Peruvian Minister of Foreign Affairs, Lima, June 17, 1868 (*El Comercio*, Feb. 27, 1869).
[6] Report, p. 200: "Igualmente se recibe á bordo la visita del Ministro de Portugal el cual práctica una ceremonia semejante al del Prefecto."

voyage on the coolies. "Thin and wan enough they look— even the stoutest of them are, sometimes, mere 'bags of bones.' "[7] Another asked pointed questions concerning the results of the official *visita*. ". . . how many Chinese have been released by the authorities at Callao, as brought here against his [*sic*] will? Has *one* ever been released?"[8] No record has been discovered that details the punishment meted out to a captain or a dealer for lack of compliance with the regulations, though, of course, there may have been some cases. It will be recalled that even in the case of the *San Juan*, which had sustained in the passage a death rate of almost 20 per cent, it was declared that the captain was thought to have acted in good faith.

The official inspection was, probably, in most cases formal and rather perfunctory. The Peruvian dealers in human flesh were as a rule men of position and means, and it is quite probable that ways were readily found for avoiding punishment for carelessness in handling this traffic. One does not have to go back three quarters of a century to discover, in countries better organized than Peru then was, cases of corruption among port authorities. (Americans would do well at this point to recall the corruption in the New York Port Authority which existed in the 1870's and 1880's and was not cleared up until the latter decade.)

The official inspection completed and the proper certificate of compliance with legal requirements furnished the captain by the officers, all was ready for the "sale." The word in this context was bitterly objected to by the defenders of the trade, but when one notes the procedure followed in effecting distribution of the coolies, it is difficult to escape the feeling that the word is a just one. For that matter, there were also those who objected to the word "trade" as we have used it.

[7] Editorial in *South Pacific Times*, May 24, 1873.
[8] "A Hater of Tyranny," *ibid.*, Sept. 5, 1871.

It was not unusual for a single person to contract for an entire shipload of coolies. In that case the procedure was simple. The coolies, along with their contracts, were simply turned over at Callao to him or to his agent and were taken to the work for which they were destined. A specimen case is that in which Henry Meiggs, the railroad builder, contracted with Candamo and Company, coolie importers, for the entire cargo of the ship *Clotilde*. The conditions were stated in a letter from Meiggs to the importer. They may be summarized in these words:

1. The ship on arrival should go to Callao or Paita (a port in northern Peru) for orders, then proceed immediately to Pacasmayo or Ferrol (ports of entry for roads which Meiggs was building in north central Peru).

2. The coolies must be debarked within forty-eight hours after they were brought to port.

3. The price to be paid for each coolie should be S/420 on the average—it being understood that none ill of contagious diseases would be accepted—to be paid in notes of four, six, and eight months, without interest, and dated from the arrival of the vessel at the Peruvian port.

4. If unforeseen circumstances should prevent the *Clotilde* from making the voyage to Macao, the contract was to be null.[9]

In the case, however, of a cargo not contracted to be delivered to a specific individual, the procedure was somewhat different. A marketing scene was then in order. In preparation for it the coolie donned the best of his three suits—probably the new one that had just been issued to him. "Their clothing," declared a contemporary, "is generally nothing more than the ochre colored wide

[9] Nov. 30, 1871, Meiggs Papers, Letter Book 5, pp. 144-145, quoted from Watt Stewart, *Henry Meiggs: Yankee Pizarro*, pp. 162-163. The Meiggs Papers were, in 1937, in the possession of the Peruvian Corporation, Ltd., in Lima.

trouser, and jacket which has served them on the voyage, & the usual Chinese clogs, the whole edifice being surmounted by a cane hat, which is most carefully tied under the chin, for fear the breeze might blow it away."[10] The coolies must also have had with them their possessions—blanket, small box, iron pot for cooking. Thus appareled and equipped they were lined up on the deck—at times, perhaps, on the pier—and the stage was set.

Sometimes, it seems, speculators in labor bought numbers of Chinese and their contracts with the aim of reselling them at a profit. At any rate, it has been declared that it was not a rare thing to see in the newspapers of Callao and Lima advertisements offering for sale a certain number of coolies, "just landed," described always as "models of health and sound of limb."[11] The great majority, however, were disposed of to plantation owners or their agents. The prospective buyer, often accompanied by an individual expert in sizing up a man's strength and character, passed up and down the line and made his selections. One writer described the process thus:

It seems to be the correct thing to squeeze the coolie's *biceps*, give him a pinch or two in the region of the ribs, and then twist him around like a top so as to get a good glance at his *physique* generally. There is often a look of bewilderment on the Chinaman's face whilst undergoing this process—that is to say as far as his Mongolian features are capable of expressing such emotion. But it is not always so, for there are some smart perky coolies who are only too anxious to show off their points—especially if some companion has just been selected and told to stand on one side. Brothers or cousins are always eager to get together, and if this doesn't suit the views of the purchaser, John is sometimes very decided, and often gains his point by dint of Celestial eloquence and signs. But by far the greater majority take things very easy indeed.[12]

[10]"Trefoil," *South Pacific Times*, May 27, 1873.
[11] *Ibid.*, Aug. 7, 1873.   [12] *Ibid.*

Another commentator on this scene says that the buyers selected those whom they wished after making "in the presence of everyone, a shameful examination which humiliates the dignity not only of the one who suffers it but also of those who witness it."[13]

It will be remembered that under the terms quoted in a former chapter,[14] the Peruvian party could at will sign his contract over to another individual and that the coolie could be put at any type of work—excepting only the handling of guano. It was thus a simple matter, the *hacendado* having decided to take a coolie, for the original contractor to endorse the contract to the new master, or "owner."

And so, the cargo is disposed of. The newly acquired laborers, in charge of an overseer, are marched off for their new scene of labor through the streets of Callao and Lima where the ever-present ragamuffins entertain themselves by shouting at the yellow, slant-eyed, and queerly dressed men the phrase "Chino Macao!" The ship that brought them is readied for a new voyage, and the dealer turns to a new *negocio*.

The price paid by Meiggs for the *Clotilde* coolies was a bit higher than was generally the case. As a rule, the sum paid ranged pretty close to $400.00, or soles, to use the Peruvian unit. At times, however, the price appears to have been as low as $350.00.[15] The sum paid in Peru covered the price of the Macao agent, transportation, the cost of the clothing and other equipment given the coolie—and, of course, the profit which the Peruvian dealer took. And that profit was a considerable one since, as we have seen, the cost of passage and other expenses could hardly

[13] Zegarra, *La condición jurídica, etc.*, pp. 127-128.   [14] See p. 43.
[15] Myers, Dennys, and King, *The Treaty Ports of China and Japan*, p. 228, quoted by Morse, *International Relations of the Chinese Empire*, II, 178.

have gone above $100.00 to $150.00. But one must not forget that many of the Chinese died en route—an item of the "overhead" which must be covered in the sale price.

At the height of this trade a dozen or so dealers with their headquarters at Callao-Lima had the bulk of it. "A Hater of Tyranny" describes them as "mostly foreigners, or sons of foreigners."[16] One of Hutchinson's list of ship arrivals, that for the first nine months of 1872, supplies the names of coolie consignees. In that list these firm names appear:

Canevaro y Compañía (Canevaro and Company).
Figari e hijo (Figari and Son).
Compañía Marítima (Maritime Company).
Juan Ugarte.
Candamo y Compañía.
Dimaly Filgueira.

The assumption seems a safe one that in 1872 these half dozen individuals or companies were handling almost all of the trade. Of the twenty-six ship arrivals listed, the cargoes of ten were consigned to Canevaro and Company. Of the 10,977 coolies brought on these voyages, 3,645 were consigned to Canevaro and Company—slightly more than 33 per cent.[17] There probably were some other dealers at the time. In the preceding twenty years or so others had had a hand in the traffic, of whom one must not forget the original monopolists, Domingo Elías, rich man, landholder, and founder of schools, and his partner, Juan Rodríguez.

Duffield, writing of these later years, declared that there were in Lima "many orthodox and highly respectable men" who owed their wealth to the traffic in Chinese and "in whose magnificent salas a conversation on China is as

---

[16] *Callao and Lima Gazette*, Sept. 5, 1871.
[17] Hutchinson, *Two Years in Peru*, I, 247.

welcome as the mention of the gallows in a family one of whose members has been hanged."[18]

It has not been possible to establish statistically the exact distribution of these ninety thousand coolies in Peru, nor to determine accurately the number engaged in different occupations. The data are incomplete, but some general conclusions can be derived from them. In the 1850's most of the Chinese were on plantations, in the neighborhood and north of Lima. That conclusion follows logically from the initial monopoly granted Elías and Rodríguez to furnish coolies for the Provinces of La Libertad and Lima, though other dealers could dispose of them elsewhere. Another fact which can be established is that —to an extent in the fifties but to a much greater in the sixties—large numbers were active in the guano beds off the coasts of central and southern Peru. The prohibition against employment in guano already noticed in the contract of the late 1860's did not obtain in the earlier period. It was the truly infernal conditions under which labor was performed in the guano beds that led to the insertion of the prohibitory clause; the news was getting about in China, it appears, and the coolies wanted nothing of that type of labor. Those brought earlier were not, of course, released from this labor by the new prohibitory clause. The Englishman Duffield, who went to Peru originally to investigate the state of the guano industry for English holders of Peruvian bonds, has a great deal to say—which we shall later note—about the horrible conditions of the Chinese engaged in it. Beginning in 1871, Meiggs used more than five thousand coolies on his railroad-building projects.[19] Toward the end of the period there was, as well, no lack of Chinese in the small factories

---

[18] *Peru in the Guano Age*, p. 43.
[19] Stewart, *op. cit.*, pp. 162-164.

of Lima, Callao, and other population centers. Duffield
has a helpful passage on this point:

"How did you manage to do all that work?" was a question
put at a dinner table one night in Lima, when I was partaking
of the awful hospitality of an English-speaking capitalist.

"Well," was the reply, "I bought half-a-dozen Chinamen,
taught them the use of the machine, which the devils learned
much quicker than I did, and in less than three months I found
that I could easily make ten thousand dollars a month," etc.

"I bought half-a-dozen Chinamen!" They might have been
so many sacks of potatoes, or pieces of machinery, and the ease
and familiarity with so repulsive a commerce which the speech
denoted, proved too well the contempt which such familiarity always breeds.[20]

Earlier in this study it was observed that lands along
the coast were held by large proprietors. A Peruvian
periodical makes the flat statement in 1871 that "These
lands are at present cultivated by Chinese."[21] While there
were, no doubt, some workers other than Chinese on these
plantations, it seems highly probable that a very large
part of them were coolies. Even the Peruvian government "bought" these laborers. A national agricultural
institute had been established on the Santa Beatriz plantation in the environs of Lima. In an estimate of expenses
for the institute for the year 1874 appears a table of the
cost and the expenses of 108 Chinese who did the labor
performed in connection with it.[22]

One may gain some idea of the distribution of the agricultural workers by studying a list of the sugar plantations
of Peru in 1875. On the authority of the National Agri-

[20] *Op. cit.*, pp. 46-47.
[21] *Callao and Lima Gazette*, Aug. 15.
[22] *Documentos Parlamentarios, 1874*, "Anexo B, Instituto Nacional de
Agricultura—Memoria del Ministro de Gobierno, Policía y Obras Públicas
al Congreso Ordinario de 1874," II, 87.

cultural Society, they numbered 235. The listing is arranged geographically along the coast from the north to the south, Lima, of course, being located near the coastal center:

Lambayeque,	29	Cañete,	9
Chiclayo,	62	Pisco,	3
Pacasmayo,	32	Ica,	2
Trujillo,	38	Samaná,	6
Santa,	7	Castilla,	1
Chancay,	15	Islay,	16[23]
Lima,	15		235

Peru had in 1875 probably somewhat fewer cotton than sugar plantations. The boom of Civil War times was beginning to decline, and many cotton planters were shifting to sugar.[24] Cotton culture was concentrated somewhat less in the northern region than was sugar. The guano beds were mainly located in southern Peru and off the coast of that section. The thousands employed by Meiggs were used in the central and northern sections. All in all, then, it is probable that considerably more than half of the coolies, in the 1870's, were laboring in the northern half of the coastal region. The largest of the haciendas in this part of Peru were those of Delgado, Elguera, Loas, Montero, Swayne, Arbrecht, Carnaval, Paz-Soldán, and O'Higgins. In the early 1870's those plantations were estimated to be producing an annual yield of sugar and spirits to the value of S/20,000,000.[25] These plantations, one readily appreciates, were definitely big business. Many of them no doubt used several hundred coolies. On his various holdings Henry Swayne employed more than fifteen hundred.[26]

[23] *South Pacific Times*, Jan. 25, 1876.
[24] J. B. Steere, *loc. cit.*, pp. 207-208.
[25] *The Railroads of Peru* (Lima, 1873), p. 25.
[26] Hutchinson, *op. cit.*, I, 137-138.

A group of government statistics, of the few that are available on this subject of distribution, details the places and the occupations to which were assigned nearly all of the 3,982 coolies that were brought to Peru just previous to June 11, 1874, very close to the end of the trade—but three weeks of it yet remained. They were brought by the ships *Rosalia* (371 coolies), *Camilo Cavour* (661), *Emigrante* (125), *Guillermo* (189), *América* (740), *Manco-Capac* (574), *Luisa Canevaro* (756), and *Nueva Providencia* (512). An indication of the distribution of the latest years of the trade is afforded by the tables. The fact that some 450 of the coolies are not accounted for is probably owing to incomplete reports from the local authorities. The tables follow:

EXTRACT OF LISTS THAT HAVE BEEN REMITTED TO THIS
DATE FROM THE DIFFERENT SUBPREFECTURES

Ship	Number of Colonists	Residence	Occupation to Which Dedicated
Rosalia	216	Chiclayo	216 agricul.
(371)	52	Trujillo	40 agricul., 12 miners
	40	Pisco	40 agricul.
	16	Lima	11 servants, 5 cigar-makers
	3	Callao	3 servants
	10	Huacho	10 laborers
	21	Ica	21 agricul.
Camilo Cavour	159	Lima	126 agricul., 5 bakers,
(661)			1 iron worker, 27 servants
	282	Trujillo	282 agricul.
	100	Chiclayo	100 agricul.
	25	Pisco	25 agricul.
	63	Chancay	63 agricul.
	1	Ica	1 servant
	3	Huarochiri	3 agricul.
	1	Arequipa	1 servant
Emigrante	74	Trujillo	74 agricul.
(125)	7	Huarochiri	7 agricul.
	15	Lima	13 agricul., 2 servants
	5	Callao	5 bakers
	24	Pacasmayo	24 bakers
Guillermo	139	Lima	129 agricul., 10 servants
(189)	8	Tarma	8 agricul.
	39	Chincha	39 agricul.
	2	Callao	2 servants

Ship	Number of Colonists	Residence	Occupation to Which Dedicated
América (740)	152	Lima	52 servants, 97 agricul., 3 bakers
	21	Callao	10 servants, 3 agricul., 2 bakers, 6 laundrymen
	38	Camaná	38 agricul.
	49	Trujillo	49 agricul.
	34	Cañete	32 agricul., 2 servants
	38	Pisco	38 agricul.
	65	Chancay	65 agricul.
	9	Ica	9 agricul.
	34	Cajatambo	34 agricul.
	80	Santa	80 agricul.
	50	Arequipa	50 agricul.
Manco-Capac (574)	125	Lima	17 servants, 102 agricul., 6 millers
	10	Trujillo	10 agricul.
	13	Chancay	13 agricul.
	30	Chincha	30 agricul.
	149	Chiclayo	149 agricul.
	40	Cañete	40 agricul.
	177	Santa	177 agricul.
	5	Callao	3 laborers, 2 servants
	1	Pacasmayo	1 servant
	2	Lambayeque	2 servants
Luisa Canevaro (756)	125	Chancay	125 agricul.
	248	Trujillo	248 agricul.
	150	Chiclayo	150 agricul.
	36	Santa	36 agricul.
	110	Lima	60 agricul., 29 servants, 21 cigar-makers
	45	Pisco	45 servants
	15	Callao	15 servants
	27	Pacasmayo	27 agricul.
N. Providencia (512)	111	Lima	100 agricul., 11 servants
	29	Moquegua	28 agricul., 1 servant
	13	Callao	4 bakers, 9 servants
	100	Santa	100 agricul.[27]

By far the largest numbers of these coolies were disposed of for work at Lima and in the haciendas to the northward. A tabular breakdown will show more clearly the occupations to which they were destined in the hands of their new masters:

[27] *Documentos Parlamentarios, 1874,* "Anexo A, Inmigración Europea y Asiática—Memoria del Ministro de Gobierno, Policía y Obras Públicas al Congreso Ordinario de 1874," II, 68-70.

TABLE OF OCCUPATIONS

Ship	Agr.	Serv.	Cigr. mkr.	Bakr.	Labr.	Minr.	Ldry.	Miller	Founder
Rosalia	317	14	5	..	10	12	..	..	..
Cam. Cavour .	599	29	..	5	..	..	..	..	1
Emigrante . . .	118	2	..	5	..	..	..	..	..
Guillermo . . .	176	12	..	..	..	..	..	..	..
América	495	64	..	5	..	..	6	..	..
Manco-Capac	521	22	..	..	3	..	..	6	..
L. Canevaro .	646	89	21	..	..	..	..	..	..
Providencia . .	228	21	..	4	..	..	..	..	..
Totals . . .	3,100	253	26	19	13	12	6	6	1

No railroad workers appear here for the reason that for lack of funds Meiggs had already begun to slow down in his activities, and he had earlier secured as many coolies as he needed. The most noticeable single fact is that so large a proportion—slightly more than 90 per cent—of all of the coolies accounted for were destined to work on haciendas. If figures for distribution and occupation were complete, however, it would undoubtedly be found that somewhat less than 90 per cent of all the 90,000 coolies went to the plantations. Meiggs used at one period more than 5,000 on his railway operations, and there must have been at an earlier time some thousands employed in getting out guano. From this breakdown of figures, it is also evident that many of the Chinese were employed as house servants, particularly in Lima and Callao, though their use in this capacity was not confined to these cities. Besides, the growing industries of Peru must not be left out of our calculations. Nevertheless, probably at no time were less than 80 per cent of the Chinese on the plantations. This harmonizes with the fact that it was, first and last, the *hacendado* who insisted on the immigration. He was by all odds the person most interested. The *hacendados* as a class profited most from the labor of the coolies.[28]

This almost universal distribution and use of the Chinese worker in the coastal region and the multiplicity of activities in which he was engaged is wittily expressed by Juan de Arona, a Peruvian poet who (in addition to writing an excellent work which touches largely on the Chinese question) composed this poem about them:

> No hay donde al chino no lo halles,
> Desde el *ensaque* del huano,
> Hasta el cultivo en los valles;
> Desde el servicio de mano,
> Hasta el barrido de calles.
> Aún de la plebe es sirviente,
> Y no hay servicio ¿lo oís?
> Que el no abarque diligente.
> —¿Y la gente del país?
> —¡Está pensando en *ser gente!*

Freely rendered in English, the poem goes something like this:

> There is no place where you do not find the Chinese,
> From the *sacking* of guano,
> To the cultivation of the valleys;
> From waiting on the tables
> To cleaning the streets.
> He is even the servant of the commoner,
> And there is no activity—you understand?—

[28] A remarkable item of the tables is that which indicates eight coolies from the *Guillermo* as having been taken to Tarma as agricultural workers. Tarma lies beyond the Andes in the humid montaña region of Peru, and it was very rarely that coolies were taken there. This is the only specific case of the sort that has been encountered.

> On which he does not diligently embark.
> And the people of the country?
> They are thinking of *becoming gentry!*[29]

The flick of the whip in the final line probably was not much to the liking of those of Arona's compatriots who were amassing wealth through the labor of the humble coolie.

[29] *La inmigración en el Perú,* p. 40.

V

THE LIFE OF THE CHINESE "COLONIST" IN PERU

THE NEWLY-ARRIVED coolies were last noticed, after the sale on shipboard, marching through the streets of the port city bound for the haciendas, factories, and homes in the Lima-Callao region. Actually, of course, many were taken on the ship that had brought them, or on another ship or ships, to more distant points on the coast of Peru, more often to the north, but frequently also to the south. The only description that has been found of the process of arriving and being absorbed into the labor corps of the plantation is that of the correspondent "Trefoil." His description is sometimes lightly satirical, sometimes humorous:

One of the oldest hands—a house-servant for instance, who speaks, or rather understands Spanish is then called for to act as interpreter, and the owner, or overseer, being seated, the new coolies are ranged in a line, though some squat about most unconcernedly, and the books of the *hacienda* are produced for the purpose of registration. One is called forward through the interpreter, who enquires his name, and he answers Afo, Asau, Atere, Achin, &c. &c., as the case may be; his paper is then examined, and returned to him, when the grave question arises as to his name.

"Oh! call him Calisto," says the owner.

"No Sir," breaks in one of the stewards, "we've got one already."

"Have we got a Samuel?"

"No Sir."

"Then call him Samuel."

I have seen the name-giver pause a moment (knowing well

that such vulgar names as Juan, Pedro, Manuel, José, &c. were out of stock), then as if seized by a bright idea ask for a calendar, and select such an out-of-the-way name as Calisto, Pancrasio, Ticiano, Zenon, Mimerto, Protasio, &c.; and the knotty point having been settled, down went the lucky *chinee* in the book as Protasio Asin—Age, 29 years—Stature, medium—Colour, yellowish-white—Forehead, high—Eyes, small—Mouth, wide (muttered ejaculation: plenty of room for rice!)—Particular marks on person, has the cicatrix of a wound on the left arm, above the elbow. This last part of the performance the men seem most eager to go [get] through and most positively protest that they have never had the slightest ailment in their lives; and if such a mark as the one just mentioned is found on them, it always happened when they were—so high,—that is about eighteen months old, from a fall or something of the sort, but never from a cut received in some of their piratical expeditions. A man struggling with his fate is said to be a sight for the gods, but a Chinaman trying to look innocent is more than Uriah Heep, Maworm, and the equally unctuous Mr. Stiggins, all three single gentlemen rolled into one.[1]

This process completed, the men, with their equipment in hand, were conducted to the quarters which they would occupy. This ceremony no doubt varied somewhat on different plantations and in different occupations. Sometimes, as in the case of those who worked for Meiggs, the individual was known by a number, registered doubtless alongside his Chinese name.[2]

There was also much variety in living and working conditions, the variations depending on the character of the owner and the type and location of the work. While house servants by no means lived in luxury and idleness, it is highly probable that—as on plantations of the South-

[1] *South Pacific Times*, May 27, 1873.
[2] See Meiggs to R. H. Penny, Lima, April 9, 1874, Meiggs Papers, Letter Book unnumbered, p. 425, in which mention is made of deductions from the pay of Chinese workers Nos. 1429, 1556, 1489, and 1069.

—the house servant fared best, both in the cities and on the
plantations. The reasons are so obvious as to require no
elaboration.

Of the tens of thousands who performed manual labor,
there is reason to believe that those "owned" by Meiggs
were rather well treated. There is a considerable body of
contemporary documentary evidence to support this generalization. Reference is made to the "large and commod-
ious houses" in process of being constructed for their ac-
commodation along the route of the Oroya line above
Lima.[3] An American visitor declared Meiggs's coolies
appeared "robust and contented."[4] The English consul-
general inspected a Meiggs camp at San Bartolomé and
wrote enthusiastically about its arrangements and the
treatment of the Chinese:

Few things on my journey up here gave me so much pleasure
as an inspection of the 480 to 500 Chinese that are working at
this camp. They have got a large galpon or wooden shed, to
sleep in; it is, in fact, a wooden house, enclosed and excellently
ventilated—their sleeping places being arranged in the style of
sailors' bunks on board a ship. It is not more than a few hundred
yards to Captain Heath's house, on the top of the hill. The floor-
ing is wooden, raised four feet above the ground; and to the
capital arrangements of this residence is due no small amount of
the contentment of the Chinamen, as well as their good condition.
Some friends of mine . . . had previously told me that San Bartolomé was the only place in which they had seen fat Chinamen
in Peru. This was not surprising, for during their dinner-time, I
saw them regaling on rice, and beef in great plenty. Before starting in the morning for their work, they all get bread and tea, and
the whole arrangements here plainly indicate, that John Chinaman would have little to complain of, if he were treated every-

[3] *Callao and Lima Gazette*, Dec. 7, 1871, Feb. 13, 1872.
[4] Steere, *United States Foreign Relations, 1873*, pp. 207-208.

where in Peru as he is on the Oroya railway line by the employees of Mr. Meiggs.[5]

While good treatment of a human being is to be commended, whatever the reason, it is nevertheless interesting to notice the motives which produced this rather unusual consideration for the coolie. It is very clearly stated in a note which Henry's brother, John G., general superintendent of the Meiggs enterprises, wrote to the director of the operations on the Chimbote railway line in North Central Peru:

Food for Chinese. Do you give them bread, with their tea in the morning before going to work?—if not it should be done as we have found on this road [the Oroya] that they need a change of diet, and liberal food, and improve on it. I would like you to be very liberal to all who are, or may be in the Hospitals, giving them bread, tea & coffee and in fact liberality will be found the best economy.[6]

The Meiggses, as this note proves, had learned a lesson in efficiency which, regrettably, very many Peruvian employers of Chinese laborers were never able to grasp.

All evidence indicates that the worst type of labor to which the coolie in Peru was condemned was that of the guano beds. Since the mid-1840's Peru had been getting out and sending abroad millions of tons of this odorous natural fertilizer. For more than a quarter of a century, measured by its place in the nation's foreign trade, it was the greatest single source of Peruvian wealth. Chinese of both the first and the second immigration were put to shoveling and sacking this bird manure. In the decade of the 1860's, thousands were imported for this work. Though the form of contract which has been quoted stip-

[5] Hutchinson, *Two Years in Peru*, II, 65-66.
[6] To A. A. Locke, Lima, Dec. 23, 1872, Meiggs Papers, Letter Book 8, p. 239. Quoted in Stewart, *Henry Meiggs: Yankee Pizarro*, p. 164.

ulated that the coolie should not be put at labor in the guano beds, nevertheless, through the period of the migration the bulk of the work in this industry was performed by the Chinese.

Climatic conditions of the region of the guano deposits would make any type of work there a matter of privation and hardship. The heat is tropical during a large part of the year, the humidity is high, and there is an absolute lack of rainfall. Duffield describes in terms of high tragedy the misery of the workers in these deposits:

No hell has ever been conceived by the Hebrew, the Irish, the Italian, or even the Scotch mind for appeasing the anger and satisfying the vengeance of their awful gods, that can be equalled in the fierceness of its heat, the horror of its stink, and the damnation of those compelled to labor there, to a deposit of Peruvian guano when being shovelled into ships. The Chinese who have gone through it, and had the delightful opportunity of helping themselves to a sufficiency of opium to carry them back to their homes, as some believed, or to heaven, as fondly hoped by others, must have had a superior to the Almighty, than have any of the money-making nations mentioned above, who still cling to the immortality of fire and brimstone.[7]

Another English observer, who viewed these works somewhat more coolly, catalogued the elements of the life of the coolie there:

I can state that their lot in these dreary spots is a most unhappy one. Besides being worked almost to death, they have neither sufficient food nor passably wholesome water. Their rations consist of two pounds of rice and about half a pound of meat. This is generally served out to them between ten and eleven in the morning, by which time they have got through six hours' work. Each man is compelled to clear from four to five tons of guano a day. During the last quarter of 1875, it is reported that there

[7] *Peru in the Guano Age,* pp. 77-78.

were 355 Chinamen employed at Pabellon de Pica alone, of whom no less than 98 were in the hospital. The general sickness is swelled legs, caused, it is supposed, by drinking condensed water not sufficiently cooled, and by a lack of vegetable diet. The features of this disease are not unlike those of scurvy or purpura.[8]

The hard lot of the coolies in the guano works was magnified by the cruelty which they suffered from hard taskmasters. As early as 1854 a group of Englishmen were publishing abroad the abuse of the coolies in the Chincha Islands. They stated that "two dozen lashes makes them breathless, and when released after thirty-nine lashes, they seem slowly to stagger over, reeled and fell, and were carried off to the hospital—in most cases, if they recovered, committing suicide."[9] Time did not soften the hearts of the guano bosses, for a United States consul to Peru, writing in 1870, gave further harrowing details of their management of the coolies and the latter's reaction to it:

Those employed on the Guano Islands have a daily task to perform of 100 wheelbarrow loads of Guano, should they fail to get that amount to the shute [by which it was conveyed to the boat], their task has to be completed on Sunday. They are indifferently fed and clothed, and as a consequence one fourth of their number, become sick, but are not admitted to the Hospital while they retain strength enough to stand. I have been informed by American Captains, trading at the Chincha and Guañape Islands that many of them too weak to stand up are compelled to work on their knees picking the small stones out of the Guano, and when their hands become sore from the constant use of the wheelbarrow it is strapped upon their shoulders, and in that way they are compelled to fulfill their daily task. . . . Life to the Chinaman under such circumstances possesses no attractive features, and death (at

[8] Fitz-Roy Cole, *The Peruvians at Home* (London, 1877?), p. 199.
[9] "Memorial of Nine English Shipmasters to the Lords of the Privy Council of Trade," London, June 27, 1854. Quoted in Morse, *International Relations of the Chinese Empire*, II, 172.

all times and in its worst phases a matter of indifference, supposing as the Coolie does, that it is the mere transition from an unhappy state to the enjoyment of all the glories of his celestial fancy) is welcomed by him as his deliverance from the miseries of his lot in life.—This feeling necessitates the constant employment of a guard around the shores of the Guano Islands, where they are employed, to prevent them from committing suicide by drowning, to which end the Coolie rushes in his moments of despair.[10]

Since, as already stated, probably four fifths of the Peruvian coolies were used on the coastal plantations, conditions there must be considered as typifying the life of the coolie in Peru.

The plantation's coolie quarters were known as the *galpón*. Sometimes the *galpón* was a large shed, sometimes a walled enclosure containing a number of buildings. Its construction was never very substantial. Indeed, owing to the general warmth of the climate and the lack of rainfall, comfort did not demand a tight, securely, roofed shelter, though nights in the winter could be uncomfortable if blankets were not adequate. Whatever the type of the *galpón*, it was usually capable of being locked at night. One Peruvian writer to the paper makes reference to the "little and usually filthy dwelling" of the coolie and says that at eight or nine o'clock he was locked up in "the galpon, commonly an enclosure without water or the most necessary sanitary arrangements."[11] The degree of comfort and decency of the *galpón* no doubt varied with the character of the owner, but it may safely be conjectured that its furnishings were minimal and that not much expense was incurred for making it comfortable. It may be regarded as a sort of barracks where each coolie had a section in which to store his small

[10] D. J. Williamson to Secretary of State, Callao, Sept. 20, 1870 (No. 11), Consular Despatches, Callao 6.
[11] "A Hater of Tyranny," *Callao and Lima Gazette*, Sept. 5, 1871.

belongings—blanket, cooking utensil, clothing, sleeping mat. The nightly locking up of the *galpón* is significant of the lack of freedom of movement possessed by the coolie.

The day's work extended normally from five to five or from six to six, with an hour of recess between ten and twelve, or thereabout, for the preparation and consumption of the day's meal. It was standard practice that the coolie himself prepare it, building a fire for the purpose in the field where he happened to be. The day's activities varied, of course, with the nature of the crop cultivated on a given plantation. An informed observer described in these terms the beginning of the day and the organization of its tasks on a cotton hacienda:

The great bell, with which all haciendas are furnished, booms out at half-past four in the morning, and is the signal for a general muster. The owner, or administrator, while smoking his cigarette awaits the arrival of the under-stewards who soon report themselves and a move is then made for the *Galpon* or enclosure where the laborers have been penned up for the night. They have had to tumble out or rather tumble off their cane beds and mats, pretty quickly, their movements being hastened by some of their fellows who have arrived at the dignity of Corporals. Fancy then, in the dim, gray light of morning, a crowd of shivering Chinamen, in every imaginable variety of raiment, being gradually drawn up into a line and answering to their names. It is not a very inspiriting sight I assure you. Whilst they are being told off into gangs the day's ration of rice is served out, and shovels, picks, and whatever implements they may require are taken out of store. Some, the more experienced ones, are sent to the plough, others to weed, others to pick cotton, others to plant or hoe, in fact the day's work is parceled out among them, and off they start, each body headed by its respective mayordomo. The invariable cooking-pot . . . is carried by each one as well as any

firewood which they may have been able to collect on the preceding day.[12]

The food staple of the coolie was rice. Commentators
mention different amounts for the ration which vary from
one to two pounds. Sometimes a quantity of meat or fish
was issued, probably on Sunday if furnished only once a
week. The coolie was at times able to secure a sweet
potato or an ear of corn to add savor to his boiled rice.
There are suggestions that the food issued was often not
of good quality and that the issuer was not overly careful
regarding the amount apportioned—"a pannikin or other
measure heaped full or otherwise, representing a ration."
Usually, on the large haciendas was to be found a shop
where the coolie, if he could afford it and so wished, could
purchase lard, tea, bread, or fish to eke out his daily
ration. Often not much of the weekly wage of a dollar
was left when Sunday came round.[13] The ration was customarily issued daily since it was found that if food for a
longer period was issued, many of the men gambled it
away and as a consequence were without food until the
next issue date, unless furnished an additional supply.
Writing of conditions on the sugar plantations, Fitz-Roy
Cole said that the laborer was allowed "two pounds weight
of peeled rice per diem and one pound of goat's flesh,
which last he sometimes barters for opium,"[14] also to be
obtained at the plantation store.

It was not usual on the larger plantations to use exclusively Chinese labor. Cole declares that the *hacendado*
followed the policy of "divide and rule." Since race
prejudice against the Chinese was very strong among the
Negroes, zambos, Indians, and mestizos, numbers of these

[12] "Trefoil," *South Pacific Times*, June 5, 1873.
[13] *Ibid.*, Aug. 7, 1873.
[14] *Op. cit.*, p. 197.

groups were employed. Sometimes Negroes and zambos to half the number of Chinese were found on the hacienda. In case of difficulty with the Chinese, the master could always count on the colored natives lining up with him against them. "Every hacienda which boasts a 'Hong-Kong,' also contains a row of zambo huts. They lie at some distance apart, and frequently a water-course divides Black Christian from Yellow Heathen." The Negroes were more robust, better fed as a rule, hence were stronger than the Chinese. In many cases these Negroes themselves had been slaves, and they are said to have regarded the Chinese as their successors and to have enjoyed cracking the whip over the yellow laborer as it had once been cracked over them. Usually, native Indians and mestizo peons were also employed in considerable number. One writer remarked that, in case of trouble with the coolies, the peons were used as a reserve, being thrown into the fray in case the Negroes proved unequal to the task of quelling the Orientals.[15]

It was not exceptional to find the owner living on and directing the operations of his plantation. However, the wealthy proprietor often preferred the comforts of the provincial city or of Lima to the relative discomforts of living on his acres. Consequently, there was much absentee-landlordism in Peru. In such cases the plantations were administered by managers employed for the purpose, or perhaps by a son or other relative. Many managers were foreigners by birth, as Europeans were thought to be best adapted to the work. They were more able to exact obedience and industry from the workers and were "more fertile in resources than their own easy-going countrymen." As an incentive for production, they were often promised a share in the profits of the plantation.[16]

[15] Cole, *op. cit.*, p. 142.   [16] *Ibid.*, p. 140.

If not of good character, these managers, in all likelihood, had little regard for the comfort or even for the lives of the coolies, or other workers, for that matter.

The contract coolie's opportunities for social activities and social relaxation were few. The contract granted him three days for celebration of the Chinese New Year. He made of them what use he could with religious ceremonies (many of the larger plantations had a joss house), firecrackers, if they were available, and gambling. Except for these three days, he worked customarily seven days in the week. A few cases are mentioned where a wise *hacendado,* appreciating the better work which resulted, gave Sunday free, or at least a part of the day, along with extra meat to break the dietary monotony. If this was done, however, the coolie was expected to work beyond his eight years a sufficient period to compensate for the Sundays of rest. It was not until very near the end of our period that anything was done to better this situation.

The long work day left little time for play and, in most cases probably, little energy for it. However, despite adverse conditions, gambling often went on in the *galpón* during the hours of daylight that remained after the day's work was finished. One of the games, probably that most played, since the necessary equipment was simple, is described by a correspondent:

It is nothing more or less than *odd and even*. The parties who play, sit down on the ground with a handful of beans &c between them, and one, taking out a few, stakes his money, or other available property, on the fact as to whether they are odd or even in number. The lookers-on invest according to their fancy, and the beans or grains of maize, or coffee, as the case may be, are carefully counted one by one; but neither player is allowed to touch them with his fingers. The operation is gone through with a bit of stick, and frequently when they are getting down to the last few, the scions of Celestial soil, indulge in further bets. The result, when once finally arrived at, seems to have very little effect on the interested parties. In this they seem to be about as fatalistic as in other matters.[17]

The coolie immigration was entirely male; no women at all were brought. Opportunities for association with women in Peru, until the end of the contract labor period, were, if not nonexistent, very rare. A natural consequence of this situation—judged by the dark and nicely Victorian references to it—was a somewhat more than normal degree of sexual perversion. Perhaps this womanless state of the coolie partially explains his addiction to gambling, to opium-smoking—also rather frequently mentioned—and his sometimes desperate efforts to escape his laborious fate.

Because of his rather cheerless lot and the heavy exactions of labor by his "owner" or overseer, a coolie not infrequently attempted to escape from the plantation and from his contract. Sometimes the attempt was individual, sometimes it was a group affair. The *hacendado*, of course, pursued such fugitives, using his Negroes and soldiers supplied by the local authorities. When, as was usually the case, the fugitive was secured, he was subjected to punishment. Imprisonment with loss of labor was not desirable, though sometimes employed. Nor would imprisonment be much of a punishment, since it would merely provide the coolie with a vacation. Some *hacendados* imposed fines which, in most cases, had the effect of extending the contract period, as it was very difficult for the laborer to save much of his S/4.00 monthly wage. Others, less humane, hobbled the runaway with heavy chains and forced him to work with this added weight until the punishment was thought sufficient. J. B. Steere declared that he saw at one

[17] "Trefoil," *South Pacific Times*, June 5, 1873.

estate between thirty and forty coolies come up from their work heavily ironed and holding up their chains with one hand to keep them from galling their ankles, while they carried their spades, with which they had been working, with the other. The owner of the estate told him that the men had attempted to run away. "Crimes committed by the coolies," declared Steere, "are generally punished by their owners, as they are too valuable to pass their time in the public prisons. This is even the case with murder, the penalty for this crime, when the victim is also a coolie, being that the murderer shall work out the term of service of his victim, added to his own."[18] A punishment for lighter offenses was flogging or curtailment of rations, or both. Beginning in 1870, it was not an uncommon occurrence for large groups to rise in rebellion and riot, burn, kill, and otherwise seek vengeance for their wrongs.

The larger and better equipped plantations had hospitals with a doctor in regular attendance either full or part time. If, however, the number of contract employees was small—even at times when large—it was the local village doctor who administered to the coolies' ills. Such a doctor was not always available. Under the best conditions, when several hundred laborers were used, some sort of medical service would be needed almost continuously.

Though most of the Chinese imported were not beyond forty years of age, in the natural course of events some deaths would occur. Because of undernourishment or other causes sustained in China or from hardships on the voyage to America, many were not in good physical condition when they commenced their Peruvian labors. Add to these factors the insufficient or bad diet and the overwork demanded of them and the insalubrious climate of the coast, and it is not surprising to find that critics of

[18] *Op. cit.*, p. 208.

the plantation labor system pointed often with a degree of horror to the high death rate among these laborers. Statistics on this point of mortality after arrival are too scattering to have much significance, but that an abnormal mortality was a fact can hardly be questioned. Steere wrote that he had heard it estimated that less than a third lived out their term of service. He added that "every estate has a Chinese burial place, which is thickly covered with little heaps, each marking the spot where a Chinaman lies a few inches under sand without shroud or coffin."[19] At the high point of the coolie trade to Peru, an editorial in Peru's leading newspaper concluded with these words: "The greatest part of those being newly contracted by the plantations are coming to replace, not those who are completing their contracts, but rather those who died fulfilling them!"[20]

Suicide was not infrequently chosen as the coolie's way out. The guards along the coast of the guano islands to prevent suicide by drowning already have been noticed. Steere, speaking of the coolies of the haciendas, declared that suicide was frequent among them, "and this often by hanging." He added, "Small trees about the buildings upon the estates were often shown me that had borne many fruits of this kind."[21]

The employer of Chinese labor did not consider it particularly cheap. Critics of this type of labor liked also to point out its cost, efficiency and other items considered. A writer in *La Patria* made a lengthy calculation the result of which was to the effect that, even estimating the cost of free labor at S/1.50 per day, everything considered, the free laborer would be cheaper.[22] Another writer calculated the cost of coolie labor in this manner:

[19] *Ibid.*
[21] *Op. cit.*, p. 208.
[20] *El Comercio*, July 24, 1871.
[22] Oct. 14, 1873.

On the average the buyer paid for his contract S/500.00[23] which, for eight years, would represent about S/62.00 per year without interest; subsistence per year ran around S/90.00; pay at S/1.00 per week, S/52.00 per year— making the total annual cost S/204.00. This does not take into consideration the cost of clothing, shelter, and medical attention.[24] The minimum was spent on shelter. The same statement could truthfully be made of clothing —many writers make reference to the "filthy rags" in which the coolie was clothed, if "clothed" be the correct word.[25] And medical care was not a major expense. However, if one calculates the loss of labor of those who died or fled with contracts unfulfilled, the cost of chasing down and restoring to the plantation those who ran away, with perhaps other minor items of expense, the cost of this labor would assuredly rise to a point considerably higher than S/204.00, perhaps to as much as S/250.00 per year. The writer in *La Patria* referred to just above, in fact, shoved it up to almost S/400.00. The factor of cost figured very importantly, of course, in the effort to get the greatest possible amount of labor from the coolie and, likewise, in the "owner's" thinking when he was trying to recover runaways and to discourage repetition of the offense.

In considering the conditions under which the Chinese labored and lived, it must not be forgotten that, while harsh and unfeeling treatment was more or less the rule, not a few masters were considerate of their workers. "Some Lovers of Agriculture," writing to one of Lima's periodicals, made mention of "the great and famous hacienda of Chocabento," the property of Don Pedro

[23] Inflation in Peru in 1873 had increased prices of everything, including the Chinese coolie.

[24] *South Pacific Times*, May 24, 1873.

[25] See, e.g., *ibid.*, Sept. 27, 1873.

Denegri, as a model of management of coolies. The manager was the owner's son, Félix, "humane and intelligent," and a "man of conscience" who did not demand of his "colonists" anything more than the fulfilment of their duties as stipulated in their contracts. He, for his part, fulfilled his duties to them with the result that "no single Asiatic complained of his treatment or ran away from the farm." Indeed, so far did the Chinese go in displaying their gratitude, obedience, and respect that they "looked after his interests as if they were their own."[26]

Another so-called model *hacendado*, cited by the English consul-general, Hutchinson, was Henry Swayne —one of the absentee landlords, by the way, for Hutchinson makes reference elsewhere to having been a guest in his Lima home. Swayne owned four estates in Cañete (a hundred miles or so south of Lima), connected by tramways and on which steam plows were used. "Besides, he has a farm near Cerro Azul [in the same region], another close to Chilial, and a hacienda at Ungara. . . . His property in this valley [of the Cañete River] includes an extent of more than ten thousand acres, and has an annual produce of more than two millions of dollars worth in rum and sugar." Respecting the Chinese employed on these properties, Hutchinson continues:-

At the quebrada I first saw Chinese labourers on the coast of Peru. Their treatment is exceptionally good, and on Mr. Swayne's different properties they number beyond fifteen hundred. They have their joss-houses, and their opium-smoking saloons, without both of which it would be as difficult to make them work as the proverbial impossibilities "to wash the blackamoor white, or make the leopard change his spots." There is a hospital for them, which is daily attended by the Doctor from Cañete town, and they seem as happy as the day is long.[27]

[26] *El Comercio*, Jan., 1872.   [27] *Op. cit.*, I, 137-138.

Under Peruvian law the coolie was not, of course, a
slave, nor was he obliged under law to endure illegal
exactions on the part of his master. It was specifically
provided in the contract that he might appeal to the
courts in order to secure the rights which under the contract were his. This looked good on paper, but in actual
practice how was he to make complaint of abuses?

Peru had a constitution; it had a plentitude of laws,
the Civil Code, and many decrees designed to protect the
individual in his rights. But, actually, neither constitution
nor laws were very well administered. This condition was
not, as any thinking person knows, uniquely true of Peru.
In no country has the man without means or influential
friends an equal chance before the machinery of government and law. In Peru, at this particular period, social
and political stability were scarcely the rule. Arbitrary
action on the part of officials and influence exerted by the
well-placed and the wealthy were widespread. The government was highly centralized; communications throughout the country—where the geography makes construction
of means of communication peculiarly difficult and expensive—were poor. These factors made the *hacendado*,
a wealthy man and often a man of rank and lineage, on his
isolated plantation pretty much a person of absolute power.
The local official, even if his intentions were of the best,
was often not sufficiently supplied with police or soldiers
to present a strength equal to that of the *hacendado*, with
his numerous following of Negroes and peons.

General Hovey, American consul-general in Peru in
1866, sent to his government information concerning the
treatment of the coolies. He enclosed copies of a number
of representations that had been made to him by Chinese
or by their sympathizers. A passage from one such document runs:

It is horrible to think of the barbarous manner in which the overseers and major domos beat the Chinese for the most insignificant faults, often without any cause whatsoever, and it is to be remembered that there is no law which sanctions this system, nor is it licit to have on each Estate a regular prison, as is the case on all the Estates here.[28]

Another representation, signed "Chinese by Birth," contains this informative passage:

Where the poor Chinese suffer the greatest abuses is most undoubtedly on the large Estates, as there is no justice to punish the owners for their horrible and criminal abuse of the Asiatic, and the Chinese is never heard by the authorities, against his patron, as said patron possesses great influence from the high social position he occupies, so that the Colonists are reduced to absolute slavery without remedy.[29]

Locked in the *galpón* by night, requiring, if he wished to leave the plantation, a pass signed by the master or his representative, the coolie's movements were severely restricted. All else aside, it was physically difficult for him to reach the ear of authority. Furthermore, the abused Chinese, subject, as he felt himself to be, to the arbitrary power of one Peruvian, had little confidence in the justice that might be expected from another Peruvian. There was, too, the language difficulty. Hence, in most cases, if abused beyond endurance, the coolie was much more apt to seek release or redress through suicide, attempted flight, or revolt than to go to an official with complaint.

Moreover, assuming he was able to get to an officer, say a justice of the peace or even the departmental prefect, what would be his situation? The prefect was appointed from Lima, the justice of the peace was locally appointed

[28] "To the North American Commander," with Hovey's No. 41, Nov. 28, 1866, Diplomatic Correspondence, Peru 21.
[29] *Ibid.*

by the prefect, and both officials were usually not in position to make cause against the interests of the "big man" of the community, the *hacendado*. It must often have been the case, indeed, that these officials were relatives of the plantation owner, if not themselves owners of plantations. The great landowners had been throughout the colonial centuries the influential men of the country. They were only slightly less so in the period of this study. Consequently, the Peruvian authorities were for long a weak reed in the matter of assuring the Chinese the rights that were legally theirs. It was not until the injustices and the cruelties practiced against the coolies became notorious, not only in Peru but abroad, not until the condemnation of those practices threatened to dry up at its source the stream of coolie labor, that a Peruvian government took the steps necessary to secure for the humble Oriental a semblance of his rights, legal and human. And then it proved to be too late.

Perhaps it will not be inappropriate to close this chapter by quoting at some length from the work of a Peruvian who, writing in the period when the controversy over the "Chinese Question" was at its height, was in a position to inform himself first-hand of the condition of the Chinese, and apparently did so. While his presentation of their lot may be considered somewhat theatrical, it must be given weight, for he was a leading Peruvian intellectual. This man, Félix Cipriano C. Zegarra, stated that the planters, by the treatment which they accorded their laborers, promoted their natural degeneration, lodging them in filthy sheds and bestowing no care upon them, while condemning them to "a ceaseless and unremitting toil, without a ray of hope that their condition will ever be better." He continued:

For the enslaved Chinese the day dawns with labor; labor pursues him through its weary hours, a labor which will bring no good fruit to him, and the shadows of night provide him with nothing but dreams of the tormenting routine which awaits him tomorrow. In his sickness he has no mother to attend him with care; he has not even the melancholy comfort that he will be decently buried when he dies, much less that his grave will be watered with the sacred tears of those who loved him. Of the meanest Peruvian the authorities know where he lived, where he died, and for what cause, and where he is buried. But the Asiatics are disembarked and scattered among the numerous private properties, their existence is forgotten, they do not live, rather they vegetate, and at last die like brutes beneath the scourge of their driver or the burden which was too heavy to bear. We only remember the Chinese when, weary of being weary, and vexed with vexation, he arms himself with the dagger of desperation, wounds the air with the cry of rebellion, and covers our fields with desolation and blood.[30]

It is a somber picture. Cole and Hutchinson, both English, make the assertion, though the former in other parts of his book qualifies it considerably, that the inhumane plantation owner was the exception rather than the rule, and Peruvian defenders of the coolie labor system join them. Duffield, also English, the editors of the *South Pacific Times* and the *Lima and Callao Gazette*, both under English management, and scores of native Peruvian critics—including the newspapers *El Comercio*, *El Nacional*, and *La Patria*—would have it that the humane "owner" was the exception. What did the coolies themselves say? "Although there are some good masters and just officials or employees who are interested in our

[30] *La condición jurídica de los estranjeros en el Perú*, pp. 130-131; as translated by Duffield, *op. cit.*, pp. 45-46.

well-being, they do not number ten, no more than one or two."[31]

The condition of the Chinese coolie in Peru was lamentable. In no case was he brought to Peru for his own betterment. He was there to serve the interests of the Peruvian master. Money-making was the spirit that ruled over his recruitment, by whatever means, in Macao; profits were the great consideration in his transport to the new land; and acquisitiveness was the chief motivation of the *hacendado* or other user of his labor. He was scarcely regarded as a human being; rather he was a machine for the production of wealth. His ills—physical, social, and psychological—were indeed appalling.

[31] *El Comercio*, Sept. 10, 1869, printing translation of a Chinese representation transmitted through American diplomatic officers to the Chinese government.

VI

THE CHINESE A NATIONAL PROBLEM

T HE COOLIE TRADE, from the very beginning, had strong critics in Peru. It has been seen that criticism, intensified as a consequence of the great mortality among the coolies in transport and on the haciendas and in the guano beds of Peru—allied with the humanitarian statesmanship of Marshal Ramón Castilla—had been strong enough to cause a discontinuance of the trade in the mid-fifties. But neither the Marshal nor adverse Peruvian sentiment was strong enough to stem the drive of the *hacendado* for reopening the traffic in the early sixties. Disturbances, chiefly domestic and foreign wars, occupied the attention of the public until late in 1867. By that date a considerable number of Chinese had been brought to the country under the new law. With the reestablishment of peace, the increasing number of Chinese workers, and a repetition of high mortality rates among them, criticism was renewed. It never from that time ceased or was weakened—developments, in fact, added to its strength and effectiveness—until the coolie trade was brought to an end, almost a decade and a half after its renewal.

The only classes among which there were no critics were the employers of coolies—*hacendados, guaneros*, and, with the passage of time, an increasing number of industrialists who had found the Chinese adaptable to their pursuits. The leaders of the attack were inspired by various motives, but perhaps the humanitarian was the strongest. Of the humanitarians, the most able were Juan de Arona (Pedro Paz Soldán y Unánue) and Félix Cipriano C. Zegarra, whose writings have been repeatedly cited. But these intellectuals were but two of many. Some who felt sympathy for the abused coolies trembled at the prospect that a continuance of unlimited importation of the lowest class of Chinese would in time make of Peru a still more mongrel society, one with lower physical and moral attributes.[1] Peruvians of the laboring class saw in the coolie in factory or elsewhere a competitor who lessened the number of jobs available for the native-born and kept down the scale of wages and living. Even the *hacendados* and other employers, fearing foreign action that would cut off the supply of Chinese hands, were glad to search for other and more desirable sources of manpower.

With very few exceptions, Peruvian newspapers and periodicals were critical of the importation of coolies and of their treatment at all stages from Macao to the Peruvian employer. The chief exceptions were government publications or newspapers closely allied with the government, though even there the voice of criticism was sometimes heard, as previous citations have shown. The English language newspapers, the *Callao and Lima Gazette* and the *South Pacific Times,* devoted much space to the subject. This was to be expected, for their editors and owners were English. Isaac Lawton was for a time editor of the former, which in 1873 was succeeded by the second-named newspaper. England was highly critical of the coolie trade, and these papers followed the English "line." But local native-owned and -edited papers were not far, if at all, behind. *El Nacional, El Comercio, La Patria, La Sociedad,* and *Paz y Progreso,* over the course of years,

---

[1] *El Comercio,* Sept. 7, 1870.

gave many, many columns of space to editorials or correspondence of private individuals condemning the trade and
the treatment of the coolies. The first-named paper was
perhaps most severe and most consistent in its criticism.
All types of critics found the columns of these papers
hospitable to attacks on importers and employers of
Chinese. Foreigners who traveled or were posted in the
country in diplomatic offices observed the situation and
wrote books which were more or less critical of the institution of coolie labor. Of those the most prominent who
wrote probably the most widely read books were Thomas
J. Hutchinson, British consul-general, Fitz-Roy Cole and
A. J. Duffield, also English, and Ephraim George Squier,
United States consul.[2] Criticism by officials of foreign
governments was naturally somewhat restrained.

The bases of criticism were many. The methods of recruitment in China and mortality and abuses on shipboard
en route to Peru were much discussed and deplored, as
was also the callous manner in which the coolies were disposed of to Peruvian masters. More attention, however,
was devoted to the trials to which they were subjected in
Peru, particularly in the guano beds and on the haciendas.

Employers were charged with giving their coolies insufficient and bad food, with failing to clothe them decently
and comfortably in accordance with their contracts, and
with obliging them to live in filthy and inadequate quarters. Enough attention has already been given those
charges; it is apparent that in many cases they could be
amply substantiated. When the value of Peruvian money
declined, as it did in the 1870's, many of the employers
of the coolies paid them in depreciated money, or merely

[2] Their books, some of them already repeatedly cited and quoted, were,
respectively, *Two Years in Peru with Explorations of Its Antiquities*, *The
Peruvians at Home*, *Peru in the Guano Age*, and *Incidents of Travel and
Exploration in the Land of the Incas*.

paid eighty centavos for each sol, whereas the contracts called for hard money. The government found it necessary to issue to the prefects a circular on the point.[3]

Another criticism was based on the contract clause in which the coolie agreed to but three days of nonwork annually—the Chinese New Year. Critics maintained that, since by Peruvian law work could not be required of Peruvian employees on Sundays and other legal holidays, it was an abuse to exact labor from the Chinese on those days and that the coolie could not contract away his rights in the matter. Nor, in case the master should decide that the coolie worked more efficiently if given Sunday as a day of rest, was he justified (as was the usual practice) in requiring the coolie to extend his period of service to compensate for those days.[4] Sociologist, humanitarian, and "efficiency expert" urged upon the employers the consideration that not only would the Chinese be less unhappy if they were given those holidays, but also that their labor would be more productive. Certain employers were held up in print as being wise enough to adopt this procedure and, according to the critics, were well rewarded by more and better labor, by a happier atmosphere among the coolies, by a lowering of the death rate, by fewer runaways, and by the absence of uprisings.[5]

Criticism on this point became so insistent that the government found itself obliged, in mid-year of 1873, to issue a decree forbidding coolie labor on Sundays in all lines except domestic service.[6] A few days later, on suggestion of the prefect of the Department of Lima, a new decree was published which permitted coolie labor on Sun-

[3] Signed by Carlos Lissón, dated Oct. 22, 1875 (*El Comercio*, Oct. 25, 1875).
[4] *El Comercio*, June 14, 1873.
[5] *Ibid.*, Jan., 1872, and Hutchinson, *op. cit.*, I, 137-138.
[6] *El Peruano; Boletín Oficial*, July 5, 1873, p. 3.

days until 10:00 A.M., where there was necessary work to be done, provided the worker were paid eighty centavos more than the regular weekly wage.[7]

Hacendados were accused of using various other pretexts for keeping their coolies an additional period beyond the eight years of the contract—such as adding the time lost through illness, the value of articles he was supposed to have stolen, and expenses incurred for bringing him back to the job when he had run away.[8] Such extensions were contrary to the specific terms of the contract, wherein it was declared that such claims must be made good before the courts.

Punishments customarily inflicted upon the Chinese for offenses such as running away were called not only inhuman but illegal as well. Whippings, chains, imprisonment, deprivation of food were mentioned in such criticisms. It was on these grounds, and others of like nature, that the importation and the use of coolies in Peru was described in the press with great frequency as "another African slave trade," as being worse than slavery in the Roman Empire, worse than serfdom in the Middle Ages, worse even than modern Negro slavery in Peru and elsewhere had been.[9] Now the traffic was not "in *ebony* but in *copper*." In all of those other cases the slave or serf could have a family. Domesticity and the family were denied the coolie. It was these ills, these inhuman exactions, that were causing the Chinese in desperation to resort to force against their oppressors.

The charge that the coolie was in worse position than the Negro slave had been in Peru was strongly made by a Peruvian writer in a point-by-point comparison of the

---

[7] *Ibid.*, July 26, 1873, pp. 85-86.
[8] "A Hater of Tyranny," *Callao and Lima Gazette*, Sept. 5, 1871.
[9] *El Nacional*, March 6, 1869, and others.

Negro's rights under the Civil Code with the denial of such rights to the coolie. He wrote, quoting and commenting:

"Masters owe to their slaves in recompense for their services, *food*, protection and assistance in their illnesses." Article 99, C.C.

There are Chinese who do not enjoy that right; because in addition to the fact that the food does not merit the name, they are charged with the cost of assistance or at least deprived of their payments during that time.

"Masters may not sell their slaves for transport from one place to another, without the consent of the latter." Article 101.

As to the Chinese their wish is not consulted in transferring them, and they are obliged to obey blindly, and to accept the residence determined by the master.

"The slave has the right of changing masters *for reason of excessive cruelty*." Article 104.

The Chinese do not enjoy this protection. If by reason of cruelty they could change masters, we are persuaded that some farms would become depopulated.

"The slave who becomes useless in the service of his master acquires his liberty." Article 105.

When the Chinese become unfit for hard labor, they are kept always busy, means being sought for utilizing the last remnant of their forces.

"The master will feed the slave who may have become useless in his service." Article 107.

The masters abandon the Chinese to die in the field or in the streets, begging public charity. There is a multitude of those unhappy ones who augment with their number the most pitiable and sometimes repugnant mendicancy.

"The slave secures his liberty if the master refrains *one year* from feeding, clothing, and educating him." Article 100.

There is no obligation to educate the Chinese; his condition is, then, inferior to that of the slave.

"That slave is free who saves his master when he is in danger of losing his life." Article 116.

Let us suppose that in the uprisings on the farms, there were loyal Chinese who could have done this at a given moment. Well, we do not know that they would have been given liberty for such cause; nor would they be able either to reap the benefit that the law conceded to the slaves.

From all of which comes what we said at the beginning of this little article: that the Chinese in Peru are in worse condition than slaves.[10]

Another commentator in *El Nacional,* after attacking the conditions of securing and transporting the coolies and declaring that many advantages could have been realized from their immigration if good principles had been observed, both as to immigration and international law, continues:

Actually more slaves than immigrants have been the individuals who have in that manner entered the body of our population and the labor of our fields: these are not elements of work, of strength, or of civilization; on the contrary, they discredit labor, demoralize and weaken the society into which they enter, and are the cause of scandal and regression. But let us not forget that this depends not on the country whence they come, but on the accumulation of faults and abuses which surround such an immigration. The slave, naturalized, made evil, full of vices and lacking all education, will always be a source of scandal and an element of disorder.[11]

An American minister to Peru wrote his government, referring to the coolies, "I have come to the conclusion that they were treated as slaves were in former times in the United States."[12] A few years earlier a consul of the United States had declared in an official letter, "Chinese

---

[10] *El Nacional,* Sept. 25, 1873. [11] Sept. 23, 1871.

[12] Gibbs to Secretary of State, Lima, Nov. 13, 1874 (No. 107), Diplomatic Despatches, Peru 28.

labor in this Republic is little less than a system of slavery."[13]

It was no doubt such severe and long continued criticisms and their widespread incidence that led the president of Peru, Colonel José Balta, when Meiggs in 1870 was considering importing Chinese for labor on his railways, to adjure him "for God's sake *not*" to do so.[14]

Another aspect of the Chinese problem became serious in 1870. While in earlier years there had been many runaways and some disturbances among laborers which could be called riots,[15] it was not until this year that an incident occurred that could properly be called an uprising. By that time the Chinese in the country numbered some fifty thousand. As time had passed, their number steadily increasing, they had become not only more conscious of the wrongs to which they were subjected but also more conscious of their numbers and thus more courageous. Moreover, the number of the Chinese who had completed their contracts and were "free" (a term widely used) was increasing. These free Chinese were better situated to appreciate the abuses of their fellow-Chinese and, it seems pretty certain, sometimes encouraged them in resisting by force unjust demands. Their activities in this respect, nevertheless, were undoubtedly exaggerated by the *hacendados*. While these uprisings, beginning in 1870, were not numerous, they were sufficiently bloody and damaging to property to cause much anxiety to employers of Chinese and to the government. Steere declared on this

[13] D. J. Williamson to Secretary of State, Callao, Sept. 20, 1870 (No. 11), Consular Despatches, Callao 6.

[14] J. G. Meiggs to J. M. Campbell, July 2, 1870, Meiggs Papers, Letter Book 1, p. 568.

[15] See in *El Comercio*, Feb. 10, 1869, account of a riot on the hacienda of San Pedro, in the Valley of Lurín a few miles south of Lima. Some 100 coolies, armed with clubs and knives, forced release of some of their fellows who had been locked up for fighting.

point, "There is a feeling of insecurity in Peru from the presence of this great number of desperate men, who have no ties to bind them with the people of the country or to keep them from taking vengeance in case of insurrection. Every one goes armed, and every farmhouse is a little armory."[16] The insurrections furnished excellent material for the agitations of the critics.

The first actual revolt, properly so-called, occurred in early September, 1870, in a region lying on the coast some 125 miles north of Lima. Here, in the valley of the Pativilca River, were a series of rich sugar plantations clustered near the coastal towns of Pativilca, Barranca, and Supe. The haciendas named in the official report as being concerned were those of Araya, Upacá, Arguay, Paramonga, las Huertas, and las Monjas. A circumstantial account of the dreadful beginning of this revolt is contained in an official letter written to his government by a foreign diplomatic agent:

The first attempt at Mutiny, occurred on the Hacienda of H. Canard, at Upacá, where there were employed some 500;—A Mr. Ballesteros had arrived at the Hacienda with a large amount of money to pay off their monthly wages, this being known to the house servants, they informed their countrymen employed on the plantation—While Mr. Carnaval and Mr. Ballesteros with two other gentlemen named Antonio Davila and Doct. Pareja were sitting at the table eating supper, they were surprised by the sudden entry through the different doors of a body of Chinamen armed with pistols, Lances, and Knives, (machetes) who commenced an indiscriminate slaughter on the party, Killing all of them and mutilating their bodies in a frightful manner, they took all the valuables that could be found in the house, they took 50 good Horses and mounted some of their men forming a squad of

[16] *Loc. cit.*, p. 208.

Cavalry, who took charge of the plunder; their force at this time numbered 600 men.[17]

After this bloody beginning, the movement spread successively to a number of other plantations, some of the coolies joining willingly, others being forced—as the Peruvian official report states. The rioters secured more firearms and gained sufficient strength for attacking the village of Pativilca. Concerning the occurrences at Pativilca, the diplomatic agent quoted above wrote his superior:

The inhabitants hearing them coming fled to the church it being the strongest building in the village; a man named Arriata with a few others nobly defended the church against the mob, killing some 50 of them and compelling the others to keep at a safe distance from the unerring aim of his rifle, those who were unable to reach the church, before the Chinamen entered the town (mostly women) suffered a terrible fate, their persons were violated, and their bodies cut in pieces, their heads cut off and placed on poles, and shown to those inside the church.[18]

Being unable to force the church at Pativilca, the coolies proceeded to the town of Barranca. But Sr. Arriata had preceded them there and warned the inhabitants of their danger. So well did the people, with Sr. Arriata's aid, prepare their defense that the attackers were repulsed and dispersed, "leaving the road covered with the bodies of Chinese." The leader was one of the slain, a fact supposed to have affected the morale of the others. At any rate, the coolies were unable to reorganize themselves after this reverse. Those who were well mounted fled up the valley of Huarmey, while the unmounted scattered into the hills where most of them were hunted down by police

[17] D. J. Williamson, United States Consul, to Secretary of State, Callao Sept. 2, 1870 (No. 11), Consular Despatches, Callao 6. Williamson states that the uprising occurred on September 4.
[18] *Ibid.*

and soldiers and restored to their haciendas, or, as in the case of the remaining leaders, lodged in the jail at Huacho. A number of free Chinese who were believed to have inspired the uprising and, perhaps, to have assisted in securing arms, were also arrested and jailed. Some 1,200 Chinese were involved in the uprising. Altogether—again according to the official report—the casualties which resulted numbered 150 Chinese killed, 16 whites killed and 7 wounded.[19] However, D. J. Williamson, United States consul, declared that "The Federal Government upon hearing of the disturbance immediately dispatched troops to the assistance of the inhabitants, who upon their arrival made terrible havoc amongst the Coolies, killing some 600 of them."[20]

The only reasons for the uprising advanced in the official report were the encouragement given by the free Chinese and the use of opium among the coolies. Peruvian critics of the system found the explanation, of course, in the cruelty of the masters, and Williamson agreed with them.

The press through September and October, 1870, carried much comment on this uprising—criticism of the *hacendados* concerned, defense by the *hacendados,* strictures on the government for its do-nothing policy and its apathy. Feeling against the Chinese ran to extremes, so much so that a member of the Peruvian congress, a Sr. Peña, proposed a bill which, if it had been approved and executed, would have forced every free Chinese in the country to make a new labor contract or leave Peru. The proposition was immediately scored as having the object of "enslaving the Asiatic perpetually."[21] One writer ex-

[19] Antonio Rodríguez y Ramírez to the Minister of Government, Police, and Public Works (*El Comercio*, Sept. 21, 1870).
[20] *Loc. cit.*   [21] *El Comercio*, Sept. 19, 1870.

pressed the belief that the Chinese were trying to make common cause with the Negroes and the native Indians of Peru against the whites[22]—a reflection of the depressed condition under which those groups, for many years, ever since the conquest, in fact, had suffered in Peru.

At this time and in the years immediately following, the free Chinese in Peru became a cause of uneasiness and received considerable attention from the press. While definite numbers cannot be established, in the natural course of events, their number would have been increasing steadily. While many coolies died in service, probably most lived to terminate their contracts. Some of these recontracted themselves for an additional period, but it appears that most did not. A few, comparatively speaking a very few, returned to China. Steere provides a bit of evidence on this point when he states that on the ship on which he sailed from Callao to China there were eleven Chinese, "all of them apparently broken in health and going home to die, though one of them was said to have with him about $25,000." He continues, "Ten or twelve Chinamen seem to be about the average number who return upon ships that take out from six to nine hundred, though a few may make their way back by way of California."[23] By 1870 there must have been several thousand Chinese in Peru who were free to do as they chose, within, of course, legal limits. And it should be emphasized at this point that the Peruvian constitution in effect at the time guaranteed to the foreigner a protection in personal rights equal to that of the native-born Peruvian.[24]

A few of the Chinese, when free of their labor contracts, probably were able to secure small plots of land

---

[22] *Ibid.*, Oct. 7, 1870.   [23] *Loc. cit.*, p. 208.

[24] Carlos B. Cisneros, *Reseña económica del Perú* (Lima, 1906), p. 221.

for farming, on a basis somewhat resembling sharecropping. It may be that a very few were able to purchase bits of land. But not many could have had money to make such purchases, and, besides, very little land was available for purchase because of the concentration of farm land in the hands of large owners. A few others remained in villages near plantations where coolies were employed and established small stores—and, it was often charged, probably with truth, sold opium to the laborers. However, generally speaking, the free Chinese preferred to go to population centers. In the larger towns in the agricultural regions, such as Pacasmayo and Trujillo, small businesses could be established, and there was opportunity for some degree of domestic service.

There was a tendency, however, for the free Chinese to go to Lima when it was possible to get there. A colony of them was growing there from the 1850's. By 1870 it was very respectable in numbers if not entirely so in attributes. A considerable fraction of these were Chinese who had become useless for work and had been cast adrift by their masters before the termination of their eight years. The Chinese colony in present-day Lima shows a decided concentration in the neighborhood of the Municipal Market, probably the continuance of an earlier tradition. The Chinese in the West have usually been much concerned with the handling and preparation of foodstuffs. This practice was early established among the free Chinese in Lima.

Not every free Chinese found work or, perhaps, wanted it. Vagrants appear to have been fairly numerous, though the point was probably exaggerated by *hacendados* and others who feared the Chinese when at large. (Does this suggest a bad conscience?) One P. J. Sevilla, writing to a departmental prefect early in 1870, declared:

There exists in this capital and its environs an increasing number of Asiatics who having finished their contracts, go about as vagrants; given over to idleness, they lend themselves to all kinds of vice and commit crimes more or less grave. This class of individuals is that which perverts the Asiatics who have not been contaminated and sow in them demoralization and bad habits.

He went on to say that these free Chinese had caused the flights and uprisings that had damaged agriculture and recommended that they be taken up under a Peruvian police regulation which was designed for the control of vagrancy and under which idle persons could be forcibly enlisted in the army and navy.[25] It is certainly true that many of the imported coolies were of a low class, and undoubtedly there were vagrants among them.

The more industrious found work. Domestic service gave employment to many, as cooks, launderers, butlers. Many became proprietors of small shops, particularly of food shops, including street stands. Others established rooming houses for their fellows. Still others became operators of small restaurants, called *chinganas* and *fondas*. From all contemporary accounts, these restaurants were anything but models of cleanliness—a statement that could have been made of most restaurants of the time, whether in Peru or elsewhere. The general distrust of the Chinese is apparent in a rumor that got about in Lima in 1872 that human flesh had been discovered in two Chinese *fondas*. "The ready credence given to the report," ran a newspaper statement in commenting on the rumor, "leaves ample room to conjecture the abject misery of the Asiatics in this country." The comment contains also the statement that medical men who made a search declared that the meat was not human flesh, but

[25] *El Comercio*, March 7, 1870.

that it was neither beef nor mutton.[26]   About the time
this rumor was afloat, a Chinese named Alán was arrested
near Lima and imprisoned for having killed a mule and
eaten a considerable portion of it; the mule was not
Alán's.[27]   This is certainly another indication of the
miserable state of some of the free Chinese.

Certain of these Chinese, as stated above, became purveyors of opium to their brethren.   There was then no Peruvian law against the sale or use of opium.   The ill effects
of the drug were recognized, however, and measures for
its control began to be discussed.   Ought its sale be
stopped?   Should it be made a government monopoly?[28]
A few Chinese became doctors—without benefit of degrees—and were forced to sustain attacks from Peruvians
of that profession.   Felipe Santiago de Cabrera wrote
and published an article of some length in which he defended such a Chinese, declaring that his herbs had cured
patients with whom Peruvian doctors had failed.[29]   It is
somewhat surprising that this type of medical treatment
should have attracted attention, for to this day herbs are
sold on the streets of Lima.   When gathering the materials for this study, the author used to see a vendor of
herbs whose daily post was located on the narrow sidewalk
opposite the entrance of the old National Library.   Herbs
were, and are, used for a variety of household remedies,
and native Indian *curanderos* who make use of them and
of magic in treating diseases are certainly not unknown.
It is another evidence of feeling against the free Chinese.

The Chinese of Lima, early in 1870, were accused by
Carlos López Aldana, a textile manufacturer who employed a considerable number of coolies, of having estab-

[26] *South Pacific Times*, May 14, 1872.
[27] *Ibid.*, May 28, 1872.
[28] See an editorial on the subject in *El Comercio*, Oct. 7, 1872.
[29] *Ibid.*, Nov. 21, 1868.

lished a "Junta of Asiatic Insurrection." Its supposed
purpose was to foment uprisings among the coolies.[30]   It
is quite probable that the free Chinese did very early
establish an organization among themselves.   Such action has been customary wherever colonies of Chinese
have existed abroad.   In the main they have been interested in self-help or philanthropic activities. The Lima
colony, following a severe earthquake of August, 1868,
turned over to the national Beneficent Society (operated
by the Catholic Church) the sum of S/205.30 as a contri-
bution to the relief of the sufferers.[31]   It is entirely possible that such a beneficent society was thought to be
mixing in the insurrections.   And, of course, it is also
possible that it was actually doing so.

It should be understood that there were in Lima a
number of Chinese merchants of good standing and considerable wealth some of whom had not been coolies.
Duffield pays compliment to a number of individuals of
this group (whose hospitality he much preferred to that of
his fellow-Englishmen)—the Wing Fats, Kwong, Tung,
Tays, etc.—in his book on Peru.[32]   Another writer declares that "Innumerable are the Chinese immigrants who,
having commenced by gaining food, clothing, and four
pesos per month, have formed capitals of 20, 30 and 40
thousand pesos."[33]   Leadership for the cause of the coolies
could readily be found among these men of means and
ability.   A former coolie who achieved a degree of wealth
and position was Manuel de la Cruz.   An article of some
length in *El Nacional* concerning this man contains this
passage:

[30] "Tres Agricultores," *El Comercio*, Feb. 25, 1870.
[31] *El Comercio*, Sept. 10, 1868.
[32] *Peru in the Guano Age*, pp. 48-49.
[33] *El Nacional*, editorial, March 1, 1869.

Having come in one of the first importations of that class of immigrants who come to fertilize our fields and to suffer at least our disdain, he finished the term of his forced contract; he devoted himself to free labor; he amassed a capital; he took, fifteen years ago, a wife in conformity with the triple law of God, heart, and honor, and devoted to her his life with a loyalty and abnegation which many wives of the most brilliantly civilized class would envy.[34]

Manuel de la Cruz's wife was, of course, a Peruvian, probably a chola, that is, of mixed Indian and white blood. Other Chinese when free were sometimes able to win Peruvian women as wives. In this manner originated that new and interesting Peruvian social group, the Chinese-Indian-white mixture.

Of de la Cruz, López Aldana said some very harsh things and accused him of having fomented trouble among the coolies of his factory and haciendas. He implied that de la Cruz had circulated inflammatory printed materials among his fellow Orientals.[35] Hence, it would appear that this free Chinese did occupy a place of influence and leadership in the Chinese colony.

It was very probably this free group in Lima that took the initiative in calling the attention of the Chinese government to the hard conditions of its nationals in Peru. A representation was drawn by Chinese subjects resident in Lima and given to General Alvin P. Hovey, the minister of the United States in Peru. He, being unable to procure a translation, sent it to J. Ross Browne, United States minister to China, whence it was passed to high officials of the Empire. The point is reserved for treatment elsewhere.

Distrust of the free Chinese was fomented by coolie employers. This feeling seems to have been rather widely

[34] July 22, 1871.   [35] *El Nacional*, Feb. 19, 1870.

entertained among the middle and upper classes. The
laboring class of Peru disliked the Chinese from the beginning. Added to a strong racial prejudice was the
feeling that they were damaging competitors in the labor
market. Prejudice of the laboring class reached a crisis
in mid-year of 1873. For some time attacks on individual
Chinese had been rather frequent. A pretext for united
and more severe action was furnished by the importation
at the time mentioned of a number of coolies from California for dock labor in the operations of the British Steam
Navigation Company at Callao. Peruvian laborers in
Callao rioted and attacked the Chinese with consequences
serious to several individuals. The rumor was spread
about Lima and Callao that the national independence
day, July 28, was to be made the occasion for an onslaught
against, perhaps a massacre of, the Chinese in those cities.[36]
The *South Pacific Times,* commenting on the rumor, supposed that perhaps only a demonstration was intended
(which fortunately proved to be the case) and made these
remarks:

> Every one is aware of the contempt in which the Chinaman
> is held in this country, however well conducted and respectable
> he may be, and those whom we should be inclined to class under
> this category are not a few. Many who affect to despise them
> could, if they were so disposed, take lessons in cleanliness, sobriety,
> self-respect, and humanity from most of the hard working eman-
> cipated coolies. But the prevailing idea among the lower orders
> in the towns has been that the Chinaman was created solely for
> their special benefit, so much lower down in the social scale than
> themselves, as to be but slightly above the brutes.[37]

The time was approaching when the government
could no longer, without inviting tragic consequences,

---

[36] See *El Nacional,* July 24, and *El Comercio,* July 25, 1873.
[37] July 22, 1873.

postpone action to find a solution of the Chinese problem. Not only was the outcry loud in Peru, where bloody incidents threatened the social order, but foreign governments were taking notice. Particularly was the Chinese government preparing measures. It might even be that the coolie trade would be halted at Macao; in 1869 it had been suspended for a time. Then where would the Peruvian agriculturist find himself? One of the directions that governmental action took was toward encouragement of European immigration.

The first effort took the form of a decree, proclaimed in 1869, looking to the colonization of the Amazonas region, that hot, humid, isolated, jungle-like trans-Andean section of northeastern Peru. Free tools and other equipment were promised, as well as a loan to assist the colonist in getting established. Either nationals or foreigners might take advantage of the conditions provided in the decree.[38] Not much could be expected from this measure in so far as solving the labor problem of the coastal plantation owner was concerned. Nor was much accomplished by it in settling the trans-Andean region until the rubber boom began not long afterward and built up Iquitos for a time to a city of respectable size and a valuable commerce.

With the great development in public works, chiefly railways, that began in the later 1860's and continued through half the following decade, the *hacendados* found themselves facing a labor crisis. Many of the natives whom they had previously employed were taking jobs with Henry Meiggs at higher pay. In these circumstances plantation owners appealed to the government for aid in the importation of Chinese. They asked a subvention of

[38] *El Nacional*, June 29, 1869.

S/2,000,000 for this purpose.[39] The response of the
government was to issue a decree for encouraging, not
more Chinese immigration, but rather European immigration.   Manuel Pardo had taken office as president in
August of 1872; he was not as favorably disposed toward
the *hacendado* as President Balta had been.   The decree,
dated December 17, 1872, provided for the formation of
a European Immigration Society.   As the name implies,
the purpose of the society was to foment in every possible
manner a movement of Europeans to Peru and to supervise their location in the country—to represent the immigrant before the government, to provide immigrants with
domestic animals, to find land for them, and to administer
such funds as congress might provide for those purposes.[40]
Congress voted S/100,000 for the use of the society.[41]
An ambitious series of committees was set up for the different regions whence it was hoped immigrants might be attracted.[42]   Early in this study it was shown that conditions
in Peru were quite unfavorable to European immigration.
However, it was widely believed that once the railways
were finished, Europeans would stream into the country.
"For it is unquestionable," declared *La Sociedad*, "that
when the Puno and Oroya Railways are finished, European immigrants will flow to our interior."[43]   Such ex-
pectations were doomed to disappointment.   No solution
for the labor problem was to be found in the operations
of the European Immigration Society.

The decree of 1868 for betterment of the conditions
of transport of coolies has previously been cited.   The

[39] *South Pacific Times*, Sept. 21, 1872.
[40] *Ibid.*, Dec. 19, 1872; *El Peruano; Boletin Oficial*, Dec. 21, 1872, p. 392.
[41] *South Pacific Times*, Dec. 23, 1873.
[42] *El Peruano; Boletin Oficial*, Dec. 21, 1872, p. 392.
[43] Quoted in *El Comercio*, June 27, 1870.

state of the laborer in Peru also demanded attention. On February 15, 1870, a decree was emitted which directed prefects to name commissions to visit haciendas and farms where Chinese were employed to observe their treatment and check on the degree to which masters and coolies were observing the terms of the contract. Small results were produced; nine months after the date of the decree the prefect of Lima Province had not yet appointed the personnel of the commission.[44]

The first positive act of the government which, it could be hoped, would better the state of the coolies after their arrival in Peru, was embraced in a series of decrees of 1873. The action may be interpreted as being, not so much an effort to meet the criticisms so loudly proclaimed at home, as one designed to affect the situation in China and forestall a complete break in the Chinese immigration. A Peruvian plenipotentiary was even then in Japan and would shortly pursue his way to China, and it was highly desirable to do something definite to regulate the place of the Chinese in Peruvian society in order to strengthen his hands. At the same time, it was hoped that the decrees would meet in some degree domestic criticisms. The decrees bear the dates of June 7, July 12, and October 14. That of June 7 concerned Sunday labor and has already been mentioned.[45] That of July 12 was designed to regulate the length of the work day and provide for overtime pay if it were exceeded.[46] By far the most important of these decrees was that of October 14. Its provisions merit a somewhat extended summary:

A new section was established in the Prefecture of

[44] "XXX," in *El Comercio*, Nov. 10, 1870.

[45] See p. 116.

[46] *Documentos Parlamentarios, 1874*, "Memoria del Ministro de Gobierno, Policía y Obras Públicas al Congreso Ordinario de 1874," II, 11-12.

Callao under the title "Registry of Contracted Asiatics."
The section was to operate under the authority of the prefect of the department. That official should have at his
orders two Chinese invested with the character of police
agents who were also to act as interpreters. The prefect
was to be in communication with the subprefects of the
several provinces where coolies were employed, and those
functionaries were to see that the labor contracts were
fairly carried out. An article of the decree provided that
on the day following the arrival of a coolie ship, the consignee must present in the registry office a list by name
of the Chinese who had come on the boat as well as the
names of those who had died on the passage or who had
been left ill at any port en route. Also, before making
over the contracts to third parties, they were required to
present a duplicate in the registry and the name of each
coolie's new master, the place where he was to reside, and
the occupation which he was to follow. The section was
also required to register the name of the ship in which
the coolie had been brought, the date and number of the
contract, the day on which each contract would terminate,
the name of the master and the hacienda, and such annota-
tions as might appear from the reports of the subprefects.

The new section was directed to remit to the subprefects a copy of the entries of laborers destined for their
provinces, and the master was not to transfer any contract
without presenting to the subprefecture the contract he
held and the duplicate in the possession of the coolie. A
separate document was then to be drawn up stating the
name of the person to whom the contract was transferred,
the place to which the coolie was destined, and the time
yet remaining of his period of service. If the coolie were
to reside in another province, the subprefect was required
to notify the subprefect of the other province, before

whom the same formalities were to be observed. That is, the new master was bound to present the documents to the authorities, giving the name of the person who made the transfer.

Other articles referred to desertion by a coolie, a matter of which the master was obliged to notify at once the subprefect for entry in his register. In case of failure to do so, no claim was afterward to be allowed for the time the laborer may have been absent. As soon as the term of the contract expired, the master was to give notice to the proper authorities, stating the number of the contract, the name of the coolie, the conduct he had observed while in service, and the occupation he had followed. Should the coolie die during the period of service, the master was equally obliged to forward the contract to the authorities, stating the date and the cause of death.

Various other clauses set forth the duties of the subprefects and contained such provisions as, it was hoped would prevent collusion between subprefects and masters. The twentieth article declared that if any of the provisions described was not complied with, the coolie concerned should be considered free.

A further clause of some importance provided for reshipment to China of any coolie who might desire to go there at the termination of his contract. In such case, the coolie was to present himself at the Registry at Callao within the period of four months after the conclusion of his term of service; after that time he could not claim transportation. The owners of coolie ships returning to China must take the number of passengers indicated to them by the Registry, the state to pay S/20.00 for each.[47]

[47] *Ibid.*, "Anexo A, Inmigración Europea y Asiática—Memoria del Ministro de Gobierno, Policía y Obras Públicas al Congreso Ordinario de 1874," II, 60-64; summary in *South Pacific Times*, Oct. 16, 1873.

It will be observed that this decree, faithfully administered and executed, would have answered many of the criticisms made respecting the management and treatment of the Chinese. The coolie would no longer have been a nameless individual, lost to sight the moment he was taken from the ship. It would also have given the authorities the means of preventing illegal exactions by the master, such as requiring the coolie to work additional time beyond the expiration of contract. Furthermore, it would have provided a complete set of statistics on arrival, distribution, and activities of the coolies.

Unfortunately, however, it was found impossible to execute the decree in the manner intended. This fact is established by the official report made by Toribio Raygada, head of the Registry Section, to the Prefect of Callao more than six months after the decree was proclaimed. The official wrote concerning his task:

In respect to truth, what up to now has been accomplished in compliance with the different articles of the supreme decree creating this office, is no great thing; . . . many of the dispositions of the decree . . . it has not been possible to put into practice. . . . little has been done by the private individuals who have Asiatic colonists in their service. . . . Up to now there are inscribed in the books of the Section no more than the insignificant figure of 1,236 of the great number of colonists who are in the Republic. . . . I regret very much to inform you that only the Sub-prefects of the provinces of Castilla and Contumaza, have complied by remitting to this office the lists of the registers which have been made in their respective provinces . . . in spite of this having been required of all the Sub-prefects of the provinces where Asiatic colonists are to be found.[48]

[48] "Anexo A, Inmigración Europea y Asiática—Memoria del Ministro de Gobierno, Policía y Obras Públicas al Congreso Ordinario de 1874," II, pp. 66-67. For "Estatutos" and "Reglamentos Administrativos," see *ibid.*, pp. 7-16.

Here we see clearly one of the reasons for the bad state of the Chinese. The national government might legislate or decree the most perfect set of regulations, but it lacked power to make them effective at the local level. It is the thesis of Zegarra's excellent work, *La condición jurídica de los estranjeros en el Perú*, cited frequently heretofore, that the evil situation of the Chinese was not owing to lack of good intentions on the part of the government, but rather to the unwillingness of the great plantation owners to give regard to national and human welfare in their use of the coolies. Though his explanation is, perhaps, a bit oversimplified, Raygada's report tends to confirm it.

At the close of the year 1873 the domestic situation in Peru with respect to the Chinese was anything but good. Criticism was bitter and growing. The government was trying to better the condition of the coolies, but its efforts were largely ineffective. The number of free Chinese in Lima and other cities was increasing, and they presented a social and economic problem of some magnitude. Gravest of all, perhaps, other nations were frowning on the coolie trade and were criticizing Peru's treatment of the coolies. The *hacendados* were deeply concerned lest the coolie trade be stopped at its source and they, consequently, be unable to operate their plantations. The government shared their uneasiness. A crisis in the whole matter was approaching. A mission, the work of which was to affect this question fundamentally, was already in China trying to negotiate with the imperial government. It is to this international aspect of the problem that attention will now be turned.

VII

THE COOLIE AN INTERNATIONAL PROBLEM FOR PERU

THE CONSCIENCE of the West rejected slavery. Liberalism in Great Britain caused the powerful British Empire to abolish slavery in its dominions in the early 1830's and to assume the lead in moving against the institution wherever it existed. Slavery in the United States had been dissolved in blood, and the American government was dominated by the antislavery section. Brazil, from the middle of the century, was moving gradually and peacefully toward freedom for its enslaved Negroes. The other independent nations of Latin America had abolished slavery, Peru itself having taken that action in 1854. The institution continued to exist in Spain's colonies in the West Indies. In Cuba it had tended to distract attention from the unenviable state of the tens of thousands of coolies who had been taken to that island and who had suffered as much as those in Peru. In the Western World, what smacked of slavery was frowned upon officially, particularly by Great Britain and the United States. It is therefore not surprising that, as stories got abroad concerning the cruelty and corruption of the coolie trade and of barbarous incidents involving Chinese laborers in Peru, the governments of those nations should have noticed them and been impelled to take corrective action.

As early as 1866, Dr. S. Wells Williams, of the American Legation in China, wrote for his government a description, by no means flattering, of the coolie trade at

Macao,[1] and reference has been made to the action of General Hovey, United States minister to Peru, in forwarding to his country's minister in China, J. Ross Browne, a representation to their home government of some Chinese in Peru. Browne had the document translated into English by Dr. Williams before presenting it to the Chinese authorities and sent a copy to Washington. The documents were published in American newspapers, and they appeared shortly in Spanish in the Peruvian press.[2] Their publication in the Boston *Daily Advertiser* elicited from one V. Pazos, presumably a Peruvian, a letter to the editor in which the charges were branded as "false and contrary to the Peruvian character"—which scarcely disproved them.[3] A quotation from the representation of the Chinese will serve to indicate its nature and content. After a polite introduction comes a statement that during twenty years thousands of Chinese had been taken to Peru, then:

They worked without ceasing both morning and night and without having any rest during cold or heat. We well know that these are the conditions for obtaining our food and clothing; but who would suppose that we are ignorant of the obligations of those who employ us? On their part, they are unscrupulous foreigners who adulate the rich and depreciate the poor, who bury all goodness and destroy all right, who have made our contracts useless paper and consider our lives as insignificant trash. Our food, our clothing, and our pay, are furnished in the most miserable manner; thus we are weakened by lack of food and nevertheless no consideration is given our fate. . . . Although there are some good masters and just officials or employers who are

[1] To Secretary of State, Peking, April 3, 1866, No. 27, Legation Archives, Williams, 1865-1866, XXXIII, 471-477.
[2] See *El Comercio*, Sept. 10, 1869, for Browne's note to Prince Kung, under date of May 27, 1869, his dispatch to Fish, American Secretary of State, dated Aug. 14, 1869, and translation of the Chinese representation.
[3] *Ibid.*

interested in our well-being, they do not number ten, no more than one or two, and in spite of everything they cannot better our condition.[4]

In his note to Prince Kung, as well as in the dispatch to his home government, Browne expressed his belief that the charges were probably based on truth; to him they had the ring of sincerity. In his dispatch to the Secretary of State, Browne conveyed Prince Kung's request that the United States minister in Lima be asked to "inquire into the details, and lend a helping hand to these people."[5] General Hovey was so instructed, and he made a representation to the Peruvian government in a note of October 19, 1869. With the note he enclosed copies of the correspondence of Browne with Anson Burlingame, then an officer of the Chinese government. The note to the Peruvian government expressed the humanitarian concern of the government and people of the United States for the suffering Chinese in Peru.[6] The Peruvian reply was to the effect that the president had received the note most favorably and had ordered the minister of government to direct the prefects of all provinces where there were Asiatics to appoint commissions of "respectable and impartial persons" to investigate carefully the condition of the Chinese and inform the government to the end that steps might be taken to correct any evils discovered.[7] Publication of this correspondence and the representation of the coolies provided further material for discussion of the Chinese problem by the Peruvian press and for in-

[4] *Ibid.* For original English translation, see Browne to Secretary of State, Peking, June 3, 1869, enclosed with No. 29, Legation Archives, Browne (China), 1868, XLVII, 937-938.

[5] *Ibid.*

[6] República Peruana, *Ministerio de Relaciones Exteriores, Años 1865-1880,* Vol. 94-A (unpaged); Diplomatic Despatches, Peru 23.

[7] Dorado, Minister of Foreign Relations, to Brent, chargé, Lima, Jan. 28, 1870, Diplomatic Despatches, Peru 23, with Brent's No. 209.

sistence in some quarters that the government issue special regulations for the rural police, empowering them to supervise relations of coolie and master.[8]

Another consequence of this correspondence was that Peru, asserting that it had been too expensive to maintain regular ministries in China and Japan, requested the United States government to authorize its diplomatic agents in those countries to act temporarily for Peru. Those agents were asked to represent to China and Japan the desirability of establishing permanent relations with the Peruvian government, the objects of which would be the development of commerce and the facilitation of emigration to Peru of the subjects of both empires. The United States government, through General Hovey, accepted the suggestion "with much pleasure" in a note of May 10, 1870.[9]

The appeal of the coolies failed to elicit any positive action from their home government. A specialist in Chinese history explains the do-nothing policy of the Chinese emperor by observing that the monarch was too busy to bother about the "stupid people" of the south. Emigration of Chinese subjects was forbidden, and for hundreds of years the rulers had "looked upon those who emigrated as unpatriotic subjects not worthy of protection."[10] The Chinese authorities were stirred somewhat from their lethargy by a second petition which reached them in June, 1871. It emanated from Peru and came by the same route as the former.[11] After leisurely con-

---

[8] E.g., editorial in *El Nacional*, Feb. 4, 1870.

[9] *Documentos Parlamentarios, 1870*, "Memoria del Ministro de Relaciones Exteriores al Congreso Ordinario de 1870," III, 39. See also Hovey to Secretary of State, March 22, 1870, No. 215, Diplomatic Despatches, Peru 23.

[10] MacNair, *Modern Chinese History*, p. 409. See also Foster, *American Diplomacy in the Orient*, pp. 278-279.

[11] Low to Fish, Nagasaki, May 13, 1871, No. 68, Legation Archives, Low, 1871, Vol. II (China).

sideration of the second representation, the emperor's government expressed sympathy for the coolies in their trials, advised patience, and suggested that they form a commission to present their wrongs in detail at the emperor's palace.[12]

Such a commission, consisting of Chinese residing in China, at least some of whom had been in service in Peru, was formed. Comment in the Peruvian press concerning it contains some interesting statements, gathered, presumably, from Chinese sources. It was understood that the commission of seven was composed of "persons belonging to the first families of China, its president being no less than the son of a viceroy." Of this son it was added, "This young man was robbed, drugged with opium, and embarked in Macao ten years ago, and he returns to his country an invalid with one foot less, after being forced to fulfil an illegal contract." The secretary of the commission had been a teacher in the family of a mandarin. Of him the story ran:

Now 16 years ago he found himself with his two students of 13 and 15 years taking a ride in a two-oared boat in the Bay of Canton, when in a fog he was stopped by an armed launch, whose men destroyed the boat, took the five persons on board a ship in Macao and in it they were brought to Peru. This teacher was thrice sold to different persons on the Peruvian coast, and obtained his liberty only after 15 years of hard labor, and when he had become completely deaf.[13]

When this teacher, now secretary, returned to China, he had to report the death of both of his former students. It was said further of the commission that, "in addition to the unquestionable proofs of maltreatment and cruelty suffered which they bear on their bodies," they had dep-

[12] Translation of reply in *El Comercio*, Jan. 17, 1872.
[13] *Ibid.*

ositions from haciendas in Peru which filled three thousand pages in Chinese characters.[14]

The Peruvian Minister of Foreign Relations, in his report to congress in 1870, had a number of things to say respecting the Chinese problem. He informed the lawmakers of the appointment of local commissions to investigate the condition of coolie labor on the haciendas. He had received some reports, but he did not summarize their contents. (Perhaps this lack of summary is in part explained by the statement of a local newspaper that nine months after the appointment of the commission for the Province of Lima, it had not yet done its work.) The minister's recommendations to congress, however, imply a realization that the existing state of affairs both with respect to transportation and treatment of coolies after their arrival was unsatisfactory. Immigration, he declared, would be better handled and would bring better results if it were so organized as to come direct from the Chinese mainland rather than from colonies on the Chinese coast. As a means of effecting such an alteration, he recommended that congress authorize the dispatch of an embassy to China for the purpose of "entering into official relations with the empire and to draw up a convention for securing robust, industrious and honest colonists, both as individuals and as families." The United States, he declared, had so proceeded and had secured excellent results. With the project of an embassy, the government associated the naming of a Peruvian commission of inspection of colonists. Its duties would be to observe and regulate the relations between the coolies and their masters as well as to set up a system of statistics and accounting respecting them.[15] Here is the genesis of the "Registry

[14] *Ibid.*
[15] *Diario de Debates*, Congreso Ordinario de 1870, pp. 72-74.

of Contracted Asiatics" which, we have seen, was established by decree of October 14, 1873. These proceedings of the Peruvian government and the publicity given representations of foreign governments are a measure of the concern felt in Peru lest the coolie immigration be made impossible.

Great Britain's position on the coolie trade became a matter of much concern to Peruvians after 1870. While that government refrained from making direct representations that would express its attitude, it was well known that Britain was very critical. No carriage of coolies from Hongkong was permitted except in British boats and to British possessions.[16] Britain was believed to be using every means other than direct action on Peru and Portugal to suppress the coolie trade from Macao. Early in 1870 the British governor of Hongkong refused to issue an exequatur recognizing as Peruvian consul at that colony César A. del Río, for the reason that del Río was thought to have been engaged in the "inhuman" Macao coolie traffic.[17] The case of the *Nouvelle Penelope* had emphatically registered the British attitude—the Hongkong court had branded the coolie traffic as "a true slave trade" and justified coolies in committing murder during shipment in order to recover their freedom.[18]

In April of 1873 England went even further in the effort to impede the coolie traffic. Every ship engaged in that traffic was forbidden to anchor in the waters of the colony or to secure any supplies whatever.[19]

[16] Pedro Gálvez, Peruvian minister to Great Britain, to Peruvian minister of Foreign Relations, London, Aug. 16, 1873, reporting a conference with Hammond of the British Foreign Office (*Documentos Parlamentarios, 1874*, "Documentos—Memoria del Ministro de Relaciones Exteriores al Congreso de 1874," I, 171-174).

[17] *El Comercio*, July 12, 1870.   [18] See above, p. 51.

[19] Ulises Delboy, Peruvian consul in Macao, to Pedro Gálvez, Macao, Aug. 26, 1873, MSS, Ministerio de Relaciones Exteriores del Peru; Año 1873; Legación en China y Japón; Anexos.

W. G. S. Jerningham, British minister to Peru, wrote a long dispatch to his government in which he paid his disrespects to the coolie labor system as practiced in Peru, a dispatch from which Zegarra quoted at length in his book.[20] This report, and others from Hongkong and elsewhere, "briefed" the Foreign Office for its campaign against coolie trade.

Guillermo García y García, a Peruvian who had participated in the operations at Macao and knew them well —he had directed a number of expeditions from Macao to Callao, either as pilot or as captain[21]—when in London was requested by the Peruvian minister, Pedro Gálvez, to provide him with a report on the subject. He complied with an extended document which bears the date of July 14, 1873. As indicated by previous references to it, Captain García y García furnished a fairly complete picture of the traffic in coolies from China to the shores of Peru. As was to be expected, he put it in the best possible light.[22] Armed with the information contained in this report and with instructions from his government embodied in a memorandum, Minister Gálvez secured an appointment for a Foreign Office conference.

Gálvez's report of the conference is enlightening, both with respect to British policy and the convictions of the Peruvian minister regarding it. In the absence of the Foreign Minister, Lord Granville, Gálvez was received by Mr. Hammond, described by the caller as an "employee whose skill is recognized and who is the key in many questions." He was also characterized as "one of

---

[20] *La condición jurídica*, pp. 137-139.

[21] Arona, *La inmigración en el Perú*, p. 60.

[22] "Informe que contiene importantes detalles sobre la conducta con los emigrantes chinos y otros datos relativos a esta emigración," *Documentos Parlamentarios, 1874*, "Documentos—Memoria del Ministro de Relaciones Exteriores al Congreso de 1874," I, 194-201.

those who has sustained most firmly the policy of abolishing all emigration of Chinese which is not for English colonies and in English boats." In the course of the conference, Hammond declared that the debates in Parliament on the subject of the coolie traffic and various administrative acts associated with it were British domestic matters and as such could not be subjects of discussion with Peru. In his report Gálvez wrote:

I found myself prepared by this argument of the Honorable Hammond, to evade every question by the same conduct which the Cabinet of His Britannic Majesty has observed in questions of this sort, and which has consisted in destroying, by all the means which a nation of such power can dispose, Chinese emigration contracted for any part of the world not under British dominance, but without ever directing a single word of reproach to any government; and when in Parliament the Cabinet has been criticised for being too tolerant with the Portuguese Government, with which it ought to employ [in the judgment of the opposition] another type of means than simple advice, the British Cabinet, through Lord Granville or Lord Enfield, has always replied that the correct policy is that of moderation. On the other hand, the fact that the English Government should not have begun a long time ago to treat this subject frankly with Peru, there being such good relations between the countries, and the Honorable Stafford Jerningham occupying himself with the subject as he does, has made me understand that the British Government wishes to avoid diplomatic questions, to go directly to its object, the suppression of the Chinese emigration, enclosing it in an iron circle.

Hammond declared that the deplorable abuses which had taken place in the Chinese emigration from Macao were unquestionable, as well as the maltreatment suffered by the Chinese in the places of their destination. He professed to believe that the Peruvian government had good will in the matter of correcting abuses, but added:

good wishes do not suffice in this matter, and he did not know whether there was in operation a system capable of preventing those abuses since some months ago two Peruvian boats destined to carry Chinese from Macao to Peru had been examined in Hong-Kong and the reports were quite unsatisfactory.[23]

Said Gálvez, "The Honorable Mr. Hammond could not take on himself the responsibility for any opinion, but the ideas expressed by him personally are a key for deducing those which dominate the Foreign Office."[24]

The content of Gálvez's dispatch indicates not only what the British policy was respecting Peru and the coolie question, it also suggests rather clearly British procedure toward Portugal and the Macao activity. It was consistent with British policy that it should avoid ultimatums and merely maintain a constant pressure on Portugal to clear up the plague spot in her colony of Macao. Gálvez read the situation correctly. British pressure in time produced results.

It seems well to inject here another point which will help to explain Peruvian sensitiveness to Britain's attitude in international matters. While Peru, in the early 1870's, was not conscious of being on the threshold of the war with Chile which began at the end of the decade, there yet existed a keen and somewhat bitter rivalry with that country for leadership in the South Pacific. In case of a war with Chile, or with any other nation, the role of the navy would very probably be decisive. And, at the time, the English controlled the mar-

---

[23] The boats in question were the *Colonia* and the *Luisa Canevaro*. Questions regarding them arose when the decree of April, 1873, referred to above, was put into effect. See Granville to Gálvez, London, Jan. 16, 1874, MSS, Ministerio de Relaciones Exteriores del Perú; Año 1873; Legación en China y Japón; Anexos.

[24] Gálvez to Minister of Foreign Relations, London, Aug. 16, 1873, *Documentos Parlamentarios, 1874*, "Documentos—Memoria del Ministro de Relaciones Exteriores al Congreso de 1874," I, 171-174.

ket in South America "for the sale of almost all the
articles necessary to supply the naval forces in the waters
of the Pacific." The foreign diplomat whose words are
quoted added that coal, then so indispensable to a navy,
was "almost exclusively" under British control in Peru.[25]

One of the first evidences of Portuguese wavering in
connection with the activities at Macao was the government's procedure following the international publicizing
of a scandal in Peru involving some coolies. From Lambayeque, under date of May 11, 1868, an individual
whose name is not announced—let us call him X—wrote
a letter to the president of the Peruvian "Society of
Friends of the Indians." On the fourth of that month,
said X, a boat had brought to Lambayeque from Callao
forty-eight Chinese. The following day X had passed
the house where the forty-eight were lodged, and he had
noticed that "all bore a mark, not entirely cicatrized, that
ran from near the articulation of the chin, and describing
a semi-circle, passed under the ear and ended behind it
in the upper part of the neck, forming a C." On questioning the coolies, X had been told, he declared, that they
had all been branded with a hot iron by the master, that
he might identify them in case they should run away.[26]

When published, as it was shortly and very widely,
the story created a sensation, as one may readily believe.
Narciso Velarde, Portuguese consul-general in Peru, in a
note to the government of June 17, demanded an investigation and, in the event the report should be found to be
true, the punishment of the responsible person. The consul, among other things, wrote, "we see the *hacendados*,
with honorable exceptions, looking at the *colono* not as

[25] General Hovey to Secretary of State, Lima, Jan. 14, 1867, Diplomatic
Despatches, Peru 21.
[26] *El Comercio*, June 10, 1868.

a man, but as an instrument and less than a slave." He
ended with the threat that

if the crime of which I write should go unpunished, the undersigned will find himself under the painful necessity of sending to
his government a copy of this note, adding to it the disagreeable
picture which the streets of Lima present, with the immense
number of Chinese mutilated in the service of their masters and
abandoned by them when they are unable to work that they may
go to live on public charity, with the object that my government,
if it should find it proper, should give the necessary orders to the
governor of Macao to forbid the emigration of Chinese from that
port to those of Peru.[27]

The minister of government, Dr. Juan M. Polar, ac-
knowledged receipt of the consul's note, with its threat of
a most unwelcome action, and turned the matter over to
the department of justice for investigation.[28] To use the
word of the minister of foreign relations, it was discovered
that the report was "inexact."[29] Before a thorough investigation could be completed, however, Velarde made
good on his threat, sending to the governor of Macao a
communication dated August 2, 1868, in which the story
of the "branded 48" was detailed. Whether as a result
of Velarde's communication or because of other reasons,
as, e.g., the pressure of the United Kingdom, the governor of Macao, on November 18, 1868, issued a decree
—and the forty-eight were mentioned in it—suspending
until further notice the emigration of Chinese to Peru
through Macao.[30] This suspension spread alarm among
the *hacendados*, who saw in it their imminent ruin, and
stimulated efforts at securing European immigrants.

[27] *El Nacional*, March 1, 1869.
[28] *El Comercio*, Feb. 27, 1869.
[29] *Memoria que presenta el Ministro de Estado en el despacho de
Gobierno, Policía y Obras Públicas al Congreso de 1870*, pp. 56-58.
[30] *El Comercio*, Feb. 27, 1869.

Jerningham did not fail to inform his government of the "scandal of the 48." He sent with his dispatch various clippings from Peruvian newspapers relating to the incident.[31] The outcry of the British press must also have been strong, since a member of the Peruvian Legation, J. Jara Almontes, on order of his superior, wrote the editor of the London *Times* a communication designed to appease it. The Peruvian government and people, Jara declared, condemned as did other civilized nations the "abuses and crimes that had been born of the Chinese emigration." He asserted that the Peruvian government had done and was doing everything in its power to suppress the wrongs of the Chinese and to secure the bases for a good and free emigration.[32] The letter is equivalent to an admission that many of the wrongs charged were actually in existence.

Though the document that renewed the traffic from Macao to Peru eludes discovery, the traffic must have been reopened by the middle of the following year, as Peruvian statistics revealed that in 1869 some 2,000 coolies were embarked at Macao for Peruvian ports.[33]

Continued criticisms of the coolie trade and the reaction to the *Nouvelle Penelope* incident produced, under date of February 24, 1872, a consular convention between Peru and Portugal with a special section on contract laborers. The convention was designed to improve conditions—or to make a motion in that direction—and to remove at least some of the bases of criticism. The Peruvian minister who negotiated it was Pedro Gálvez, minister to England and France. In a dispatch to his government he stated that it was designed to be so broad as to cover not the Chinese alone, but Portuguese and

[31] *Ibid.*, Sept. 14, 1871. [32] *Ibid.*, Sept. 19, 1871.
[33] See above, p. 75.

Peruvians as well. Since China had forbidden the emigration to Peru, the Portuguese did not wish to make a convention frankly covering only the Chinese emigration.[34]

The most important stipulations of the convention were these: (1) the emigrant should have the right to rescind his contract at any time, with indemnity to the master and with six months previous notice; (2) questions that might arise between the parties to the contract should be decided by arbitration; (3) diplomatic and consular agents of either country should have the right, in the country of destination, to watch over the fulfilment of the laws and regulations pertaining to the making of labor contracts, the transport of laborers, and the faithful execution of their contracts, and the officials named should be provided with all the facilities necessary for so doing.[35] This convention may be considered a mere palliative rather than an approach to the root of the question. About all that its provisions meant, circumstances considered, was that Portuguese officials in Peru were empowered more explicitly to do what we have already seen them doing, as when Velarde protested in 1868 respecting the "branded 48." The convention was approved by the Peruvian congress on April 19, 1873.[36]

An occasion for another such protest arose in mid-year of 1872. The Portuguese chargé d'affaires was the recipient of accusations of abuse of Chinese on certain haciendas in the Province of Chancay, those of Molino, Ingeniero, and Retes being mentioned. He made a representation to the government, and the charges were at

[34] Gálvez to Minister of Foreign Relations, Lisbon, Feb. 27, 1872, *Documentos Parlamentarios, 1872*, "Documentos—Memoria del Ministro de Relaciones Exteriores al Congreso de 1872," I, 55-57.

[35] *Ibid.*, I, 25-27.

[36] Riva-Agüero, Minister of Foreign Relations, to García y García, Lima, April 19, 1873, *ibid.*, I, 87.

once investigated, Sr. Soria, prefect of Lima, going to Chancay for the purpose. Soria reported that, except for one case, the charge that coolies were being held to work beyond their contracts was false. Some were forced to work an additional period in compensation for time lost when they ran away, but he considered that requirement justifiable. In the case of the one just complaint, the prefect set matters in train for correction through judicial action.[37]

We now approach the *María Luz* affair. Related somewhat to that of the *Nouvelle Penelope,* it was much more widely publicized. The incident occurred in a place not previously associated with the coolie traffic and was of such nature and produced such reverberations that it constituted a crisis in the history of Peru and the Chinese coolies.

The *María Luz,* a ship of Peruvian registry, commanded by a Peruvian, Captain Ricardo Herrera, sailed from Macao on May 28, 1872.[38] She had on board 225 coolies under contracts made for Tanco Armero, an agent for Emilio Althaus, of Lima, and a dozen minors under contract with the captain himself. The contracts had been made in the usual manner and had been validated by the Portuguese authorities and a Peruvian consul.[39] Weather and the damage caused thereby compelled the ship on July 10 to put into the Japanese port of Yokohama. A day or so afterward one of the coolies of the *María Luz* leaped overboard and swam to the *Iron Duke,* a British ship, by which he was picked up "in a state of great pros-

[37] *Ibid.,* I, 162-163; *South Pacific Times,* Oct. 14, 1873.
[38] The governor of Timor gave it (if printed correctly) as the twentieth. Different coolies of the boat gave it as May 22 and May 24. May 28 is the date as printed in an official Peruvian document.
[39] Aurelio García y García to Japanese Minister of Foreign Relations, Yedo, March 3, 1873, *Documentos Parlamentarios, 1874,* "Memoria del Ministro de Relaciones Exteriores al Congreso de 1874," I, 91.

tration." The coolie begged protection, declaring that, with others of his emigrating companions, he had been badly mistreated. The captain of the *Iron Duke* sent him ashore to the British chargé d'affaires, R. S. Watson.[40] Watson at once addressed a note on the subject to the Japanese Foreign Minister, Soyeshima Tane-omi. He asserted that the coolie traffic between Macao and the western coast of South America had been characterized by barbarousness and had "with justice excited the greatest disapprobation in Europe and the other civilized nations." He urged the Japanese government to protect the coolies of the *María Luz*.[41]

Japanese officials took charge of the escaped coolie. Captain Herrera appeared shortly to claim him, declaring that he had a complaint against this coolie and several others who had attempted to escape the ship. When Herrera promised to inflict no further punishment, the coolie was handed over to him and taken on board the *María Luz*. Whereupon, it appears that, contrary to his pledge, Herrera flogged the returned coolie and some others that had attempted to escape, their cries being heard on the decks of the *Iron Duke*. Watson, on being advised of this new development, went aboard the *María Luz* to investigate. He was refused any communication with the coolies but was able to see them, and he felt convinced that Herrera had punished them—some had had their queues cut off and others had been flogged. Believing that such procedure was not justifiable on the part of the captain of a merchant vessel toward his passengers, he

[40] "Japanese Memorandum on the *María Luz* case," *El Comercio*, Dec. 24, 1872. This memorandum, prepared to explain Japan's action to other governments, in Spanish translation fills four closely-typed pages. It will hereinafter be cited as "Japanese Memorandum," and the cited number of *El Comercio* will be understood.

[41] *Documentos Parlamentarios, 1874,* I, 65-67.

suggested as much to the Japanese government and expressed his belief that an investigation should be undertaken to establish the actual situation.

By this time other coolies had made their way to the *Iron Duke*—which must have seemed to all of them a haven of refuge—and still others had been seized by Herrera while attempting to leave his ship. The Japanese government, in these new circumstances, decided that an investigation was in order. The authorities, when they examined the escaped coolies, became convinced that they had been abused. They arrived at this conclusion not only by questioning the Chinese who had got ashore by way of the *Iron Duke*, but by questioning likewise those that were yet on the *María Luz*. An official, Hayashi Gotenji, accompanied by G. W. Hill and an interpreter, Ching Shing, went aboard the *María Luz* on July 14. The group spent there three and a half hours in the course of which they examined most of the coolies. Various of them declared that they had been kidnaped, that they had been forced to sign their contracts after the boat had left Macao (though the contract had been read to them earlier), and that they had had insufficient food. The fact that a number of the coolies had been flogged was established. Coolie No. 8, showing a club, said, "This is the club with which I punished No. 5. The captain ordered me to do so." The Japanese official concluded his report with these statements:

While I was making these notes [on the facts mentioned above] the other coolies surrounded me shouting loudly and vehemently and begging protection. I was so deeply impressed that I saw myself obliged to tell them that their petition would be attended to. I was scarcely able to free myself from their importunity.[42]

[42] "Translation of Japanese minutes of the visit to the boat," *Documentos Parlamentarios, 1874*, I, 100-101.

Captain Herrera was in great need of recovering the escaped coolies. His procedure toward them, however, was considered by the Japanese authorities to constitute an offense under their laws, some of the alleged offenses having been committed under Japanese sovereignty. If, therefore, he were to recover them, it would be necessary to prove his rights in court. There was difference between the captain and the Japanese concerning those coolies that had escaped to the *Iron Duke*. Herrera argued that if they were given entire liberty, he could not recover them, even if the court should find that he had a right to do so, because in all probability they would have made their way back to China before the case could be determined. This point had validity, and the authorities consented to hold those coolies, on condition that Herrera bear the cost of their food. He was obliged to assent; he would have had to feed them had they been returned to his ship.

The case was tried in the court of the Kencho of Kanagawa, the superior authorities at Tokyo having refused, when their views were asked, to order the return of the Chinese to the *Maria Luz*. From the day when the ship anchored in the Bay of Yedo to that of the final judgment, more than six weeks passed. In the course of the trial, Herrera declared that the Chinese were not properly passengers, since their passages had not yet been paid; that they had been insubordinate and that he, as captain of the ship, had a right to maintain discipline by whatever means were necessary; that the coolies were under contract and that in law and right they should not be permitted to break their contracts by escaping.[43] The outcome of the case is revealed in these words from the sentence pronounced by the Kencho on August 26, 1872:

[43] "Japanese Memorandum."

The charge made against the captain of having maltreated the passengers and prevented their leaving the boat, is fully proved; since the captain himself does not deny many of the acts with which he is charged, such as having cut off the queues of three of the Chinese, detained them by force, etc. The charge made by the greater part of the passengers of having been detained on board by force, he himself admits. . . . These offenses, for they are thus proved, having been perpetrated by the captain in the Bay of Yokohama, and within the jurisdiction of this Kencho.[44]

The customary Japanese punishment for such offenses was severe, being no less than one hundred lashes or one hundred days detention, depending on the rank of the offender. The tribunal could, if it thought proper, pardon the offender. In this case, considering the circumstances and everything that had been deduced in the captain's favor, also that he had been detained for a long period and had suffered many inconveniences, the tribunal decided to pardon him and permit him to depart with his boat. The ship's papers were restored. The tribunal coupled with this act of grace a severe censure of the captain for his conduct toward the coolies.[45] As to the coolies, they were turned over to a commission sent by the Chinese government to take charge of them.[46]

While the case was running its course, several representatives of foreign governments had expressed doubt of the jurisdiction of the Kencho of Kanagawa. It was to answer those doubts that the "Japanese Memorandum," several times cited, was published. Likewise, before a decision was reached, the governor of Macao and Timor, who was at the same time Portuguese plenipotentiary to the Japanese court, registered a protest. The governor understood the action of the Japanese court, he asserted, to

[44] Translation of sentence in *Documentos Parlamentarios, 1874,* I, 62-63.   [45] *Ibid.*   [46] "Japanese Memorandum."

be based on the supposition that the traffic in which the
María Luz was engaged was "illegal and illicit or in
abuses and crimes which might have been committed on
board." As to the territoriality of the ship, that matter
concerned the Peruvian government, but as to the Chinese emigration from Macao, it was "free and spontaneous,
regulated and protected by special laws, which in no respect injured the humanitarian character of the government" which the minister represented. Documents accompanied the note to prove the truth of the Portuguese
minister's asseverations.[47] The Japanese reply was that
the court's judgment was a matter which concerned only
the governments of Peru, China, and Japan. It denied
also any intention to discredit the Portuguese government.[48]

Sufficiently indicative of the attitude of the Chinese
government in this affair is the fact that to Captain Arthur,
of the *Iron Duke*, it presented a decoration, the Kung-pai
of the first class. It also formally expressed its thanks to
the Japanese government for its intervention.[49]

The government of the United States was also concerned, though not deeply. It will be remembered that in
1870 Peru had requested that government to act for it in
matters touching relations with China and Japan and that
it had assented. On August 19, 1872, C. E. DeLong,
minister of the United States to Japan, addressed a note
to the foreign minister of Peru imparting the information
that he was urging prompt action in the case of the *María
Luz*.[50] In another note he stated that the Japanese government had refused to recognize his right to ask for in-

[47] *El Comercio*, Dec. 24, 1872.
[48] Soyeshima Tane-omi to Visconde de San Januario, Aug. 18, 1872, *ibid.*
[49] *South Pacific Times*, May 24, 1873.
[50] *Documentos Parlamentarios*, 1874, I, 56-57.

formation in the case on the part of Peru. However, it latter presented him with copies of the act of the tribunal.[51] Acting for his government, DeLong also assumed responsibility for the expenses of caring for the *María Luz* and paying the crew.[52] Captain Herrera had not possessed sufficient funds to meet the expenses of this long delay in his voyage. (Herrera abandoned his ship and left Japan on October 3 by the mail steamer en route to Hongkong and Peru.)[53] While discharging these courtesies for the Peruvian government, DeLong was careful to make it clear that his government was "decidedly opposed to the traffic in which Captain Herrera was engaged," and that his instructions definitely forbade him "to do anything which tended to favor it."[54]

The international furor raised by the *María Luz* affair had wide repercussions. Details of the Japanese investigation and judgment were published around the world. There can be little doubt that its influence was a determining factor in producing the decrees emitted by the Peruvian government in 1873, culminating in that of October 14, for the amelioration of the condition of the coolies in Peru.

Its greatest immediate effect, however, was on Portugal. That nation felt itself definitely "on the spot." This scandal was the culmination of the pressure that had long been growing in opposition to the coolie traffic. Here was the crisis; Portugal could stand no more. By a decree of December 27, 1873, the governor proclaimed the end

[51] *Ibid.*, I, 61-62.   [52] *Ibid.*, I, 133.

[53] See "La 'María Luz,' Relación que hace su Capitán D. Ricardo Herrera," MSS, Ministerio de Relaciones Exteriores del Perú; Año 1874; Legación en Rusia y Alemania; also Lavalle's "Exposición" to the Russian czar in the arbitration of the affair later conducted, in *El Peruano; Boletín Oficial*, July 27, 1875, p. 33.

[54] DeLong to Peruvian Minister of Foreign Relations, Tokyo, Sept. 28, 1872, *Documentos Parlamentarios, 1874*, I, 69-70.

of Chinese coolie emigration through Macao, to become effective three months from that date.[55] Supplementary decrees of January 2 and 9, 1874, established the new conditions that would govern the movement of passengers from that colony after March 27. No contract labor coolie could be numbered among them.[56] The content of these decrees has already been noted at the conclusion of Chapter II.

Gálvez, Peruvian plenipotentiary to Portugal, attributed the action to the "constant hostility of England" to the traffic. He quotes the governor of Macao respecting the "ease with which the English and the Chinese could do away with the Chinese emigration through Macao." The governor concluded with the observation that "no matter how well organized the emigration might be, it could not continue without involving the colony of Macao and Portugal in very disagreeable conflicts with the English and Chinese governments."[57] These statements of the governor, thought Gálvez quite correctly, gave the key to the actual situation.

With these Portuguese decrees, the calamity long feared in Peru, particularly by the employers of Chinese coolie labor, fell upon the country. No more Chinese could be introduced under pre-existing conditions. To establish other conditions, satisfactory to China, to Peruvian critics, and to international critics, which would permit a continuance of the importation of Chinese laborers became a great objective of the Peruvian government. No longer could the mission to China, for some time projected, be delayed. It must be on its way forthwith, and it must succeed in its objective, else irreparable harm to the Peruvian economy would result.

[55] Translation in *El Comercio*, March 24, 1874.
[56] *Ibid.*; also in *Documentos Parlamentarios*, *1874*, I, 237-238.
[57] Gálvez to Minister of Foreign Relations of Peru, Lisbon, April 22, 1874, *Documentos Parlamentarios*, *1874*, I, 241-242.

VIII

THE GARCIA Y GARCÍA MISSION—
INSTRUCTIONS; JAPAN

THE NECESSITY of sending an embassy to China was clear to the Peruvian government as early as mid-year of 1870. In an interpellation which he sustained in the Cámara de Diputados on November 17, 1876, José Antonio García y García, the minister of foreign relations, made some revealing declarations on the subject. The laws of China, he stated, had made it impossible to secure laborers from that country in a direct manner. They were brought through Hongkong as long as the English permitted it, and later through Portuguese Macao. The government of President Balta had become anxious lest the movement through the Portuguese colony become impossible through pressure of the Chinese and the English. In July, 1870, declared the minister, and again in February, 1871, President Balta had offered him the headship of a Chinese mission. Personal and political reasons had prevented his accepting. Positive action at the time did not ensue because of the disturbed condition of internal politics consequent to the approaching end of Balta's term in early August, 1872.[1]

Those political troubles led, just at the conclusion of Balta's presidency, to the attempted barracks revolution of July 22-26, headed by the Gutiérrez brothers, which resulted in the assassination of Balta.[2] Thus his administra-

[1] "Apéndice," *Diario de los Debates*, Cámara de Diputados, Congreso Ordinario de 1876, pp. xxi-xxii.
[2] For a brief account of this insurrection, see Stewart, *Henry Meiggs: Yankee Pizarro*, pp. 283-287. A longer account appears in the work

tion accomplished actually nothing in the matter of the proposed diplomatic mission.

When the succeeding president, Manuel Pardo, took office on August 2, it was already fairly certain that the movement of coolies through Macao would not for long continue. Moreover, the procedure of the Japanese government respecting the *María Luz* had caused the Peruvian government much concern; the national honor was involved. The establishment of good diplomatic relations with both of the Oriental Empires seemed highly desirable, if not absolutely necessary, particularly as concerned China. The Pardo government acted with commendable dispatch. On November 6, 1872, it appointed Naval Captain Aurelio García y García as envoy extraordinary and minister plenipotentiary to the governments of both China and Japan.[3]

García y García, in addition to enjoying prestige as a high officer in the Peruvian navy, was a member of a family of excellent standing.[4] He was also author of "important publications on navigation of the coasts of Peru and other scientific works," which had earned him some recognition in Europe and the United States. He had been for some years commander of the armored frigate *Independencia*, a ship whose construction he had supervised in London in the years 1865-1866.[5] In the course of the interpellation alluded to, the foreign min-

of Pedro Dávalos y Lissón, *La primera centuria* (Lima, 1919-1926), IV, 295-308. Lima's newspapers of late July, particularly *La Patria* of the twenty-seventh, contain extended accounts.

[3] Instructions in *Documentos Parlamentarios, 1874*, I, 76. The instructions, with two brief omissions, are to be found on pp. 76-83, *ibid*. The complete original is in MSS, Ministerio de Relaciones Exteriores del Perú, 126-A.

[4] A grandson, Dr. Enrique García Sayán, was, in 1947, Peruvian Minister of Foreign Relations.

[5] *El Americano* (Paris), II (April 21, 1873), 65.

ister stated that the broad purposes of the mission were, as respects China, "to remove in a definite and suitable manner" the two grave obstacles which were embarrassing the immigration of Chinese to Peru: (1) the lack of treaties between Peru and China which would open Chinese ports to free emigration from China to Peru, and (2) the absence of a sure and rapid means of communication between the two countries, such as would be afforded by a line of steamers.[6]

The instructions of Captain García y García bear the date of December 3, 1872. The minister of foreign relations, at the time José de la Riva Agüero, began by surveying briefly Peru's experience with immigrants for agricultural labor. In the course of this survey he declared, "The Asiatic immigrant has been, as regrettable and as strange as it may seem, the sole one compatible with the peculiar exigencies of our agriculture, and with the ardent climate of our coast."[7] Respecting the abuses charged against that immigration, he made the interesting statement that "if they exist, they can emanate only from the first contractors or runners in the ports and in the interior of the empire and from the secondary runners or agents who present the emigrants in Macao for contracting."[8] The envoy was instructed that the great object of his mission was to promote the establishment of direct, frank, and cordial communication between the government of Peru and the governments of China and Japan and to establish the bases for such communication in treaties. As any pact made by the envoy would be *ad referendum*, only general principles were laid down.

García y García must insist on including in these treaties "the same advantages, the same practices, and

[6] *Loc. cit.*, p. xxii.   [7] *Documentos Parlamentarios, 1874,* I, 77.
[8] *Ibid.*

AURELIO GARCIA Y GARCIA

the same reservations" which had been inserted in treaties made with the most favored nation, especially with the United States, England, France, Russia, Austria, Italy, Spain, and Portugal, which had treaties with China and Japan. He was to insist also, as an essential clause in the treaties of friendship, commerce, and navigation, on a provision for "the liberty of the citizens of each of the contracting parties to emigrate to the territory of the other." (It must be remembered that China and the United States in 1868 had drawn and ratified the Burlingame Treaty; it established very liberal provisions for mutual immigration, putting the parties on a basis of complete equality.) The government, declared the minister, considered it indispensable "to celebrate a special convention on emigration with China," and with Japan as well, if Japan were so disposed. The end in view in making such conventions was to assure to the subjects of those nations who might transfer themselves to Peru "positive guarantees of liberty in contracting, good treatment and comfort on the voyage, and morality and respect in the exercise of the labors to which they might obligate themselves." The envoy was referred to the conventions of similar nature made by England and France with China in 1866 and promulgated as law by China on March 22, 1868, for the norms which he should follow. The envoy was reminded that while Spain had made a convention with China respecting emigration similar to that of England and France, difficulties had been put in the way of its full execution; he must endeavor to avoid a similar history for the conventions which he should make. He might propose the sending to Peru of an agent especially charged with assuring the exact fulfilment of conditions stipulated in labor contracts.

It was suggested to Captain García y García that he

would do well to put himself in contact with one or more Chinese companies that might establish the business of fomenting free emigration to Peru, "as has been done in the case of California." If he could make such an arrangement, the minister asserted, a direct steamship line would be established immediately between Callao and the ports of China. He added, "I do not doubt that the Pacific Steam Navigation Company at once will furnish boats suitable to this service."

The instructions contain an extended section on diplomatic and consular agents with emphasis on the latter. "Very high and very delicate are . . . the functions which our consuls are called upon to discharge, and, for this reason, it is indispensable to employ the greatest care in their appointment." The governments of China and Japan had adopted the principle of not admitting as consuls persons engaged in commercial operations in their countries. Because of this, other nations had named and were maintaining in those countries salaried consular officials. García y García was empowered to appoint provisional consuls where he thought them most needed, provided he could make the necessary treaty arrangements. If the importance of official relations, or of commerce, or the movements of emigrants warranted setting up a permanent mission in Peking or Yedo, the envoy was empowered to appoint as chargé d'affaires ad interim and consulgeneral the secretary of the legation, Don Juan Federico Elmore.

The minister provided García y García with the various documents relating to the *María Luz* affair—to "the improper and hostile interference of the diplomatic agent of His Britannic Majesty in Yedo," and to the action of the Japanese court. In the view of the Peruvian government, the voyage of the *María Luz* was made under the same legal conditions as the voyages of those ships that left Macao for Peru and Cuba, or the ports of China for the English and French colonies. The procedure of the Japanese authorities had constituted "an insult to our flag and grave injuries to the masters and the outfitters of the vessel." On his arrival in Yokohama, the envoy would carefully investigate the antecedents of the case and act in such manner as to secure reparation for the injustice and violence of which Captain Herrera had been the object, and indemnity for damages as well as satisfaction to the Peruvian flag.

Gifts for the sovereigns and high functionaries of China and Japan were provided. The envoy would make such use of them as he should think proper. They were not considered as having any value for their utility or richness "but as a moral sign of the high value placed on relations with those people" who were for the first time being saluted by the people and government of Peru.

In the final paragraph of the instructions these words appear:

It will contribute greatly to the success of your mission if you can persuade the cabinets of Pekin and Yedo and foreign diplomats that the Peruvian government in promoting the drawing of treaties, especially conventions of emigration, is obeying the same high inspirations of justice, the same humanitarian interests, which are moving the European nations and the United States, to work toward the reform of systems adopted for the contracting and transport of the Asiatic emigrants. On the other hand, it is to be hoped that you will find friendly support in the representatives of the United States and France and to whose governments I have addressed myself, asking their moral aid to facilitate the success of your laudable propositions. I have as yet not had official response, which, in my judgment, cannot fail to be satisfactory.[9]

[9] *Ibid.*, I, 83.

The Peruvian government thus clothed Captain García y García with ample powers and left him a wide field for initiative. The captain's abilities, as the sequel will show, justified the trust placed in him.

In addition to the chief, the mission consisted of the following persons: Secretary, Dr. Juan Federico Elmore; adjuncts, Emilio Guiroy, Julio Benavides, Almanzor Paz Soldán, Joaquín Delgado, Tadeo Roa Tudela, and Gerardo Garland; military aide, Sergeant Major Francisco Ramos Pacheco; naval aides, Second Lieutenants Octavio Freyre and Nicanor Aramburú.[10] The minister's instructions obliged all the members of the mission to live together. The chief of the mission was urged to give the young men the most positive injunctions to observe that "worthy and circumspect conduct which belonged to the mission" that they were fulfilling. If any one of them should commit a fault, García y García was authorized to put him on the next boat for Peru, giving him only the cost of his passage.[11] One concludes that these were young men of high spirits and that their superiors may have anticipated some difficulty in controlling them.

The original intention was to send the mission to China under convoy of two warships. However, when the *María Luz* incident led to the inclusion of Japan, the idea of warships was dropped "in order to avoid doubts concerning its pacific ends."[12] The rumor had, in fact, got about in Japan that Peru was planning war in satisfaction of its wounded honor.[13] The mission, therefore, traveled in commercial passenger boats.

[10] Riva Agüero to García y García, Lima, Dec. 19, 1872, MSS, Ministerio de Relaciones Exteriores del Perú, 126-A, 28.

[11] Same to same, Lima, Dec. 21, 1872, *ibid.*, p. 29.

[12] *Documentos Parlamentarios, 1874*, I, 75.

[13] DeLong to Peruvian Minister of Foreign Relations, Feb. 18, 1873, MSS, Ministerio de Relaciones Exteriores del Perú; Año 1873; Legación en China y Japón; Anexos.

Captain García y García did not long delay his departure after he had received his instructions. He was in Panama in late December,[14] and in late January a San Diego, California, newspaper was describing the visit of the mission to that city where its members were taken· for a tour of local places of interest. The reporter was impressed by their youth—none of them seemed to be more than thirty years old.[15] On February 1 Captain García y García and his young men made their exit from San Francisco's "Golden Gate" in the ship *Colorado.* The vessel anchored in the port of Yokohama on the twenty-seventh of the same month.[16] On instructions from the United States minister, DeLong, the captain of the U. S. S. *Idaho,* then in port, sent a boat to carry the Peruvian party ashore. They debarked immediately.[17]

The Japanese government placed at the disposition of the visiting diplomats the Imperial Palace of Hamagoten. Formerly a palace of the shoguns, it was a magnificent residence, sumptuously furnished and well supplied with objects of art. Its beautiful gardens and extensive parks extended to the shore of the Bay of Tokyo. There the mission found itself comfortably, even opulently, lodged.[18]

It was logical to attempt first the Japanese portion of the mission. Japan was geographically nearer than China. Moreover, the problem here was simpler, and it could be hoped that it might be solved in a comparatively short time. Too, as a preliminary, the Japanese negotiations

[14] *El Nacional,* Feb. 6, 1873, quoting *Estrella de Panamá,* Dec. 31, 1872.

[15] *South Pacific Times,* March 15, 1873, quoting an unidentified California periodical.

[16] Ricardo Aranda, ed., *Colección de los Tratados, Convenciones, Capitulaciones, Armisticios, y otros actos diplomáticos y políticos celebrados desde la Independencia* (Lima, 1907), II, 48.

[17] Jorge Bailey Lembecke, "La primera misión diplomática del Perú al Japón," *El Comercio,* Oct. 26, 1941, p. 16.

[18] *Ibid.*

would provide valuable experience for the main event in China. DeLong, instructed from Washington on the coming of the mission, did what he could to prepare the ground. Late in December he wrote a note to the Japanese minister of foreign relations announcing that the Peruvian government proposed sending a mission to make a treaty of friendship and commerce. He invoked an agreeable reception and expressed the hope that the mission might be successful in gaining its end. The minister replied:

The Government of His Imperial Majesty the Emperor will receive the Representative of Peru with great pleasure; and will listen with respect and consideration to such proposals as he may be instructed to make; and when he arrives he will receive a hearty welcome and such success as shall appear consistent with justice and the interests of the Empire.[19]

The emperor received the Peruvian minister on March 3, and the same evening his foreign minister, Soyeshima Tane-omi, was host at a state banquet in the Hamagoten Palace.[20] Probably shortly after his arrival, Captain García y García presented to the emperor the articles which he had brought for that purpose. These gifts consisted of a large photograph of the Peruvian president in a gilt frame; specimens in a crystal urn of all the modern coins of Peru and of the principal medals in gold and silver commemorative of national public works;[21] a complete set of silver toilet articles for the bathroom, in a leather case; two albums bound in velvet with silver clasps, one

[19] DeLong to the Peruvian Minister of Foreign Relations, Yokohama, Jan. 18, 1873, enclosing copies of correspondence with the Japanese government, MSS, Ministerio de Relaciones Exteriores del Perú; Año 1873; Legación en China y Japón; Anexos.

[20] Bailey, *op. cit.*

[21] The coins were 4 of gold, 5 of silver, 2 of copper; the medals, 18 of gold, 18 of silver (*ibid.*).

of photographic views of Peru, the other of photographs of distinguished Peruvians, each in its case; two maps, one of South America, the other of Peru; a box with works on Peru—geography, history, statistics, antiquities, law, agriculture, public works—sixteen books in all; two boxes of coffee from Carabaya; one box of chocolate from Cuzco; and a collection of Peruvian wines and *aguardientes*. Other officials with whom the mission had contacts received gifts of a similar sort in a descending scale of their importance. Minister DeLong, for instance, was given three geographical works on Peru, including a map, one box of Carabaya coffee, one cask of Falconi sherry, and half a dozen bottles of Locumba *aguardiente*.[22] To square the bill, as it were, before the mission departed, the emperor presented President Pardo with a portrait of himself, a casket of Japanese coins, five of gold, five of silver, two Japanese lacquer boxes, two rolls of silk, two boxes of Japanese tea in a case, and two albums.[23]

A detailed discussion of the Peruvian envoy's activities in Japan is not required here. Only their larger aspects demand attention, particularly those associated with the *María Luz* controversy. After discharging the social amenities, the captain and the Japanese foreign minister began their discussions. To employ the captain's phrase, they were carried forward "in truly complicated circumstances." Since each government felt itself in the right in its attitude toward the *María Luz* happenings, and as neither would yield its point, their representatives finally arrived at the conclusion that the only solution was arbitration. Their choice of arbitrator fell upon the Russian tsar. This decision they reached on June 22, protocols for

[22] García y García to Minister of Foreign Relations of Peru, Yokohama, July 7, 1873, *ibid.*

[23] Same to same, Yokohama, Sept. 7, 1873, *ibid.*

the arbitration having been signed on the nineteenth.[24] As to the *María Luz* itself, we have seen that Captain Herrera had been constrained to abandon it in the Bay of Yokohama in the care of the United States minister. The two governments agreed that the ship should be sold at public auction. From the proceeds, the costs of its care should be paid, and Japan would retain the balance until the conclusion of the arbitration.[25]

With the arbitration agreed upon, the "truly complicated circumstances" were not sufficient to keep the captain from reaching his goal of a treaty of friendship, commerce, and navigation. One of these circumstances was Japan's desire to relieve itself of the obligation of extraterritoriality embodied in its treaties with European nations. At the time when García y García and Soyeshima were negotiating, a Japanese mission was in Europe endeavoring to alter those treaties according to Japan's desires. Japan did not wish to include in the Peruvian treaty the clauses that it was trying to remove from the existing treaties. Yet García y García was instructed to insist on the inclusion of those clauses.[26] "After many difficulties which only a pertinacious patience was able to vanquish," the Peruvian envoy gained his point. However, the Japanese negotiator, by insisting on dubbing the resulting treaty "preliminary," emphasized what Japan hoped would be its temporary character.[27] An agreement on the terms of the treaty was reached on August 18, but

[24] *Documentos Parlamentarios, 1874,* I, 125-126, 133. The original of the protocols is in English and is encountered in MSS, Ministerio de Relaciones Exteriores del Perú; Año 1873; Legación en China y Japón; Anexos, No. 9.

[25] *Ibid.*, p. 133.   [26] Bailey, *op. cit.*

[27] For the text of the treaty, see *El Peruano; Boletín Oficial,* Oct. 2, 1875, p. 133. The official English version—a four-page pamphlet on bluish-purple paper—is filed in MSS, Ministerio de Relaciones Exteriores del Perú; Año 1873; Legación en China y Japón; Anexos.

the treaty signatures were affixed on the twenty-first; consequently, that is the official date of the treaty. As a manifestation of the sincerity of the relations which Japan was thus establishing with Peru, the forts of Kanagawa, on the day of signing, raised the Peruvian flag and fired a twenty-one-gun salute. Reporting the fact to his home minister, the captain informed him of his pledge to Japan that within twenty-four hours of receipt of news of the signing of the treaty, the forts of Callao would return the courtesy.[28] The Peruvian envoy was careful to enclose a description and a drawing in color of the Japanese flag for the information of his government. The Peruvian pledge was fulfilled faithfully on September 20, 1873.[29] Presumably, this exchange represented a compromise pursuant to a demand by the captain for an apology and a salute.

A social event of the mission's stay in Japan was the celebration on July 28 of the fifty-second anniversary of Peru's independence. Hamagoten Palace was the scene of another banquet, the guests being the entire diplomatic corps and the foreign minister and other functionaries of Japan. The chief toast of the occasion was given by the dean of the corps, the Britisher, Sir Harry Parkes. In most friendly terms, he toasted the day, the prosperity of Peru, and the health of its president, while expressing satisfaction at seeing in the midst of the corps the representative of the "young and progressive Republic."[30] The occasion was all the more satisfactory and enjoyable as the end of the negotiations was in sight.

[28] Yedo, Aug. 21, 1873, MSS, Ministerio de Relaciones Exteriores del Perú; Año 1873; Legación en China y Japón.

[29] Peruvian Minister of Foreign Relations, to García y García, Lima, Sept. 20, 1873, MSS, Ministerio de Relaciones Exteriores del Perú; Vol. 126-A, 40.

[30] García y García to Peruvian Minister of Foreign Relations, Yedo, Aug. 5, 1873 (*ibid.*, Legación en China y Japón).

The Peruvian minister of foreign relations, in acknowledging his envoy's news of the completion of the treaty, spoke of the agreeable surprise of the government and the entire country, and felicitated the captain on "the brilliant result" which he had obtained in the "two most important matters" which were commended to him before the Japanese government.[31] The treaty was ratified by the Peruvian congress on September 5, 1874.[32]

The *María Luz* incident was soon disposed of, once for all. The Russian arbitrator announced his decision in June, 1875, after the governments concerned had stated their respective cases in voluminous documents. The case of Peru was drawn by Joseph Antoine de Lavalle y Saavedra, envoy extraordinary and minister plenipotentiary to Russia and Germany.[33] The tsar pronounced in favor of Japan, declaring that the Japanese authorities had acted in good faith and in the conviction that they were discharging an unpleasant duty when they seized the ship. No treaty between Peru and Japan existing, the Japanese government was not bound to indemnify Peru for losses sustained in the seizure of the vessel. One Peruvian publication, when announcing the decision, expressed the belief that Peru, notwithstanding the adverse decision, was the gainer, since the incident had led to the making of a satisfactory treaty with Japan and had "caused the country to acquire a reputation in the East it had not possessed before Señor García y García visited it in the character of Peruvian ambassador."[34] The decision did not, however, please Sr. Lavalle y Saavedra. Under date of June 15, 1875, he wrote an extended note to his government denouncing

---

[31] Sept. 20, 1873, *ibid.*, 126-A, 40.

[32] *El Peruano; Boletín Oficial*, Sept. 18, 1874.

[33] For the text of the "Exposición," see *El Peruano; Boletín Oficial*, of July 27, 1875, pp. 33-36.

[34] *South Pacific Times*, Aug. 7, 1875.

the "injustice" of the decision and declaring that the arbitrator had not even given himself the trouble of studying the formidable document which he had drawn for the tsar's instruction.[35]   The arbitrator's lot, as well as the policeman's, is not a happy one.

In accordance with the agreement of the negotiators, Minister DeLong proceeded to advertise the *María Luz* for sale, a "dodger," and, perhaps, the newspapers as well, being used for the purpose.   An interesting item of the dodger is that which catalogues the equipment of the "Chinese Galley"—"1 Lot Cooking Utensils, 1 Lot Dippers, 100 Tin Pans, 230 Tin Cups"—not an overly adequate equipment, it would seem, for providing food for 237 persons.[36]   This list contrasts with a listing of ten classes of items under "Galley," presumably the equipment of the galley that served officers and crew.   The certificate of sale describes the *María Luz*: British built, by Whiteharm; sails; two decks; three masts; length, 109 feet, 2 inches; breadth, 26 feet, 8 inches; depth, 18 feet, 5 inches; weight, 370 tons.[37]   The ship was purchased by L. Haber, Esq., a German, for the sum of $7,250.00 (Mex.).   After deducting costs of the sale and the sums which DeLong had spent in caring for the vessel, there remained for later disposal $4,713.28 (Mex.).[38]   This sum was turned over in 1877 to Herrera and Sauri, the original owners, Herrera being the same who was captain of the vessel when it encountered trouble.[39]

Captain García y García judged that Peru needed a

---

[35] Bailey, *op. cit.*
[36] A specimen of the dodger is filed in MSS, Ministerio de Relaciones Exteriores del Perú; Año 1873; Legación en China y Japón; Anexos.
[37] *Ibid.*
[38] The corresponding documents are in *ibid.*
[39] John A. Bingham, United States minister to Japan, to Secretary of State, Tokyo, May 7, 1877, Diplomatic Despatches, Japan 34, No. 554.

consular organization in Japan. Consequently, in exercise of authority contained in his instructions, he appointed Oscar Heeren as consul-general in Yedo. The Japanese government at once granted the necessary exequatur.[40]

In the autumn of 1873 Captain García y García had some reason for feeling that he had done rather well in Japan. While he could get nothing better than arbitration in the matter of the *María Luz,* yet arbitration did provide for a definitive settlement, and he could hope that the judgment might be favorable to his country. He had, moreover, secured a treaty—"preliminary" though it was—which gave satisfaction to his superiors. He could, perhaps, face the far more difficult Chinese part of his mission with better morale and with increased efficiency, the result of his experiences in negotiating with the Japanese. So, with hope and courage, he turned his face from the "Land of the Rising Sun" to that of the little known, recently opened, and still somewhat mysterious Chinese Empire. He had succeeded in making Peru's first treaty —the first, in fact, of any American nation other than the United States—with an Oriental country. Would he be able to make its second?

[40] García y García to Peruvian Minister of Foreign Relations, Yedo, Sept. 7, 1873, MSS, Ministerio de Relaciones Exteriores del Perú; Año 1873; Legación en China y Japón.

IX

THE GARCÍA Y GARCÍA MISSION— CHINA

THE CIRCUMSTANCES under which Captain García y García negotiated his treaty with China were decidedly more "truly complicated" than those which he had confronted in Japan. For almost a quarter century the coolie traffic had been "one of China's great griefs," as an American minister declared about this time. "Both government and people feel that it is a great wrong and injustice, forced upon them against their will by foreign nations. This feeling . . . is universal."[1] Dr. S. Wells Williams, of the American legation, a man of long experience in China, writing to García y García, asserted that "The atrocities and wrongs connected with this business have left the impression on the minds of those who know anything of the matter, that it is equivalent almost to a living death for one of their countrymen to be taken away as a coolie."[2] The Chinese rulers considered Peru to have been one of the worst offenders in this traffic. "In the estimation of the Chinese, a Peruvian was little better than a *kidnapper*."[3] The situation of the Peruvian envoy was made worse by the fact that at the moment China was engaged in an acrimonious controversy with Spain regarding the coolie trade and the treatment of its nationals in Cuba. In Chinese popular opinion, Peruvians were

[1] F. F. Low to Secretary of State, June 24, 1872, No. 166, Diplomatic Despatches, China 32.
[2] Peking, Sept. 22, 1873 (encl. with No. 11), Despatches, China 35.
[3] Eli T. Sheppard, United States consul, Tientsin, to Williams, July 15, 1874 (encl. with Williams' No. 49), Diplomatic Despatches, China 36.

pretty much identified with Spaniards, an error made easy because many of the Macao agents of Peruvian coolie dealers and numbers of the captains of Peruvian ships engaged in the traffic were Spaniards.[4] The Peruvian captain might well feel that he was attempting one of the more difficult labors of Hercules in negotiating with the Chinese dragon.

García y García had not even been able to learn what was going to be the official attitude toward his mission. From Japan he had directed letters to the representatives in China of Great Britain, France, and the United States —the Messrs. Wade, Geofroy, and Low, respectively— soliciting their aid with the Chinese authorities and asking for their opinions regarding his reception.[5]

Minister Low, shortly after he received the captain's request, addressed the Chinese emperor's chief minister, Prince Kung, informing him of the intended arrival of the Peruvian mission and expressing the hope that it might be received "in the same spirit which animated Peru in sending it."[6] Prince Kung's reply was prompt. He referred to the mutual good will which existed between China and other nations with which treaties had been made, then, referring to Peru, continued:

But the manner in which that country has acted towards China is so different from the conduct of other nations that she cannot be regarded in the same light; and I am obliged to enter into some details to explain it to your Excellency. The only

[4] Juan F. Elmore, chargé, to Peruvian Minister of Foreign Relations, Hongkong, Sept. 11, 1874. MSS, Ministerio de Relaciones Exteriores del Perú; Año 1874; Legación en China y Japón.

[5] García y García to Peruvian Minister of Foreign Relations, Shanghai, Oct. 11, 1873. *Documentos Parlamentarios, 1874,* I, 205. For letter to Low, dated Yedo, June 15, see MSS, Ministerio de Relaciones Exteriores del Perú; Año 1873; Legación en China y Japón; Low's reply in *ibid.*

[6] July 5, 1873. (Encl. No. 3 with No. 276 to Secretary of State), Diplomatic Despatches, China 34.

traffic which Peru has heretofore carried on is getting coolies and carrying them away, so that there are now several myriads of Chinese in that land. These people are treated with such injustice and cruelty, and suffer such extreme misery, that it cannot be adequately made known.

Prince Kung made reference to the notes he had received some time since from Browne and Williams enclosing representations from the Chinese in Peru, and went on:

This government has also heard from other sources of the harsh treatment of Chinese laborers by the Peruvians, who never stop their oppression till death ends it, and whose plan is just to sell human flesh for money. The evidence of their barbarous dealings with the coolie is plain and explicit; and this Government has no desire to make a treaty with that country.
. . . this Government considers that it will not be meet to repel the Peruvians too harshly or too finally; but they ought to be plainly informed that until they return all the coolies to their own country, and agree not to hire any more no treaty can be made with them. If they decline this, it will be impossible to enter into any arrangements with them.[7]

The two other ministers proceeded as did Low and received replies of similar tenor. Their responses to García y García's notes were not encouraging. They indicated, in the captain's interpretation of them, that for the time "nothing could be hoped from the Chinese authorities, and very little from the group of foreign legations in Pekin."[8] However, the envoy wrote again to Wade and Low (Geofroy's reply had not yet been received), invoking their best efforts to secure an alteration in the severe Chinese attitude. He decided to go to Shanghai in

[7] Tungchi, July 6, 1873. English translation in *ibid.*, Diplomatic Despatches, China 34 (encl. 5 with Low's No. 276).
[8] To Peruvian Minister of Foreign Relations, Shanghai, Oct. 11, 1873, *Documentos Parlamentarios, 1874*, I, 206.

the meantime and await further developments. He could not afford to enter Tientsin until he felt assured he would not receive a diplomatic rebuff.

García y García's position in China was further embarrassed by a domestic incident. From Yedo, on June 3, 1873, he had notified his superior in Lima that he had separated from the mission one of his young men, Tadeo Roa Tudela, for being "quarrelsome and not conducting himself as a gentleman." The captain had wished to send him directly back to Peru with Elmore, who was carrying dispatches, but Roa Tudela balked. Whereupon, having no other recourse, the chief of the mission summarily dismissed the young man.[9] Roa then struck out on his own to see China. Attaching himself to a complaisant French traveler, he started for Peking. But, as he lacked a passport, his character of "friend" of the traveler was not sufficient to carry him through, and he was stopped at Tientsin by Chinese officials. Forced to turn back, he went to Hongkong. While there he became incensed at a report concerning his activities that had appeared in the Shanghai *North China Daily News*. In a letter to the editor—in his own English, presumably—he denied that he was a Peruvian official, as had been stated. He continued in a high tone:

I am only a Peruvian gentleman travelling round the world, as the same manner of the Editor of the *North China Daily News* a writer without material to his journal, and without respect and consideration for the persons, as strange in this country as the Editor himself. Should I seen there, your journal, I would answer to you in another way—as present, I advise you to take notice of the things before giving it to the public.[10]

[9] No. 43 in MSS, Ministerio de Relaciones Exteriores del Perú; Año 1873; Legación en China y Japón.
[10] García y García to Minister of Foreign Relations, Shanghai, Oct. 11, 1873, No. 67 (newspaper clipping enclosed), MSS, Ministerio de Relaciones Exteriores del Perú; Año 1873; Legación en China y Japón.

Roa Tudela's effusion is dated September 20. The newspapers represented this incident as a defeat for the Peruvian mission, assuming that Roa was still attached to it.[11]
While the incident proved the wisdom of the Peruvian
government in conferring on the chief of the mission full
power over his subordinates, it certainly did not make
easier the mission's task.

García y García and most of his assistants reached
Shanghai on October 7.[12] He learned shortly that it
would be safe to proceed to Tientsin. Dr. Williams had
had a conference with Prince Kung on September 16.
He had carried with him a twenty-page communication
from the Peruvian minister in which that official had set
forth Peru's reasons for wanting a treaty and had done
his best to show the falsity of current Chinese ideas concerning the Peruvian coolies.[13] In conformity with the
Peruvian's request the American chargé imparted to
Prince Kung the chief items of this document. In the
course of the conference Williams insisted on "the im-
propriety of refusing to receive and confer with an envoy
sent with the most friendly intentions, from a foreign
country, and dismissing him without even hearing what
he had to say even if the Chinese objected to making a
treaty."[14] Dr. Williams' efforts, joined with those of the
British and French ministers, finally elicited from the
authorities the declaration that "no minister of a foreign
state, even of those that have not made treaties, was ever

[11] *Ibid.*

[12] To Peruvian Minister of Foreign Relations, Shanghai, Oct. 11, 1873,
ibid. Freyre, ill, had been left behind in Yedo at the home of Consul Heeren
(*ibid.*).

[13] Yedo, Aug. 25, 1873, *ibid.* Also English translation (enclosure 1
with Williams' No. 11, Peking, Nov. 20, 1873), Diplomatic Despatches,
China 35.

[14] Williams to García y García, Peking, Sept. 22, 1873 (enclosure with
No. 11 to Secretary of State), *ibid.*

received in China with discourtesy." The three ministers, after securing this concession, were unanimous in recommending to the Peruvian envoy that he proceed to Tientsin. There, in accordance with Chinese custom, he would be received by the viceroy or governor-general, Li Hung Chang. But, in making this concession of courtesy, Prince Kung restated the government's basic policy respecting Peru—China would make no treaty with that country until all the coolies that had been taken to Peru should have been returned to Chinese soil.[15] Nor would the prince listen to Dr. Williams' suggestion that a special commission be appointed to talk with the Peruvian envoy in Tientsin.[16] Notwithstanding the unfavorable auspices and with nothing more than the slight encouragement embodied in Prince Kung's statement regarding Chinese courtesy, the captain determined to continue to Tientsin.[17]

The Peruvian mission arrived at Tientsin, a city situated some eighty miles from Peking, on October 23.[18] It encountered considerable difficulty in finding suitable quarters. Finally, through the agency of the United States consul, a house was located, though an empty one which had to be furnished at much expense. Here the legation of Peru was installed, and the minister was able to receive visitors with some degree of dignity.[19]

Viceroy Li Hung Chang, with whom García y García negotiated, was China's most famous general; he had victoriously put an end to the Great Taiping Rebellion. He was said to recognize no superior save the emperor him-

---

[15] García y García to Minister of Foreign Relations, Shanghai, Oct. 11, 1873, *loc. cit.*; also in *Documentos Parlamentarios, 1874*, I, 205-207.
[16] *Ibid.*   [17] *Ibid.*
[18] García y García to Pedro Gálvez, Tientsin, Dec. 11, 1873, MSS, Ministerio de Relaciones Exteriores del Perú; Año 1873; Legación en China y Japón.
[19] *South Pacific Times*, April 9, 1874, quoting letter from Peking, Dec. 23, published originally in Lima's *Opinión Nacional*.

self.[20] In a passage of one of his official letters—suppressed when published originally in 1874—the Peruvian plenipotentiary said of him, ". . . he has the reputation of being an enemy of foreigners and of possessing a character excessively vain and proud, as well as violent and discourteous."[21] In other items of his correspondence, García y García described some of Li Hung Chang's ideas as "puerile" and stated that he gave proofs of "the most crass ignorance" respecting everything Peruvian.[22] Li Hung Chang was one of China's two viceroys or captains-general. These officials were superintendents of commerce in their respective jurisdictions—North and South China—and had as one of their duties that of dealing with foreign representatives who for the first time came to China. Li Hung Chang exercised the superintendency of the ports of the north to which the Peruvian minister, when given a choice by Prince Kung, had decided to go because it was nearer Peking.[23]

On October 24 Li Hung Chang received Captain García y García, courteously and in considerable style. The viceroy, accompanied by several mandarins, advanced to the outer patio of his residence to receive his visitor and immediately seated him at a table "profusely prepared beforehand with fruits and sweets of the country, tea, and liquors." On the twenty-sixth the viceroy returned the visit, with a numerous following. Both calls turned into discussions of the coolie question, their content being much the same. The viceroy spoke of the cruel

[20] *Ibid.*

[21] To Minister of Foreign Relations, Tientsin, Oct. 31, 1873, MSS, Ministerio de Relaciones Exteriores del Perú; Año 1873; Legación en China y Japón.

[22] To Gálvez, Oct. 23, 1873, *ibid.*, Anexos; to Minister of Foreign Relations, Dec. 23, 1873, *ibid.*

[23] García y García to Minister of Foreign Relations, Tientsin, Oct. 31, 1873, *Documentos Parlamentarios, 1874,* I, 209.

treatment the coolies had received in Peru, the effect of which, he declared, was that nine out of ten of them died. He made repeated references to the representations which the Chinese in Peru had made to their home government in 1869 and 1871. He declared emphatically that no treaty with Peru could be negotiated until it should have returned to their country all the Chinese who had been taken there. The viceroy did not conceal his "pronounced animus" against Peru.[24]

To the charges launched by the viceroy, García y García replied as best he could. That the Chinese did not by any means die in Peru in the numbers of the viceroy's declaration was clearly proved by the fact that there were nearly 100,000 of them in Peru at that very time; a fact which also indicated that their treatment was not such as the viceroy believed it to be. The representations of 1869 and 1871 were not worthy of serious attention, for they consisted only of generalizations and listed the name of not a single individual who had suffered cruelty or been wronged in Peru. As to the return of the Chinese then in Peru, that was not possible; it would amount to a deportation contrary to the Peruvian constitution. Only the tribunals of justice could order a deportation as punishment for proved wrongdoing. Moreover, not all the Chinese would wish to return. Many of them had become prosperous merchants or farmers or had secured advantageous employment after working the period of their contracts. To deport them in a body would be a great injustice.

[24] *Ibid.* The interpreter for these talks was John A. T. Meadows, a merchant of Tientsin who had formerly served China. He had been thirty years in the country. The American consul, Sheppard, believed the Peruvians unwise in employing Meadows for the reason that he was not liked by Li Hung Chang. See Sheppard to Williams, July 15, 1874 (enclosure with Williams' No. 49), Diplomatic Despatches, China 36.

Such reasoning did not convince Li Hung Chang, though in the second interview, more or less the same charges and arguments being repeated, the Peruvian believed he saw a favorable modification in his words and manner. The captain, while contradicting many of the charges of the viceroy, declared that, in any event, those matters referred to an epoch that was past; that the existing government of Peru was greatly interested in improving the position of the Chinese colony and had put out a number of decrees designed to effect a betterment. The viceroy requested copies of the decrees, and García y García promised to furnish them.[25] He also suggested that after diplomatic relations should be established, if any abuses such as charged existed, they could be adjusted by the Chinese official in Peru. "Then," runs the Peruvian's report:

Mr. Li Hung Chang answers with great assurance, that if *foreigners* went to Peru, *their statements could not be believed;* that if Chinese Commissioners went, they *would be detained* there by the Peruvians and prevented from coming back; and that no Chinese mandarin would go. Finally, the Viceroy ended as he began, by doubting all I said.[26]

It appeared to the Peruvian plenipotentiary impossible to talk seriously on such bases as those on which Li Hung Chang insisted. Nevertheless, the conferences ended courteously.

Commenting on these visits, a Peruvian on the ground said of the viceroy that "he became convinced that humility was not a quality to be found in Señor García y García; and truth to say the relations of both persons have been

[25] García y García to Minister of Foreign Relations, Tientsin, Oct. 31, 1873, *Documentos Parlamentarios, 1874,* I, 209.
[26] To Williams. English translation in Diplomatic Despatches, China 35. It is dated "Shanghai, Oct. 10, 1873," an error probably made in copying, since it had to postdate Oct. 26.

very cordial, and have proved the sagacity and circumspection of our Minister."[27]

The decrees to which García y García had referred were those of midyear, 1873, which have been described in Chapter VI.[28] Faithful to his promise, he secured translations in Chinese and forwarded them to Li Hung Chang on the twenty-eighth.[29] The decree of October 14 he did not yet, of course, have in his hands. It was later to be put to a very effective use.

After he had received and, presumably, studied the copies of the decrees, Li Hung Chang wrote a strong note in reply. He confessed that the regulations seemed to him to have been dictated by "a spirit of justice and equity," but he feared that Peru's government would not have sufficient power to change the abuses established in the past. He again made reference to the petitions of 1869 and 1871. He remarked that, though the contracts provided for the return of the coolies at the end of their period of service, not one had been returned. "Consequently, the Peruvian regulations for the protection of the Chinese workers cannot be cited as proof that the government of Peru has protected them."

The viceroy made reference to the facts disclosed by the *María Luz* investigation, which proved arbitrary conduct toward Chinese workers abroad. He spoke of the numbers of Peruvian boats that had taken Chinese from Macao in 1870, 1871, and 1872, and the many workers that had been crowded into them. Regarding those countries that had treaties with China, the viceroy declared that they were not permitted to contract Chinese laborers in Macao. Peru, with no treaty, had proceeded in a clan-

[27] *South Pacific Times*, April 9, 1874.   [28] See p. 133.
[29] García y García to Minister of Foreign Relations, Tientsin, Oct. 31, 1873, *Documentos Parlamentarios*, *1874*, I, 212.

destine manner to take Chinese through Macao by force. "The Chinese people are, consequently, greatly irritated at the conduct of the Peruvians." In taking the 100,000 Chinese that were in Peru, the viceroy charged, Peru had violated the Rights of Man. He repeated the charge of cruelty in Peru. "The condition of those Chinese is truly deplorable!" He concluded his note with the statement that, owing to the reputation Peru had gained because of its treatment of Chinese coolies, he feared he would have difficulty in entering into negotiations for a treaty.[30]

These were serious charges, and they could not be permitted to go unanswered. García y García requested a conference with the viceroy. His request brought a reply indicating November 7 but fixing as a condition previous to discussion the return of all coolies to China. As a means of showing his displeasure, the Peruvian minister did not appear on the date set. Finally, however, an interview was arranged for the thirteenth.[31] On that date García y García spent three and a half hours in an effort to change the Chinese view. He got nowhere, unless an advance be seen in the viceroy's proposal for sending a commission to Peru—perhaps because of Dr. Williams' insistence on the point in talks with Prince Kung[32] —and the suggestion that after three years a treaty might be discussed. Repatriation continued to be the big point with the Chinese. In these circumstances García y García thought it time to play his trump card. He manifested to Li Hung Chang his intention to leave China immediately if the Imperial Government had resolved to make im-

[30] *Ibid.*, I, 217-219.
[31] García y García to Minister of Foreign Relations, Tientsin, Dec. 3, 1873, No. 78, MSS, Ministerio de Relaciones Exteriores del Perú; Año 1873; Legación en China y Japón.
[32] Williams to García y García, Peking, Oct. 31, 1873 (copy in Spanish with García y García's No. 78), *ibid.*

possible the establishment of permanent official relations between the two countries. "On hearing me, the Governor-General," he declared, "visibly changed face." The astute Peruvian took immediate advantage of this facial slip and proposed that, since the viceroy was operating under instructions from Peking, he, García y García, should draw up in detail his reply to Li Hung Chang's charges and that the reply be sent to Peking with the hope that it would produce a rational change in the original instructions. This solution was received with "great complacency" by the viceroy, and once again an interview terminated amicably.

The "exaggerated pretensions" of the Chinese government, the Peruvian envoy believed to be decidedly supported by the principal foreign legations in Peking.[33] In a section of his dispatch of December 3 (also omitted from the original Peruvian publication), he wrote:

Dr. Williams, replying to my note from Shanghai and the long letter from Tientsin . . . wrote me a communication, which I received the first week in November, in which he announced to me that "he did not believe it possible, asking another interview, to produce any modification in the opinions of Prince Kung or of the members of the Tsung-li-Yamen," and "it is not possible under the existing circumstances, that this Legation be invited or given permission to visit Peking." In the same note he details with rare originality, the bases for an arrangement, which he believes would serve as a beginning of international relations between Peru and China. This exceedingly curious piece merits special study; in it he is not in the least concerned with the dignity of our flag nor with the well understood national interests which I ought to cement here. The dominant idea of the North American Representative and which he presents as one of its warmest proponents, is that no contracted emigrant should leave

[33] To Foreign Minister, Tientsin, Dec. 3, 1873, *Documentos Parlamentarios, 1874,* I, 215-217.

China. Everything causes me to presume that the Cabinet in Pekin today agrees.[34]

Undaunted by the numerous difficulties which hedged him about, the Peruvian minister applied himself to drawing up the note of refutation as agreed with the viceroy. The resultant note bears the date of November 26. In some parts of it the argument is rather legalistic, but, on the whole, the job was well done. The bases of all the Chinese government's charges he saw as (1) the supposed unhappy state of its subjects in Peru, and (2) the manner in which it was believed the Chinese emigration to Peru was carried on. He discussed these points in detail, repeating at greater length the arguments he had already used verbally with Li Hung Chang. He was most legalistic in his remarks on the Chinese appeals of 1869 and 1871. "It is not said who were maltreated, by whom, when or where, and they cite not a single case in which a complaint of abuse made to a Peruvian official was disregarded." He quoted from a dispatch of Dr. Williams to Washington to indicate that the Chinese government was completely incapable of attending to the complaints of the Chinese nationals in Peru.[35]

Various of the statements of Li Hung Chang would be considered offensive were it not that the envoy was convinced that they arose from lack of information, a consequence of the isolation in which China had lived with respect to Peru. In two or three places in the document this barbed point was insinuated with some skill and force.

As to the conditions under which the emigration was

[34] To Peruvian Minister of Foreign Relations, MSS, Ministerio de Relaciones Exteriores del Perú; Año 1873; Legación en China y Japón. For text of Williams' suggested arrangement, see enclosure with his No. 11, Diplomatic Despatches, China 35.

[35] *United States Foreign Relations, 1871*, pp. 149-150.

carried on, according to the minister's exposition, they were clean and honorable, every Chinese having contracted quite willingly and understandingly for his period of Peruvian service. The viceroy's charge that men had been taken by force, that they had been bought, was not accompanied, as it should be if it were to have force, by a single specific instance. "In Peru there are not nor can there be slaves; slavery was abolished ten [*sic;* actually eighteen] years ago by a solemn declaration of the Peruvian government and human liberty is solidly guaranteed by our constitution and our laws." If it were admitted that some abuses had occurred abroad in the places where emigrants were embarked beyond the protection of Peruvian laws, it was precisely to correct such abuses that Peru had, at much cost and against many difficulties, sent a mission charged with making a treaty to eliminate them.

The captain repeated his argument respecting the impossibility of returning all the Chinese and cited chapter and verse of his country's constitution to support it. Then followed a long paragraph detailing the reasons for the Chinese wishing to emigrate—excess of population with an accompanying lack of means of subsistence; bad crops and famine; "moreover, though no country is found free of rebellions [and here, certainly, García y García could speak with authority!] in China they have been many and disastrous." (One must here remember the Taiping Rebellion.) "All this is in conformity with the laws of nature, and without prejudice to China." The charge that the Chinese were crowded into Peruvian boats in too great number the envoy did not find substantiated by facts. The mere fact that thirty-three Peruvian boats had in three years carried from Macao to Peru 15,681 Chinese was no proof that the boats had been overcrowded; the tonnage of the individual boat and its total of passengers were needed to determine overcrowding. "At present the English rule is in operation with us, according to which not more than one passenger per two tons of registry is permitted."

The note closed with a significant section in which García y García enumerated seven points as representing the "elevated designs" that animated the Peruvian government. They read as follows:

1st. The Peruvian Government in its desire that the Chinese emigrants should enjoy the greatest protection and that whatever abuses introduced in the course of time should disappear, has recently dictated special dispositions in their favor.

2nd. As a means of realizing in their totality these humanitarian ends, it has accredited a mission of the highest rank near His Majesty the Emperor of China, to whom His Excellency the President of Peru sent an autograph letter. The undersigned is in fact fully authorized to negotiate with the Chinese Plenipotentiary the treaties which will assure the interests of all sorts between the two people.

3rd. The condition previous to treating which His Imperial Highness Prince Kung has expressed, that is, that my Government must first repatriate en masse all the Chinese living in Peru, is inacceptable.

4th. The employers of the colonists in whose contracts repatriation has been stipulated, will be obliged to return them to China, when the emigrants solicit it, once their respective contracts are terminated.

5th. Also the employers will cancel all contracts of Chinese who may ask it, provided the colonists indemnify the employers for the losses due to cancellation.

6th. The Peruvian Government wishes that only immigrants who come of their free and spontaneous will should arrive at its coasts; and that there should also be established a movement of emigration similar to that which today exists between China and California.

7th. In Peru they would welcome with the greatest pleasure

the naming of an agent or agents accredited by the Chinese Government to watch over the interests of its nationals, to represent them before the authorities in case it were necessary, and report to the Imperial Government respecting their condition in the country.[36]

When the Peruvian envoy wrote his minister the dispatch of December 3, winter had come in North China and Tientsin was about to be cut off from communication by sea. The envoy saw himself completely isolated in that "inhospitable place, during a winter almost polar because of its rigor."[37] It was at this point of low morale that Captain García y García received, perhaps somewhat to his surprise, an invitation to go upriver and spend the winter in Peking. The arrangement resulted, declared Dr. Williams, from the good offices of Mr. Wade, the British minister, and "was calculated to promote the end which all the Legations desired to see—the negotiation of a treaty between China and Peru."[38] The Peruvian minister explained the invitation as arising from the fact that Li Hung Chang was at last convinced that he would not meet his conditions. He accepted it, as he said, "for the honor of Peru." And he accepted with some alacrity, for he entered Peking with his subordinates on December 21.[39]

The American consul at Tientsin, Eli Sheppard, later summarized rather neatly the character of García y García's two months of conversations and correspondence with Li Hung Chang at Tientsin. They consisted, he stated, largely of complaints by Li of the ill treatment of Chinese subjects in Peru which were met by the Peruvian's repeated denials of the truth of the charges:

[36] *Documentos Parlamentarios, 1874,* I, 219-230, the entire note.
[37] *Ibid.*
[38] To Secretary of State, Peking, July 25, 1874, No. 49, Diplomatic Despatches, China 36.
[39] García y García to Minister of Foreign Relations, Peking, Dec. 23, 1873, *Documentos Parlamentarios, 1874,* I, 230-231.

"How can China treat with Peru," asked Li, "while such things exist?"

"But they do not exist," urged the Minister again and again.

"Then let us send a Commission to Peru," said the Viceroy, "and ascertain the true condition of the Chinese there."

"No," rejoined the Minister, "if I cannot receive what I came after, I must return as I came, and your Government must take the consequences."

Li-Hung-Chang: the coolies must be returned.[40]

Actually, García y García had advanced slightly in the course of those two months. He had been unyielding in the matter of the return of the coolies en masse, and despite this attitude, he was being permitted to go to Peking. Furthermore, this period of exchanges with Li had afforded him an opportunity of stating clearly and at length the Peruvian ideas concerning the content of a treaty.

The Peruvians were vastly pleased at their reception in the Chinese capital. One of them, writing home about the big event of the entry into Peking, said:

The impenetrable and vast holy city, hidden from all those who do not find favor in the eyes of the "Sons of Heaven" has been freely, and quickly opened to the Peruvian representative. Yesterday, at half past two in the afternoon Señor García y García, on a Mongolian steed, and followed by sixteen vehicles containing the members of the Embassy, the luggage, and provisions etc., passed the outer gate of the mysterious Chinese capital. Half an hour afterwards we saw the internal walls of the Tartar city, into which we penetrated in the same order, as far as the house that had been prepared for us, situated in the quarter occupied by the foreign ambassadors.[41]

It was Prince Kung who did the honors. Captain

[40] To Williams, Tientsin, July 15, 1874, Diplomatic Despatches, China 36.

[41] *South Pacific Times*, April 9, 1874.

García y García called on the prince on December 31
"with emotion and curiosity." The affair began rather
coldly, the captain reported. But after he had made some
flattering remarks to the prince, one of them being that
"his name was known and appreciated by all the states-
men of Peru," he thawed decidedly and "gave the most
expansive and happy character to his words. He filled our
two cups, asking that we drink it all and saying to me on
finishing it that I would see him soon." The Peruvian
envoy took his departure. Shortly after he gained his
residence, Prince Kung returned his call in state, accompanied by a numerous following dressed "de gala y en
todo aparato."[42]   Prince Kung let the Peruvian minister
know that China would be glad to make a treaty which
would establish relations of mutual friendship and advantage to both countries.[43]

The Peruvian envoy and his staff spent the remainder
of the winter in Peking. During this time García y García
did not advance in his affair. When he tried to negotiate,
he was referred to Li Hung Chang,[44] who was not then
available for conferences. However, the Chinese authorities had become convinced that he would not yield on the
point of repatriation. Moreover, in December, Portugal
had proclaimed a closure of the coolie emigration from
Macao after March 27, 1874. Consequently, there seemed
to be no good reason for refusing longer to negotiate a
treaty. Though Chinese law forbade it, actually the
Chinese government had no objection to the emigration
of its subjects under conditions which it considered proper
—a point sufficiently proved by the emigration that had

[42] To Minister of Foreign Relations, Peking, Jan. 6, 1874, *Documentos
Parlamentarios, 1874*, I, 231-232.
[43] *El Comercio*, editorial, April 25, 1874.
[44] Williams to Secretary of State, Peking, July 25, 1874, No. 49, Diplomatic Despatches, China 36.

been in progress without friction and for several years between China and the west coast of the United States and various portions of the British Empire. Viceroy Li Hung Chang was named to continue treating with García y García, and for that reason the minister in May moved back to Tientsin.[45] There the final negotiations were conducted.

The terminal discussions were not without their stormy interludes. Assistance at various crises was rendered by Mr. Mayers, secretary to the British Legation at Peking, and by the American consul, Eli Sheppard. Mayers was sent to render what aid he could as interpreter, but he ventured to make to Li some helpful suggestions respecting the treaty terms. Sheppard's aid was of particular importance, if his own report can be fully credited. On June 12 he was informed by the viceroy's secretary that negotiations had been broken off by the Peruvian minister. The next day the viceroy sent for him. Before Sheppard called on Li the following day, he paid a visit to García y García, who confirmed all the consul had heard concerning a rupture. The captain declared that he intended to leave Tientsin the following week. There had been an angry discussion between him and the viceroy on the main points of difference, and neither showed any signs of compromise; they had parted in bad humor with the understanding that their negotiations were terminated. Sheppard's circumstantial account of the last stages of the negotiations is interesting and revealing. In part it runs:

The main points of difference were substantially as follows: The Viceroy refused—1st To permit this preliminary convention to be called by the Chinese name signifying Treaty. 2d. To allow the insertion of the favored nation clause. 3d. To allow

[45] García y García to Minister of Foreign Relations, Tientsin, May 18, 1874, *Documentos Parlamentarios, 1874,* I, 253.

the insertion of an article proposed by Captain García binding China to conclude a convention of emigration as soon as the Commission to be sent to Peru should present its report. And 4th. He insisted that this present preliminary Agreement, Convention, or Treaty, should expire upon the report of the Commission without binding the Government of China to enter into any treaty in the future.

Sheppard states that when he called on the viceroy, he was received with great cordiality, and the treaty subject was freely discussed. Li Hung Chang, he says, was "evidently disconcerted at the abrupt turn of affairs." In the circumstances Sheppard concluded that his friendly mediation would be acceptable. He wrote:

I therefore suggested to him that all civilized governments felt an interest in the result of the present negotiations. I pointed out that the ratification of the Special Agreement by the Peruvian Government depended upon this result; and consequently the advantage accruing thereby to China must be lost unless a treaty were concluded. When his attention was drawn specifically to the above four points of difference, he said that he would not consent to any agreement, or in any way stipulate for a convention with the Peruvian Government regulating the emigration of coolies to that country. He therefore objected to one of the articles proposed by Capt. García, which bound China to "conclude a Convention for emigration laborers" upon the report of the Commission to be sent to Peru. He also objected to the insertion of the favored nation clause, because he regarded it as conceding to the Peruvian Government the same privileges, rights, &c. which had been granted to the Govt. of Spain regarding the coolie traffic, and which the Chinese Government now desired to abrogate.

I then proposed an adjustment upon the following basis which seemed to me to be alike fair and honorable to both parties:—

1st. That the name of the preliminary treaty should be the same (in Chinese) as that used in the text of the American and British Treaties of 1858.

2d. The insertion of the most favored nation clause.

3d. That the preliminary treaty should remain in force until a permanent treaty should be concluded.

4th. That the objectionable article referred to above, binding the Chinese Government to conclude a Convention of Emigration laborers at a future time, should be struck out, and the substance of Art. V of the Burlingame Treaty, providing for *free emigration only,* inserted in its stead.

When the viceroy expressed approval of Sheppard's proposal, the latter went at once to the Peruvian legation and talked to the minister:

As the Viceroy had yielded every other point, I felt confident that Capt. García would readily assent to my proposition as a substitute, in place of the objectionable emigration clause, the American Article providing for *free* and *voluntary* emigration only. I was therefore a little disappointed at receiving from him an equivocal answer. However Li's overtures were kindly received, and a good understanding was arrived at. Negotiations were resumed on the 26th.[46]

Li Hung Chang displayed in the course of these discussions some fear of censure from the Chinese people if he did not secure something in favor of his compatriots in Peru. There had been, naturally, a great deal of critical publicity in China concerning the Peruvian coolies. When this fear of the viceroy came out, García y García, fortunately, had been informed of the content of the decree of October 14, of the previous year.[47] This decree, when the captain communicated its terms to the viceroy, gave

[46] Sheppard to Williams (enclosure No. 4 with Williams' No. 49 to Secretary of State, Peking, July 15, 1874), Diplomatic Despatches, China 36.

[47] See pp. 133-135.

the latter much satisfaction. The envoy believed that without its aid it would have been impossible to establish at that time relations with China. He believed also that without it he would have been unable to secure conditions that would permit even free emigration of Chinese to Peru.[48] However correct Captain García y García may have been in his judgment, it is a fact that on June 26, 1874, immediately on resumption of negotiations following the threatened break, he and Li Hung Chang signed a treaty of friendship, commerce, and navigation, as well as a convention on emigration. In summary, the treaty was as follows:

Articles I-IV provided for mutual protection of the citizens and subjects of the parties and for exchange of diplomatic and consular agents with the immunities usually associated with such functionaries. In view of the history of the coolie traffic, Article VI, an adaptation of Article V of the Burlingame Treaty mentioned by Sheppard, is of such importance as to merit quotation in full:

The Republic of Peru and the Empire of China cordially recognize the inherent and inalienable right of man to change his home. Their citizens and subjects respectively may consequently go freely from one country to the other for the purpose of curiosity, trade, labour, or as permanent residents. The High Contracting Parties therefore agree that the citizens and subjects of both Countries shall only emigrate with their free and voluntary consent; and join in reprobating any other than an entirely voluntary emigration for the said purposes, and every act of violence and fraud that may be employed in Macao or the ports of China to carry away Chinese subjects. The Contracting Parties likewise pledge themselves to punish severely, according to their laws, their respective citizens and subjects who may violate the present Stipulations, and also to proceed judicially against their respective

[48] García y García to Minister of Foreign Relations, Tientsin, May 18, 1874, *Documentos Parlamentarios, 1874,* I, 253.

ships that may be employed in such unlawful operations, imposing the fines which for such causes are established by their laws.[49]

Article VII obliged Peru to name official interpreters of the Chinese language in those regions of the country which were centers of Chinese laborers. As to shipping and mercantile rights, mutual most-favored-nation treatment was provided by Articles VIII and IX. Article X provided for the customary treatment of visiting warships, while Article XI laid down liberal bases for treatment of the ships of either that might be forced to put into port or be wrecked on the shores of the other.

Articles XII-XIV granted to Peru a slightly modified form of extraterritoriality. The modification lay in the provision that if the Peruvian consul, in a cause that concerned a Peruvian and a Chinese, could not make a satisfactory settlement, he should ask the assistance of the proper Chinese authority "and in common accord they will decide the case, in conformity with the principles of

[49] Official English version from a Shanghai pamphlet (1875), *Tratado y Convención entre el Perú y la China*, p. 5. The official Spanish version of the treaty is in the same pamphlet and may also be found in *Documentos Parlamentarios; Colección de los Tratados del Perú*, I, 159-163, and in Aranda, *Colección de los Tratados, etc.*, IV, 795-807. For comparison, the text of Article V of the Burlingame Treaty is given: "The United States of America and the Emperor of China cordially recognize the inherent and inalienable right of man to change his home and allegiance, and also the mutual advantage of the free migration and emigration of their citizens and subjects respectively from one country to the other for purposes of curiosity, or trade or as permanent residents. The high contracting parties therefore join in reprobating any other than an entirely voluntary emigration for these purposes. They consequently agree to pass laws making it a penal offence for a citizen of the United States or Chinese subjects to take Chinese subjects either to the United States or to any other foreign country, or for a Chinese subject or citizens of the United States to take citizens of the United States to China or to any other foreign country without their free and voluntary consent, respectively" (Wm. M. Malloy, ed., *Treaties, Conventions, International Acts, Protocols and Agreements between the United States and Other Powers, 1776-1909* [Washington, 1910], I, 235).

equity." Articles XV and XVI stated clearly that Chinese subjects in Peru should have equal rights with Peruvian citizens to appeal to the tribunals for protection of their rights, and that Peruvians in China should enjoy all the rights conceded to other nationals on the most-favored-nation basis. In Article XVII it was agreed that the treaty should be drawn in Spanish, Chinese, and English, nine copies to be signed, three in each language. In case of difference on interpretation of the Chinese and Spanish, the English version should be decisive. Article XVIII provided that either party might ask for alterations in the treaty after ten years, notification to be given six months before the expiration of ten years. In case no such notification were given, the treaty should continue in force for an additional ten-year period. The final articles provided for exchange of ratifications in Shanghai or Tientsin as early as possible.

The most important provisions of the convention on immigration related to (1) a commission which China should send to Peru and (2) return of those Chinese who desired it. As to the first, it was stated that the commission was to go to Peru for the purpose of establishing "a complete and amicable understanding" regarding the coolies in that country. Peru obligated itself to facilitate in every way the work of the commission. Its members were empowered, in case they should discover a Chinese who had been abused, to take the case to the authorities, even to the highest courts. As to the second point, it was provided that the Peruvian government would oblige employers of Chinese contract laborers, when their period of service expired, to return them to China—provided their contracts so stipulated, and provided, further, that the coolies desired to return. In the case of those whose contracts contained no stipulation for return passage, if they wished to return and were unable to do so, the Peruvian government would repatriate them at public expense.[50]

His task of treaty-making concluded, Captain Aurelio García y García set sail for Peru on August 1, via Suez, accompanied by an adjunct, Octavio Freyre. He left behind, in pursuance of powers granted in his instructions, the secretary of the legation, Juan Federico Elmore as chargé d'affaires ad interim before the governments of China and Japan. Said the minister of Elmore: "The circumspection, elevated intelligence and distinguished gifts which Señor Elmore possesses, give the most solid guarantees for the good discharge of the duty commended to this outstanding functionary of the Nation."[51]

The Peruvian congress promptly gave its approval to the treaty and the convention on October 6, 1874, and the president proclaimed them on the 13th of the same month.[52] News of ratification was slow in reaching China. In explanation of the supposed reluctance of Peru to ratify, Benjamin P. Avery, minister of the United States at Peking, conjectured that

Peru, dissatisfied with the restricted nature of the emigration clause, . . . withholds ratification until the result of the Cuban dispute is known, and contemplates, should Spain carry her point and the old traffic be reopened, availing herself of the same privilege and abandoning her treaty. Of course this conjecture is merely based on suspicion. . . . Yet there seems to be too much evidence of mutual understanding between the Spaniards and the

[50] *Documentos Parlamentarios; Colección de los Tratados del Perú*, I, 164-167; Aranda, *op. cit.*, IV, 809-811.

[51] To Minister of Foreign Relations, Tientsin, Aug. 1, 1874, MSS, Ministerio de Relaciones Exteriores del Perú; Año 1874; Legación en China y Japón.

[52] *Documentos Parlamentarios; Colección de los Tratados del Perú*, I, 164-167. Copy of presidential proclamation is in Diplomatic Despatches, China 39 (encl. Elmore to Avery, copy with Avery's No. 103).

Peruvians to leave it altogether improbable.[53]

Avery's conjecture, in the circumstances, had logic. The facts prove him to have been wrong, but his statements indicate that in China there was lack of confidence in Peru's good faith.

Exchange of ratifications was yet to be effected. This ordinarily routine matter presented, in this case, some difficulties. Elmore was commissioned to act for Peru in making the exchange. The Chinese opposite number was Ling Jih Chang, lately governor of Kiangsu. The edict appointing him reached Tientsin on July 16.[54] Delay ensued.

In the year that had elapsed since the signing of the documents, the officials of the Tsung-li-Yamen, China's Foreign Office, had experienced a change of opinion regarding them; they were now opposed to ratification.[55] This reversal was caused in part, probably, by the trouble with Spain over coolie labor which was not yet resolved. The report of the commission sent to Cuba to ascertain the true condition of the coolies there had received wide publicity and had horrified its readers. Another cause, and probably the most influential one, was a report that had come to China from Peru itself.

About the time Li Hung Chang and García y García were engaging in their acrimonious exchanges in June of 1874, the Chinese viceroy, on his own initiative, had asked one of his friends, Yung Wing, who was then in the United States, to go to Peru, make a survey of coolie labor

[53] Avery to Secretary of State, Peking, Feb. 4, 1875, No. 26, Diplomatic Despatches, China 37.

[54] Sheppard to Avery, Aug. 1, 1876. (encl. with Avery's No. 95), Diplomatic Despatches, China 39.

[55] Avery to Sheppard, Peking, July 13, 1875 (encl. with Avery's No. 95), *ibid.*

there, and report to him.[56]   Accompanied by two North Americans, Dr. T. M. Kellogg and J. H. Troichell, Yung spent some time in Peru in September, 1874.   He called on the minister of foreign relations, Riva Agüero, then visited the coolie labor section of Northern Peru.   The minister deduced that Yung was "not dissatisfied with his visit," though he complained of the treatment of the coolies on certain haciendas.[57]   The report which Yung Wing made to Li Hung Chang was not so polite in its terms as his conversation with Riva Agüero.   In the words of Consul Sheppard, to whom Li gave a copy, the report "showed that Chinese laborers in Peru were suffering great outrages for which no redress seemed possible."[58] When Elmore reached Tientsin on July 8, he called on the viceroy.   The Chinese brought up the subject of Yung's report, and the interview became "unpleasant and profitless."[59]   The report contained the testimony and statements of many Chinese, together with accounts given by eyewitnesses, all furnishing particulars as to time, place, and individual names.   Li did not fail to quote them, making frequent reference to García y García's note of November 26, 1873, in which he commented on the very general terms of the Chinese petitions of 1869 and 1871.[60] (How well the Chinese had learned the lesson García y García had given them in this matter!)   Li declared that unless Elmore should give him a dispatch promising redress and better treatment of the coolies for the future,

[56] Yung Wing was head of the Chinese Educational Mission in the United States, with its headquarters in Hartford, Connecticut.   Yung was himself a Yale graduate (Foster, *American Diplomacy in the Orient*, p. 272).   See also Sheppard to Avery, Tientsin, Aug. 18, 1875 (encl. with Avery's No. 95), *loc. cit.*

[57] To García y García, Lima, Oct. 27, 1874, MSS, Ministerio de Relaciones Exteriores del Perú; Años 1872-1876; Tomo 126-A, 72-73. See also *La Patria*, Sept. 18, 1874.

[58] Sheppard to Avery, Aug. 18, 1875, *loc. cit.*

[59] *Ibid.*   [60] *Ibid.*

the treaty should not go into effect.[61]   He even threatened
that unless Elmore complied, he should not go to Peking.
Elmore committed the error of discussing these propositions with Li instead of simply standing on his right to an
exchange of ratifications without a condition precedent
and requesting to know if Li, or another, had authority to
this end.

On learning of this state of affairs, the American,
Russian, and German ministers rallied round and did
what they could to aid Elmore, "representing," as one
of them later wrote,

that good faith required the prompt exchange of ratifications, and
urging upon them the importance of complying with international
law, especially at a time when they appeal to its principles and
rules for the benefit of China in a matter at issue with Spain,
relating to the same question of emigration, which is settled on
such a just basis in the Peruvian Treaty.[62]

The Tsung-li-Yamen recognized the force of these
arguments and issued a direction to Li Hung Chang for
the appointment of a plenipotentiary to make the exchange.   Ling was then appointed.   The American minister expressed the conviction that it was only the earnest
arguments addressed to the Chinese by himself and his
colleagues that led them to reconsider their original ob-
structive policy, "the result of great soreness on the whole
question of Chinese emigration to Spanish-American
countries, and of that singular want of tact which they
evince in most of their dealings with foreigners."[63]   Minister Avery asked Sheppard at Tientsin to bring his views
to the knowledge of Li.   Sheppard did so, and Li ceased

[61] Avery to Secretary of State, Peking, Sept. 1, 1875, No. 95, Diplomatic Despatches, China 39.
[62] *Ibid.*
[63] *Ibid.*

opposing the treaty as such but continued to demand a pledge from Elmore.[64]

That young diplomat was in a very unhappy situation. At one point he declared he saw nothing better to do than to leave at once for Japan. But both Avery and Wade, the British minister, who appeared opportunely at Tientsin on August 1, urged him not to act precipitately. They advised him also to refuse consent to the previous condition demanded by Li. At length, however, Elmore weakened on the point and consented to draw up such a letter as he was willing to sign in reply to one from Ling.[65] Elmore's letter, dated August 7, 1875, after acknowledging Ling's communication asking him to bring to his government's attention the content of Yung Wing's report, consisted of this statement:

In reply, I beg to state that it is the earnest desire of my Government to afford the most active protection to the Chinese immigrant laborers in Peru, and to prevent their being exposed to ill treatment in the slightest degree. I can give the full assurance that so soon as a Minister shall be appointed on the part of the Chinese Government to proceed in a representative capacity to Peru, my Government will enter with him upon the most serious consideration of all matters relating to the Chinese immigrant laborers, with a view to securing for them the entire removal of all abuses whatsoever; and of ensuring their well being and the entire protection of their persons and property, in fulfillment not alone of the stipulations of the Treaty and Convention, but also of the duties imposed by good faith. It will be my duty to forward to my Government a copy and translation of the document enclosed in Y. E.'s despatch, in order that it may inform itself of its contents, and take such action as may be necessary.[66]

[64] *Ibid.*   [65] *Ibid.*
[66] An enclosure with Elmore to Avery, Tientsin, Sept. 20, 1875, Diplomatic Despatches, China 39.

The exchange of ratifications was made, though incompletely, on the same day, August 7. A difficulty arose from the fact that the Chinese text had not been brought back from Peru and, under Chinese practice, it was required. A special protocol was drawn to cover the lack, other copies were "processed," and it was agreed that there should be no public proclamation of the treaty by China until the Chinese text arrived.[67] The missing text appeared in China some months later. The American minister, Seward, reported in a dispatch dated March 21, 1876, that ratification had been completed "within the last six weeks."[68]

Elmore had established his legation in Peking. Not long after the completion of exchange of ratifications he went to Japan. From there he wrote to Seward toward the end of May, informing him that he had obtained a short leave of absence and was proceeding to Peru for a few months, "via San Francisco and New York, in order to be present at the centennial celebration of the Great Republic."[69]

Thus the long process of negotiating and making official the Peruvian treaty with China was completed early in 1876, almost two and a half years after the opening of negotiations. The treaty did not kill the coolie traffic. That traffic was dead when the Portuguese closed Macao to it. The treaty did, however, insure that the trade would not be reopened as far as Peru was concerned. In the negotiations that had preceded the drawing of the two documents, the Peruvian may be said, perhaps, to have had a bit the better of it. Li Hung Chang had

[67] *Ibid.*
[68] To Secretary of State, Hongkong, No. 31, *ibid.*, China 40.
[69] Yokohama, May 23, 1876 (encl. with Seward's No. 77), Diplomatic Despatches, China 41.

backed down on the demand for repatriation of coolies as a condition precedent; however, he forced into the convention a provision that appeared to assure that those coolies who wished to return to China would eventually be able to do so. Every one of the seven points that García y García had sketched in his note of November 26 was realized by him in the final negotiations. He had shown skill in the management of his mission. He had been patient when patience was required, impatient when impatience would further his ends. While it must be admitted that he was greatly aided by members of the foreign diplomatic corps, in the final analysis credit must go to the captain.

When the mission's work was finished, Peru had the kind of treaty the government had wanted (though perhaps not what the *hacendados* desired)—one that appeared to make possible the resumption, in a free manner, of the emigration of Chinese laborers to Peru. The treaty also removed from the Peruvian government and nation the taint of slavery under which they had so long lived because of the coolie traffic and the abuses associated with it.

X

"NEW" CHINESE IMMIGRATION; PERUVIAN COOLIES

THE TIENTSIN TREATY was hailed in Peru by all classes. The *hacendados*, badly frightened by the Portuguese closure of Macao, could see in the treaty the promise of a continuance of Chinese immigration, though under different conditions, and a continuance, consequently, of their capitalistic agricultural operations. The critics of the coolie trade and of the treatment of the Chinese in Peru hailed the treaty as marking the end of the shameful trade and saw in it a promise of better conditions for the Peruvian coolies. The treaty was represented as a decided victory for Peru on the international stage, as indeed it was. "We have been recognized as having almost the right of extraterritoriality."[1] It was believed beyond doubt that the treaty had placed on a very good footing Peruvian relations with China. Government circles were not less pleased. The ending of the coolie trade gave ground for hope that eventually the very bad odor associated with Peru in international circles would be eliminated and that a "new" immigration would supply Peru's labor necessities. No group in the country was opposed to a continuance of Chinese immigration if it were free. True, most Peruvians would have much preferred a European immigration, but almost everyone recognized the impossibility of having it and was willing to continue bringing Chinese as the next best thing. "The Chinese are bad colonists, that we recognize; but on the

[1] *El Comercio*, Sept. 28, 1874.

other hand, they are excellent peons for the tasks of the field."[2]

An English view on the treaty is derived from an article of the *European Mail*. It could not be doubted that the Peruvian government possessed strong persuasive powers. "After the revelations which have been made in recent years respecting the Macao coolie traffic, nobody would have imagined that the Chinese government would have adopted a policy of forgetfulness and pardon as it has done in making a treaty of commerce and navigation with Peru." Quite evidently, Peru had gained a victory and obtained a substantial concession. "She has been happier than we who have been dealing with China for a long time. She has gained what she needed without burning the Summer Palace." This was seen as a "curious proof" of the incompetence of English diplomacy in China.[3]

Indeed, Peru *had* won a diplomatic victory. It remained now to make effective the treaty terms and to secure an exchange of ministers. Juan Federico Elmore, after exchanging ratifications with the Chinese representative at Tientsin in 1875, remained in China for some months as Peruvian agent.[4] He was much concerned with trying to establish conditions for starting a "new" immigration. Returning to Peru somewhat less than successful, he was appointed as the first minister resident of Peru in China.[5] On May 20, 1878, he set sail for his post.[6] Arrival of a Chinese minister at Lima was greatly delayed.

[2] *Ibid.*, May 15, 1875.   [3] *Ibid.*, Oct. 3, 1874.
[4] *South Pacific Times*, Feb. 8, 1876.
[5] *Diario de los Debates*, Congreso Ordinario de 1878, "Memoria que el Ministro de Estado en el Despacho de Relaciones Exteriores presenta al Congreso," p. 138.
[6] Arona, *La inmigración en el Perú*, p. 76.

In April, 1876, Peruvian newspapers were making reference to the Chinese commission "about to be dispatched" to Peru to investigate the condition of the country's Chinese residents, as provided, it will be recalled, in the Tientsin Convention.[7] However, that commission never arrived because of the tragedy that descended upon Peru with the War of the Pacific, begun early in 1879 and continued for four years. The only Chinese commission which Peru received was that headed by Yung Wing, whose work has already been noted. Yung's report may well have exerted a determinative effect on later policy of the Chinese government in the matter of the "new" immigration.

A Peruvian paper stated in April, 1876, that it was believed a Chinese minister was already on his way to Peru and expressed the hope that no "foreign adventurers" would be allowed to form a part of the mission.[8] The activities of the two Americans who had accompanied Yung Wing seem not to have pleased the Peruvian public. Two days later the same paper quoted the Hartford *Courant* to the effect that two Chinese, Chin Lan Pin and Yung Wing, had been appointed as joint ministers to the United States, Peru, and Spain.[9] The first Chinese minister to Peru did not arrive, however, until 1883, after the War of the Pacific had been ended by the Treaty of Ancón.[10]

The efforts to encourage a European immigration which produced the organization of the European Immigration Society had come to naught. Though it operated for a time and brought some colonists, it found, as in

[7] *South Pacific Times*, April 11, 1876.
[8] *Ibid.*, April 11.
[9] *Ibid.*, April 13. See also F. Seward to Secretary of State, Hongkong, Feb. 29, 1876, Legation Archives, No. 266, Seward 1-60, 1876.
[10] Arona, *op. cit.*, p. 76

previous similar attempts by other groups, that these immigrants would not submit to the conditions of labor on the haciendas. They wanted more of reward and less of peonage. By 1875 it was generally recognized that the Society was dead. The necessity for some form of subsidy to encourage the establishment of a steamship line to bring Chinese colonists began to be spoken of and the idea supported.[11]

On April 21, 1875, Aurelio García y García, now a cabinet minister, made a strong recommendation on the subject to the Peruvian congress. He referred to the need of agriculture for labor and spoke of "the evil threatened by that paralyzing of Asiatic immigration which has existed, and been strictly executed, for nearly a year past." He outlined the changes which the Peruvian government wished to make in the manner and conditions of the Chinese immigration:

Firstly. That the emigrants should leave China direct for Peru, without necessity for the slow and costly intermediate passage by the Portuguese colony situated on the coast of the empire.

Secondly. That the emigrants should leave their country with entire freedom to dispose of their services in the manner they might voluntarily determine.

Thirdly. That this emigration should take place with the full consent and permission of the Government, so that the emigrants could count at all times on the protection to which they are justly entitled from their Government.

The minister referred to the lack of adequate transportation as the only barrier to the development of the new immigration and declared that the only way to obviate the lack was to grant the co-operation of the State in the establishment of a line of steamers fitted for trade between

[11] *El Comercio*, April 24, May 15, 1875.

the two countries.[12]   After some discussion, the Senate
passed a bill to provide an annual subsidy of S/160,000
for such a line of steamships.[13]   In addition to establishing the amount of the subsidy, the bill empowered the
president to make the necessary contract with the proviso
that its term should not extend for more than five years
from the date of the first voyage.[14]

On June 1 a group of wealthy plantation owners held
a meeting to express approval of the Senate bill and to
draw a memorial urging the Chamber of Deputies likewise
to approve the bill.[15]   The Chamber finally did so.

Several months passed before a suitable party could
be found to enter into contract with the government under
the terms of the legislation.   However, on November 2,
1876, a contract was made with Olyphant & Company, an
American firm which had operated in China for many
years.   An American diplomatic agent in China said of
them, "They are merchants of high standing, and will
have nothing to do with emigration to Peru, or any other
country, unless satisfied that it can be carried on in an
honorable manner, and with security to the emigrant."[16]
The contract was made through Olyphant's representative,
H. Seymour Geary.[17]   As this contract failed to receive
congressional approval,[18] its terms need be given little
attention.   Criticisms were based chiefly on the belief that
the contract was too favorable to the shipping company,
failing properly to protect national interests.[19]   For the
following five months or so, there was much discussion of

[12] *South Pacific Times,* April 24, 1875.
[13] *El Peruano; Boletín Oficial,* June 18, 1875, p. 409.
[14] *Ibid.;* see also *South Pacific Times,* June 15, 1875.
[15] *South Pacific Times,* June 15, 1875.
[16] F. Seward to Secretary of State, Peking, June 16, 1876, No. 80,
Diplomatic Despatches, China 41.
[17] *El Nacional,* Nov. 7, 1876.   [18] *Ibid.;* March 27, 1877.
[19] *Ibid.,* Nov. 17, 1876.

the Olyphant contract, in the press, in congress, and in government circles. At length Olyphant & Company agreed to a contract with different conditions. This contract was approved in April, 1877.[20] In brief, its terms were these:

Olyphant & Company would establish a steamship line between Peru and China for the transport of Chinese emigrants to Peru. Each ship used would be capable of carrying one thousand men. The contract would run for five years, twenty-eight round trips to be made in that period—three the first year, four the second, and seven in each of the other three years; the first ship should arrive in Peru within six months after the signing of the contract. The government would make Olyphant & Company its special emigration agent in China and Hongkong; only those Chinese who came freely should be brought; the government would lodge them eight days in Callao at its own expense. The Peruvian government would pay a subvention each year of S/160,000 Peruvian silver money, or in nitrates if the government preferred. If the first year's experiment showed the company losing money, it should have the right to suspend operations unless the government increased the subvention so as to make possible profitable voyages. If the company should fail in making the number of trips agreed on for any year, it should forfeit S/5,000. The Company should introduce into Peru at least five hundred Chinese each trip. The government should provide for return trips cargoes of guano to the extent of at least six thousand tons per year at £3 per ton. The Company should have preference in the matter of a renewal at the end of the five-year period.[21]

The outcome of this contract was pretty sad for all

[20] Arona, *op. cit.*, p. 75.
[21] *El Peruano; Boletín Oficial*, April 27, 1877, p. 98, full text with emendations; *South Pacific Times*, Nov. 11, 1876, for English translation.

parties concerned, excepting, possibly, the Chinese. Peruvian newspapers announced early in January, 1877, that the *Perusia*, Olyphant's ship, had left China bringing Chinese laborers and suggested that measures be organized for properly receiving and distributing them.[22] But when the *Perusia* reached Callao, it was found not to have brought a single Chinese. The governor of Hongkong had refused to permit the embarkation of Chinese without express authorization from his home government. Instead of receiving such authorization, his action in refusing was officially approved.[23]

The second Olyphant effort was made at Canton, where the same difficulties were confronted. Either because of British pressure, as many Peruvians thought, or because of a "natural suspicion" on the part of the Chinese, as others suggested, a cargo of Chinese laborers could not be obtained. Moreover, the ship had ill fortune on the voyage and did not reach Callao until October 16, 1878. It put out again for China on November 1, carrying eighty Chinese who were being repatriated under the provisions of the Tientsin immigration convention. Minister Elmore in Peking worked hard to straighten matters out and make it possible for a free emigration to get under way, but he worked without effect.[24]

The reason—or perhaps the device—used by the Chinese government for refusing to consent to the carrying of Chinese by the Olyphant company was that the passage money for the Chinese was being furnished them. This was not believed to correspond with the principle of a "free" emigration. Peruvian commentators suggested

[22] *El Comercio*, Jan. 4, 1877.
[23] *El Comercio*, Aug. 12, 1878, for British official correspondence on the subject; also Arona, *op. cit.*, pp. 75-76.
[24] Arona, *op. cit.*, pp. 76-77; *El Comercio*, Sept. 17, 1878, for an article from the *China Mail* on the subject.

other reasons for the failure. The choice of an agent, they declared, had been bad. While Olyphant & Company were thought to be honest, yet it would have been better to work through one of the Chinese companies that for a long time had been managing the emigration to California. Another cause of failure was the fact that Geary, of Olyphant & Company, had been named Peruvian consul in Hongkong, perhaps for the sake of economy; the consul should not have been associated with the emigration business. Furthermore, even Elmore, the minister, was known to have connections with the Olyphant company. Whether explanations or excuses, these points were put forward by critics as helping to explain the failure.[25] It would appear that remembrance of the "coolie catchers" was still too vivid among the Chinese for this venture at once to attain success.

El Comercio, on August 19, 1878, carried a strong and very sensible editorial on the subject of British activities and the verities of this matter. A few of its passages deserve quotation:

> As for us, let us speak frankly, it is simply a vulgarism to attribute to selfish motives the attitude of the British government. . . . If the British government is trying to prevent Chinese coming to Peru, it does so only because it believes that here they are always treated with the cruelty of which, unfortunately, so many cases have been afforded in previous years. . . . But no one has taken the trouble to discover that for some time past there has been no notice of a single act of this kind that merits serious censure. . . .

> The Chinese authorities instinctively will oppose obstacles to the fulfilment of the treaties of 1874. Their beliefs, their habits, and the predisposition which they have against Peru, need but a slight stimulus to cause them to deny departure of the subjects

[25] *El Nacional*, March 16, 1878.

of the empire for a country whose name alone is sufficient with
them to frighten children.

The contract with the Olyphant company was effective-
ly brought to an end by the company's failure late in
1878.[26] This was merely an anticipation by a few months
of the effect which undoubtedly the war with Chile would
have produced.

About the time that the coolie crisis reached its height
in Peru, the situation of the tens of thousands of Chinese
in California became precarious. The completion of the
transcontinental railroad in 1869 had thrown many Chinese out of work, and they sought employment in the
cities and wherever it might be found. American laborers
did not like their competition any more than did the
Peruvians, and the San Francisco anti-Chinese riots were
the result. These riots and lack of employment of the
California Chinese gave a ray of hope to Peruvians; perhaps these Chinese could be induced to come to Peru. As
early as 1874 members of the Peruvian press had discussed California as a possible source of Chinese labor.[27]
Effective action was undertaken only with the new developments in California.

Noel West, a representative of the Pacific Steam Navigation Company, early in 1877 put out in Callao and
Lima a circular in which he proposed that Peruvian *hacendados* arrange with his company to bring Chinese to
Peru from or through California. Williams, Blanchard
& Company would be the agents in San Francisco; they
had long operated there and had good standing with the
Chinese in California as well as in China, and West asserted his belief that they would be able to secure emi-

[26] *El Comercio*, Dec. 11, 1878.
[27] See *South Pacific Times*, March 12, 1874, for an article on the subject.

grants. Williams, Blanchard had, in fact, initiated the idea. It was estimated that the passage from China to California would cost $55.00 and from California to Callao an additional $50.00, including all costs, even that of lodgment on some island in the Bay of Panama for delays in making connections. The *hacendados*, if interested, should indicate the terms on which they would contract for such Chinese.[28]

Interest in the California Chinese increased to such an extent that a commission of the Peruvian congress was appointed to examine the results of the Chinese immigration in California.[29] About mid-year the Peruvian consul in San Francisco reported that many Chinese there were "wishful to emigrate," and that this surely presented "a favorable opportunity for Peruvian estate owners and sugar cultivators" to procure the labor they so much needed. The consul called attention to the economy involved in getting Chinese from California rather than from China.[30] Moreover, Chinese houses in San Francisco, such as that of Lee Yam & Company, became interested in furthering the movement. Lee Yam went so far as to send a representative to Peru and Demarara to investigate and report on possibilities.[31]

With the growing crisis in 1877, the government became convinced that serious attention should be given the California opportunity. Late in that year a delegate was sent there to see what could be done. He and La Fuente, consul-general in San Francisco, drew up the terms of a contract that might be used. The Chinese so moved were to be employed in a variety of occupations, guano excepted; they should work but ten hours a day with no

[28] The circular, dated Feb. 23, in *El Comercio*, Feb. 27, 1877.
[29] *La Bolsa*, May 21, 1877.
[30] *South Pacific Times*, Sept. 8, 1877.
[31] *El Comercio*, April 3, 1877.

work on Sundays, Good Friday, or the three days of the Chinese New Year, and if they were worked overtime they should be paid ten centavos silver per hour. The contract would run for three years with possible extension to five; if dissatisfied, the laborer might terminate his contract on two months' notice. He should have free passage to Peru, with a month's wage paid in advance in San Francisco; the S/24.00 cost of passage to be returned by him in small monthly payments. Each laborer should be paid at the end of each month S/16.00 Peruvian silver, and should be given, besides, free food, lodging, medical attention, and clothing (two pairs of trousers and two blouses per year). No such Chinese employee should be whipped or degraded. The Chinese would pledge himself to work faithfully.[32] These terms contrast very favorably with those of the contracts under which the coolies formerly were brought to Peru. They may also be taken as indicating the advantages which the Chinese in California had enjoyed over those that labored in Peru.

Operating under the terms of this contract, Grace Brothers & Company conveyed to Peru on the steamer *Islay* twenty-three California Chinese. They were accompanied by Ah Chong, agent of the Chinese house of Hong Tik, and were placed on the hacienda of Guillermo Alzamora in the Valley of Chicama. The Grace Brothers and Ah Chong were confident that one or two thousand other Chinese could be brought from California at that time and that they could introduce from China through California all the laborers that Peruvian agriculturists needed.[33] The Grace company calculated that the advance cost to the employer of such Chinese would be

[32] *South Pacific Times*, Feb. 9, 1878.
[33] *El Comercio*, Aug. 26, 1878.

$88.60 United States gold, $13.60 of which represented one month's advance pay which eventually would be repaid by the recipient.[34] At least one other group of California Chinese was taken to Peru by the Grace Brothers before the War of the Pacific interrupted the movement.[35]

A Peruvian newspaper commentator placed at four thousand the Chinese in California at the time without employment, many of whom it was thought might be induced to emigrate to Peru. The same writer made this significant declaration:

> The first step which the agriculturists should take on the road which we should like to see them enter resolutely, is to abolish the *galpón,* imprisoning their peons not within the walls of an insupportable barracks, but within the conveniences of a prosperous situation and one as happy as may be compatible with their humble condition.[36]

It may well be that if war with Chile had not interrupted Peru's connections with the exterior and entirely disrupted its political and economic life, a considerable number of Chinese would have been transferred from California to Peru. In that event, Grant Street, San Francisco, might be less populous today. But the war was a fact, and speculation is vain. The number actually taken could hardly have been more than a few hundred.

Something further must be said of the condition of those thousands of Chinese in Peru who had still to terminate the eight years of their contracts after the Treaty of Tientsin was made, as well as of those who had finished their labor obligation but remained as members of Peruvian society. It will be recalled that the last ship bearing contract coolies (369 of them) anchored at Callao on July 2, 1874. In conformity with the Treaty of Tientsin, the

[34] *Ibid.,* Sept. 7, 1878.   [35] *Ibid.*
[36] *Ibid.,* Aug. 28, 1878.

last coolie contract would have expired by 1882. After 1874, progressively, former contracts would expire in such manner that year by year, or month by month, the number under contract would grow smaller. It was, of course, the realization of this inevitable fact that gave such concern to *hacendados* and government.

Did this realization cause the *hacendado* to alter his attitude toward his coolies? The editors of the *South Pacific Times* seem not to have thought so. Early in 1878 an editorial included this paragraph:

> That the condition of the poor people [contract coolies] had been one of actual slavery or very like thereto, we presume will not be denied, nor will it be disputed that such, at the present moment, is the condition of many of them. It is but truth to say that hundreds of Chinamen who, according to their contracts are free men, are now kept in a condition of servitude though years have expired since their contracts ceased to be binding.[37]

In 1876 there was considerable excitement in the country because of another outbreak of coolie uprisings. In October of the preceding year, as a prelude, the Chinese laborers of a Sr. Loas, at Huacho, had risen and killed him. The reasons were not publicized, but one newspaper declared that "it might be safely attributed to revenge."[38] Some support is given this explanation by the fact that very shortly the government issued a circular to department prefects stating that information had been received that some employers of Chinese were not paying them the S/4.00 monthly provided by contract.[39] Here again is seen the negligence of subordinate authorities who feared to act against the powerful *hacendado*.[40]

The uprisings of early 1876 occurred in the region of

[37] Feb. 16.   [38] *South Pacific Times*, Oct. 28, 1878.
[39] *Ibid.*
[40] For an elaboration of this point, see *El Comercio*, Oct. 26, 1875.

Trujillo and north and south of that city where were located many large sugar plantations. In February the
Chinese of the Pampas plantation, owned by a Sr. Barira,
arose, killed two of their overseers, and fled to the cane-
brakes of the neighboring Sansal plantation. There 160
of them were later apprehended. Six Chinese were killed
in this affair.[41] A month later a similar uprising occurred
at the hacienda of Chiquitoy to the north. Some 340
Asiatics were concerned. Two were killed, but most of
the others were taken by the military and returned to
their labors.[42]

About the same time much uneasiness was felt in the
Valley of Chicama. Certain *hacendados* asserted that the
Chinese of the valley were plotting a veritable revolution
designed to seize all of the region and then march on
Lima. A free Chinese from Lima, one Afú, was accused
of being the leader of the movement. On orders of the
hacendado, one Sr. Arrieta, when Afú visited the Chacra
Cerro plantation, he was seized and delivered to the local
authorities, charged as indicated above. The local authority sent him to the prefect of the Province of Lima. That
official, having no proof of the charges against Afú and
urged by the prominent Chinese of Lima, released him.
Later, when Francisco Canevaro, big landholder and employer of Chinese as well as the largest operator in the
coolie trade in earlier days, protested, the Lima prefect
wrote a sharp letter to the subprefect on the subject and
refused to act further against Afú.[43] The uprising, if
one was actually planned, did not occur. The action of the
authorities suggests that their view of the matter was that
it was a charge made by the *hacendados* concerned, either
in panic fear of an uprising or that it was a charge trumped

[41] *South Pacific Times*, Feb. 15, 1876.
[42] *El Comercio*, March 14 and 15, 1876.
[43] See documents in *El Comercio*, March 17 and 18, 1876.

up to justify their abusive treatment of the Chinese. A statement in Steere's report of three years earlier may well be recalled here:

There is a feeling of insecurity in Peru from the presence of this great number of desperate men, who have no ties to bind them with the people of the country or to keep them from taking vengeance in case of insurrection. Every one goes armed,, and every farmhouse is a little armory.[44]

The whole series of occurrences was regarded by friends of the Chinese as one more proof that Chinese were mistreated and that the national laws for their protection were not being enforced. One paper mentioned as a reason for nonenforcement the "clannish spirit" among employers of Chinese. Such employers "in all cases cover the offences or crimes of their neighbors, however much they may condemn their perpetration."[45]

As a consequence of these disturbances, a promising step was taken in the Province of La Libertad. Sr. Tizón, prefect, called a meeting of the largest employers of Chinese to discuss the best means of creating a better feeling between masters and men. The meeting was held on March 30. Sr. Tizón declared that the recent troubles had been caused by severe treatment of the Chinese and induced the *hacendados* to agree to a set of regulations to govern their conduct toward their employees. The most important points were these: (1) They should observe similarity in the food given the men and give them more and of better quality; (2) the system of correction should be modified; (3) a fixed hour should be followed in beginning and ending the day's work; (4) employers would pay 10 cents a week more to enable the Chinese to purchase meat; (5) a fine was established for

[44] *United States Foreign Relations, 1873*, p. 208.
[45] *South Pacific Times*, April 8, 1876

the plantation owner who should employ a Chinese without the presentation of the proper papers; (6) manner of recovering money expended on regaining control of laborers who beat their contracts was regulated; and (7) the *hacendados* pledged themselves to comply strictly with the regulations of the government concerning monthly payments and work on Sundays.[46]

A thoughtful editorial in *El Comercio* of March 20 noted some of the fundamentals of the problem:

> We all know what are the real causes of this unrest which the agricultural group feels concerning the Chinese colonists on our coast. Everyone knows that these frequent uprisings are bloody and impotent protests against horrible wrongs. . . .
>
> Only foolishness or malevolence can attribute to the public administration the responsibility for a state of things which have their origin in a social vice, and which is sustained by habits, preoccupations, and feelings which have for more than three centuries been rooted in the agricultural life of our coast.

The same newspaper, possibly through the pen of the same editorial writer, spoke even more plainly in an editorial of March 22. The regrettable evils which were then affecting the Chinese coolies were the logical consequence of past errors which had "centralized property ownership, making impossible free labor" in Peruvian fields. "Accustomed to the easy service of the slave laborer, our *hacendados* have constantly rejected every system that is not based on the absolute submission of the peon, on the complete denial of their natural right."

Solf & Company, early in 1877, tried an experiment with a new system of Chinese labor. This company operated the hacienda of Tumán, a property of Manuel Pardo, recently president of the republic. The system was designed to attract back into agricultural labor the free

[46] *Ibid.*

Chinese of Peru. A Chinese, called a corporal, acted as intermediary in securing the laborers, and two hundred were brought to the hacienda. The elements of the system are clearly shown in this quotation from a letter approving the system and recommending its use by other plantation operators:

> The Messrs. Solf & Co. pay 20 soles for each Chinese, money which represents their deposit in the power of the corporal, and a sol a day as wages, half paid to the peon, half to the corporal. The corporal, on his part, obliges himself to provide Chinese entirely satisfactory to Messrs. Solf & Co., changing them in all cases in which, either through uselessness, bad character, illness, or other circumstance, they become unsatisfactory to Messrs. Solf & Co. . . . The corporal provides their food, clothing, and all necessities.[47]

This publication brought an immediate letter of rebuttal from "Agricultores," dated Lima, February 6. One should have no illusions, declared "Agriculturists"; the Chinese who had concluded their contracts would not work—all they wanted was a few days work occasionally to enable them to enjoy the pleasures of Capón Street. Besides, if wages were increased, prices would have to go up in proportion; and so on.[48] It is perfectly evident that this group of *hacendados,* if their words may be taken at their face value, were without hope of bringing back to the plantations the free Chinese of Peru. No more information is available on this matter. How successful the venture of Solf & Company was is not known. Lack of comment on the system's adoption elsewhere indicates that the experiment did not encounter wide acceptance.

It is probable that by early 1879 the condition of the Chinese had been somewhat improved. Certainly the

[47] *El Comercio*, Feb. 5, 1877.   [48] *Ibid.*, Feb. 8, 1877.

terms of the Treaty of Tientsin were favorable to them, and they must gradually have learned of their rights under that instrument. The government was disposed to enforce them, as its actions prove. The agreement of the *hacendados* of La Libertad should logically have brought an improvement in the treatment of the coolies there. The probability of losing all of their Chinese laborers when their contracts were terminated unless they were decently treated, in itself, should have operated as a powerful deterrent to continued ill treatment . The opinions quoted above, however, suggest that no fundamental reversal of attitude on the part of the agricultural capitalists had supervened. They were still blind to the logic of the Tientsin Treaty and to the failure of every official attempt or private effort to supply the labor vacuum left when the Portuguese government closed Macao to the coolie traffic.

XI

THE COOLIE AS PERUVIAN

MOST PERUVIANS, in the period of our study, regarded the Chinese as an indigestible element in the social body. Indeed, there are those who entertain that view today. Historical facts do not support it. By 1879 probably much more than half of the Chinese still living in Peru had fulfilled the terms of their labor contracts and were free. Even before that date, social integration had begun.

It will be recalled that upon arrival at the plantation where he was to work a Chinese coolie, for the convenience of master and overseer, was given a Spanish name. Items here and there in the Peruvian press prove that many of them, when they became free men, retained the new name or, perhaps, adopted another in the Spanish form. An eminent Peruvian stated in a recent publication that, "as in the Colony, the use of the family names of wealthy masters began, not now by obscure slaves, but by pale serfs or coolies."[1] This practice surely indicates a tendency toward cultural assimilation.

From early years the Chinese moved slowly toward acceptance of the Christian religion. Sufficient evidence of this fact is a statement in the *South Pacific Times:* "A Chinaman is about to take holy orders in Lima. Upwards of one hundred Chinamen are regular attendants at Santo Tomás church."[2] From another source it is learned

[1] Luis Alberto Sánchez, *La Literatura Peruana; derrotero para una historia espiritual del Perú* (Lima, 1946), p. 90.
[2] Jan. 11, 1876.

that in the Santo Tomás church a French priest had been for some time giving Chinese regular instruction in the tenets of the Christian religion.[3]   Richard Gibbs, minister of the United States to Peru, declared of the coolies, "Great numbers have become converts to Catholicism and they are apparently very fervent in their devotions, and attentive to the ceremonies of the church.   In the cemetery I noticed several niches in the costly part of the ground with Chinese inscriptions."[4]   Interment in "holy ground" would not have been permitted except to Catholics.

Cases of marriage between Chinese coolies and Peruvian women have already been noted; they continued to take place.   On this matter Gibbs wrote:

They [the coolies] intermarry with the lower class of whites, mestizas, and cholas, and by these are looked upon as quite a catch for they make good husbands, industrious, domestic, and fond of their children.   While the cholo (Indian) husband is lazy, indolent, often a drunkard and brutal to his wife.

I often meet children in the streets whose almond shaped eyes show their Chinese origin.[5]

In these mixed marriages, usually, if not always, the groom in question had accepted Christianity before the ceremony—unless, of course, it was a common-law marriage.   The mixed-blood offspring would almost certainly grow up as Christians.

The Chinese colony in Lima had grown to such an extent by 1878 that a number of Chinese theaters were operating there.   They had permission to function all night, though a fugitive newspaper item states that "last night the manager of the Odeón was notified that he

[3] *El Comercio*, March 28, 1876.
[4] To Secretary of State, Lima, Nov. 13, 1874, No. 107, Diplomatic Despatches, Peru 28.
[5] *Ibid.*

must close at midnight."[6] Gibbs declared that "the second theater of the city," which a Chinese company had leased for four years, was filled nightly.[7]

An evidence of awareness of and participation in Peruvian life by the Chinese is found in the statement that "the sons of the Celestial Empire" took part in the ceremonies of the national independence day, July 28. They also sent a committee to felicitate the president of the republic on the second of August, anniversary of his assumption of office, as well as on his birthday on the following ninth of August.[8]

It was in commerce that the Chinese showed greatest ability. The Englishman Duffield has been cited respecting the high-class Chinese merchants of Lima. Many of these had not been coolie laborers. However, others had been such and eventually attained mercantile success. A newspaper statement concerning the merchants Wing on Ching & Company declares that "they have made themselves truly notable, as much for the abundance, richness, and variety of their stock as for the cheapness of their sales and the fine treatment which they accord their patrons."[9]

Chinese continued to be food purveyors in grocery shops and restaurants. At first their services were chiefly for their fellows, but with time their restaurants began to make an appeal also to the general public of Lima. Capón Street (*Calle Capón*) became the center of the Chinese section, as it continues to be today. Of that section Gibbs stated:

> Streets fronting on the large markets or those leading to them are filled by Chinese grocers, tailors, shoemakers, bakers, butchers, and other tradesmen so much so that walking around

[6] *El Comercio*, Jan. 21, 1878.   [7] *Loc. cit.*
[8] *La Patria*, Aug. 11, 1874.   [9] *El Comercio*, Aug. 27, 1877.

seeing the people, their shops and signs you could easily imagine that you were in a Chinese town.[10]

Calle Capón, as fascinating today as it must have been in the 1870's, constitutes but two blocks of Jirón Ucayali, the 600 and the 700 blocks. The first runs alongside the Municipal Market, built about the time Gibbs wrote, which is soon to be torn down and replaced with a better. The second Chinese block continues beyond the market to the eastward. It is today lined on either side by Chinese restaurants, which the Limeños call "chifas." Most of them display on their modern neon signs the descriptive "Gran"—Kuong Tun, Men-Gut, San Joy Lao, Kam-Lem, Chung-Kuo, Tonfo, Ton Qui Sen. And they do indeed provide grand food for one who has a preference for this type of gustatory enjoyment. Judged by contemporary statements of the earlier time, these two blocks probably presented much of their present-day aspect, though without neon lights and with less of sumptuousness. Today, as when Gibbs walked there, the observant stroller may note a great variety of human types, representing mixtures of yellow, red, white, and black.

At least a part of the Peruvian public appreciated the good qualities of the Chinese. An editorial writer, under the heading "The Morality of the Chinese," made these assertions:

To their mercantile skill, to their tireless industry, to their astuteness (*cálculo*) and to their profound knowledge of our people, is owed the fact that they [the Chinese] have prevailed over them, becoming their purveyors and routing in many industries the native Peruvians who have not known how to compete with them. These poor disinherited ones of eight years, have made themselves men who possess their own capital, who have

[10] *Loc. cit.*

their own establishments, and who represent perhaps millions in public wealth.[11]

Gibbs declared roundly of the Chinese merchant, "He sells cheaper and gives a better article for less money than shopkeepers of other nationalities."[12]   A Peruvian writer of recent date declares that they contributed "in an effective manner to change many old industrial habits and to cheapen prices of a great number of consumer articles."[13]

The contemporary and neutral witness, Gibbs, made one further significant statement concerning the Chinese: ". . . in all, they seem to assimilate themselves to the habits and customs of the country."[14]   The facts presented above go far toward sustaining this assertion.

"East is East and West is West," but the twain *had* met in Peru.   In general the meeting cannot quite be said to have been mutually profitable.   Undoubtedly, the Chinese added much to Peruvian wealth, but comparatively few Chinese became wealthy in the process. Through no fault of their own, they added to Peru's problems.   However, as far as the Chinese are concerned, those problems gave some evidence of disappearing by 1879.   Peru's international standing had been much improved by the abolition of the coolie immigration, even though the step was taken after others had made the immigration impossible.   Comparatively a *very* few Chinese had returned to China.   The remainder yet alive were quietly and efficiently adjusting themselves to Peruvian society, either as free workers in agriculture and industry or in some other occupation.   The time could be foreseen when that adjustment would be completed,

[11] *El Comercio*, Jan. 18, 1877.   [12] *Loc. cit.*
[13] Ulloa Sotomayor, *La organización social y legal del trabajo en el Perú*, p. 45.
[14] *Loc. cit.*

through adaptation and assimilation, and when, even socially, the former Chinese coolie would no longer be a problem.

It is traditional among Peruvian writers who touch on the subject to speak of the coolie immigration as a "national calamity." The theme of immigration has engaged the attention of many Peruvian writers and has frequently been used as a subject of doctoral theses at the Greater University of San Marcos.[15] Authors of such works treat in some fashion the Chinese phase of that immigration and almost always in the terms mentioned above. A single quotation will suffice for illustration:

> . . . as a real and beneficial condition one may cite his [the coolie's] habits of economy and order and his constant desire to hunt productive work and to build up a small capital which will make him independent; but on the other hand he introduced in the centers where he operates, the practice of highly objectionable vices, such as gambling, sensualism, filthiness, the use of opium.[16]

Actually, it does not appear that this thesis of "national calamity" can logically be sustained. The present writer agrees with the Peruvians that a European immigration would have been better for Peru. But it has been shown that under the conditions existing in that country in the quarter century 1850-1875, such immigration in any appreciable numbers was impossible. Except for some thousands of Chilean *rotos* whom Meiggs introduced for

[15] E.g., J. F. Pazos Varela, *La inmigración en el Perú* (Lima, 1891); Luis N. Brayce y Cotes, *Resumen Histórico acerca del Desarrollo de la Inmigración en el Perú* (Lima, 1899); Carlos Larrabure y Correa, *Colonización de la Costa Peruana por medio de la Inmigración Europea* (Lima, 1900); Juan Angulo Puente Arnao, *Inmigración y Medios de Adquirirla* (Lima, 1907); Mario A. del Río, *La Inmigración y su desarrollo en el Perú* (Lima, 1929). All the foregoing are theses, ranging in length from 27 pages to 315 pages. See also Hildebrando Fuentes, *La Inmigración en el Perú; Proyectos de ley y colecciones de artículos publicados en "El Comercio" de Lima* (Lima, 1892).

[61] Ulloa Sotomayor, *op. cit.*, p. 23.

work on his railways, no source of immigration but China
was available in those years. Without the humble coolie,
agriculture would have languished, the guano beds would
not have yielded their wealth, and railroad building and
industry would have been gravely hampered. Despite his
lack of robustness and the vices which he brought, or was
said to have brought, with him, the coolie with his labor
performed a great service for the country.

As to those alleged vices, some further observations
should be made. It is true that the Chinese introduced
opium-smoking. However, it is not evident that the
Peruvians themselves adopted this vice to any considerable
degree. Moreover, it would be very difficult to sustain
the view that the opium used by the Chinese was as great
an evil to the country as was the inveterate and age-old
devotion of the Peruvian Indian to the chewing of the
harmful coca leaf. As to social vices, to accuse the Chinese
of inventing or introducing them would be ridiculous.
Social vices certainly were not unknown in Peru before the
arrival of the coolies. Sexual perversions, it is quite probable, existed among the Chinese to a greater degree than
among the native Peruvian males. But this was a natural
consequence of an exclusively male immigration, together
with the social ostracism and physical restraint to which
the Chinese were subjected. It is hard to believe that
this vice increased among native Peruvians because of its
practice among the sex-starved Chinese. It would logically
decrease as the coolies became free men and formed unions
with Peruvian women.

The Chinese was charged with being lazy and unclean
in his person. As a semi-slave when under contract, he
was probably inclined to shirk his work when possible;
this is commonly the history of the human being under
servitude. As to his uncleanliness, how could he be clean

in his person in the circumstances in which he was compelled to live? The majority of objective observers of the
coolie agreed that when free he was industrious and that
when conditions made it possible, he was perhaps more
cleanly than the native Peruvian worker. It seems, .in-
deed, probable that in the long run the Chinese laborer
exerted a beneficial influence on the Peruvian worker.
He was frequently a capable individual whom his competitor might well emulate.

It can even be argued that in the ultimate analysis
Peru benefited culturally from the coming of the Chinese.
Luis Alberto Sánchez states that as the coolie was poor
and mixed only with the poor mestizo class of Peru, his
influence on general culture was not felt for a considerable
time. But this brilliant Peruvian adds, "With the passage
of time, nevertheless, this 'inert one' began to acquire
social and cultural prestige. Today he has it, undoubtedly,
in our universities and in professional life." Sánchez declares that "the Chinese *mestizo* excels in his application
to study, in his smiling acceptance of things, and in his
propensity to silence, which confuses the native. He
stands out, moreover, because of his fine analytical sense."
Sánchez believes also that the Chinese has exerted an
influence on the language of Peru, even greater than that
of the Italian.[17]

The immigration of some ninety thousand Chinese
coolies to Peru was in most respects a forced immigration.
The conditions surrounding it were pathetic for the Chinese as, in the main, were also the conditions of his life in
Peru. For those engaged in the coolie traffic and those
directly connected with the Chinese laborer in Peru, it
was brutalizing if not criminal. While the movement
may be deplored, the historic conditions that produced it

[17] *Op. cit.*, p. 90.

must be understood. The life of the coolie in China was not an enviable one; it may be that in Peru it was not much worse. He was exploited, and he was miserable in both places. It is permitted to the Peruvians to regret, even to deplore, this phase of their history, and, to their credit, most of them do. But, in the light of the years that have passed since the signing of the Treaty of Tientsin, it may be said that introduction of the Chinese was not a calamity for the country. Rather, it should be pointed out that Peru profited from their labor and that, in time, a fraction of the Chinese themselves attained to a much better status than they had formerly enjoyed.

With the passing of time the humble Chinese generally has come to be regarded as a human being deserving of treatment as such. The marching years have even brought to Peru the "new" Chinese immigration that was so ardently desired in the decade of 1870. Its conditions and the status of the thousands of free Chinese involved in it are different from those in the earlier decade. This, however, is not a part of the present story. The coolie immigration ended in 1874, and the descendants of those early Oriental immigrants are now almost indistinguishable from the mass of Peruvian citizens—be they white, black, red, yellow, or mixed.

BIBLIOGRAPHY

Source Materials—Manuscript

Peru

Meiggs Papers—
Letter Books 1, 8, one unnumbered.
Ministerio de Relaciones Exteriores—
Años 1865-1880, Tomo 94-A.
Años 1870-1876, Tomo 126-A. Contains "Legación en China y Japón," with the correspondence of Aurelio García y García with the Foreign Minister, José de la Riva Agüero.
Año 1873; Legación en China y Japón; Anexos.
Año 1874; Legación en China y Japón.
Año 1874; Servicio Diplomático del Perú; 5-32 Legación en Portugal; 5-33 Legación en Rusia—*Reservado*; 5-11 and 5-18 Legación en China y Japón.
Año 1874; Legación en Rusia y Alemania.
Año 1875; Legación en Rusia y Alemania.

United States

State Department National Archives—
Consular Despatches, Callao 4, 6.
Diplomatic Despatches
China 32, 34-37, 39-41.
Japan 34.
Peru 21, 23, 28.
Legation Archives—
China XXXIII (Williams, 1865-1866); XLVII (Browne, 1868); (Low, 1871, II); No. 266 (Seward, 1-60, 1876).
Miscellany LXXVII (1873-1875).
Notes, Peru 6.

SOURCE MATERIALS—PRINTED

China

The Cuba Commission. *Chinese Emigration; Report of the Commission Sent by China to Ascertain the Condition of Chinese Coolies in Cuba.* Pp. 236 (English version, pp. 1-91; French version, pp. 94-198). Shanghai, 1874. Of great value to this study.

China. *Tratado y Convención entre el Perú y la China; firmados en Tientsin, 26 de Junio, 1874, por Aurelio García y García y Li Hung Chang; canjeados en Tientsin, 7 de Agosto, 1875, por Juan Federico Elmore, LL.D., y Ling Jih Chang, etc.* Pp. 16. Shanghai, 1875. Contains also text of Special Agreement between Peru and China and Certificates of Exchange; official Spanish and English texts, but not the Chinese.

Peru

ARANDA, RICARDO, ed. *Colección de los Tratados, Convenciones, Capitulaciones, Armisticios, y otros actos diplomáticos y políticos celebrados desde la Independencia hasta el día, precedida de una Introducción que comprende la época colonial.* 10 vols. Lima, 1907.

Diario de los Debates; Congreso Ordinario de 1870; Cámara de Diputados, Congreso Ordinario de 1876; Congreso Ordinario de 1878.

Documentos Parlamentarios: 1870, "Memoria del Ministro de Relaciones Exteriores al Congreso Ordinario de 1870," III; 1872, "Documentos—Memoria del Ministro de Relaciones Exteriores al Congreso Ordinario de 1872," I; 1874, "Anexo A, Inmigración Europea y Asiática—Memoria del Ministro de Gobierno, Policía y Obras Públicas al Congreso Ordinario de 1874," II; 1874, "Documentos—Memoria del Ministro de Relaciones Exteriores al Congreso Ordinario de 1874," I; *Colección de los Tratados del Perú.*

Exposición presentada al Emperador de Rusia, Arbitrio en el caso de la "María Luz," por el Plenipotenciario del Perú. Publicación oficial. Pp. 22. Lima, 1875. This document is also to be found in *El Peruano; Boletín Oficial,* July 27, 1875, p. 33.

LAVALLE, J. A. DE. *Exposición presentada al Emperador de Rusia, Arbitrio en el caso de la "María Luz," por el Plenipotenciario del Perú.* Pp. 22. Lima, 1875. Same as item above.

Memoria que presenta el Ministro de Estado en el despacho de Gobierno, Policía y Obras Públicas al Congreso de 1870. Lima, 1870.

Memoria del Ministro de Hacienda y Comercio al Congreso de 1864, 1868.

Mensaje y Memorias, 1874: "La China y el Japón" occupies pp. 55-254; the "Memoria" of Pedro Gálvez to Count Granville in 1873 is on pp. 175-193; the "Informe" of Guillermo García y García is on pp. 194-201.

El Peruano; Periódico Oficial, later called *El Peruano; Boletín Oficial.*

Resumen del Censo General de Habitantes del Perú hecho en 1876. Lima, 1878.

United States

MALLOY, WILLIAM M., ed. *Treaties, Conventions, International Acts, Protocols and Agreements between the United States and Other Powers, 1776-1909.* 2 vols. Washington, 1910.

Papers Relating to the Foreign Relations of the United States, Transmitted to Congress, with the Annual Message of the President, December, 1873. Washington, 1873.

Papers Relating to the Foreign Relations of the United States, Transmitted to Congress, with the Annual Message of the President, December, 1874. Washington, 1874.

United States Foreign Relations, 1871, 1873, 1874.

United States Statutes-at-Large, 1859-1863. Boston, 1863.

SOURCE MATERIALS—NEWSPAPERS AND PERIODICALS

El Americano, Paris. Quarterly review, Spanish; founded 1872 and edited by Hector Varela.

La Bolsa, Lima.

Callao and Lima Gazette, 1871-1872; English and Spanish.
El Comercio, Lima, 1839———; Peru's oldest and leading daily.
El Nacional, Lima, 1865-1903.
La Patria, Lima, 1871-1883; originally part in Italian.
El Porvenir, Lima.
South Pacific Times, Lima, 1873-1879; successor to *Callao and Lima Gazette*.
El Trabajo, Lima.

SECONDARY MATERIALS—BOOKS AND PAMPHLETS

ARONA, JUAN DE (JUAN PEDRO PAZ SOLDÁN Y UNÁNUE). *La inmigración en el Perú.* Pp. xxi, 160. Lima, 1891.

BAILEY LEMBECKE, JORGE. "La primera misión diplomática del Perú al Japón," *El Comercio*, October 26, 1941.

BASADRE, JORGE. *Historia de la República del Perú.* 2d ed. revised and augmented. Lima, 1940.

BORJA, CÉSAR. *La inmigración china.* Lima, 1877.

BRAYCE Y COTES, LUIS N. *Resumen Histórico acerca del Desarrollo de la Inmigración en el Perú.* Pp. 27. Lima, 1899. Thesis, Greater University of San Marcos.

BRINE, LINDESAY. *The Taiping Rebellion in China.* Pp. 294. London, 1862.

CAHILL, HOLGER. *A Yankee Adventurer: The Story of Ward and the Taiping Rebellion.* Pp. 296. New York, 1930.

CISNEROS, CARLOS B. *Reseña económica del Perú.* Pp. 284. Lima, 1906.

COLE, FITZ-ROY. *The Peruvians at Home.* London, 1877 (?).

COSTA Y LAURENT, FEDERICO. *Reseña histórica de los Ferrocarriles del Perú.* Pp. 279. Lima, 1908.

DÁVALOS Y LISSÓN, PEDRO. *La Primera Centuria; causas geográficas, políticas y económicas que han detenido el progreso moral y material del Perú en el primer siglo de su vida independiente.* 4 vols. Lima, 1919-1926.

DUFFIELD, A. J. *Peru in the Guano Age; being a Short Account of a Recent Visit to the Guano Deposits with some Reflections on the Money they have Produced and the Uses to which it has been applied.* Pp. 120. London, 1877. Severe strictures on the Peruvian government and public men; sympathy for the Peruvian people and the Chinese.

ELÍAS, DOMINGO, Y JUAN RODRÍGUEZ. *Inmigración de Chinos, ventajas que proporcionan al país.* (Una representación de la Empresa a la H. Cámara de Senadores: "Colonos chinos.") Pp. 50. Lima, 1851. Chiefly a collection of letters written by masters who were employing Chinese coolies.

Enciclopedia Universal Ilustrada, XIX.

FOSTER, JOHN W. *American Diplomacy in the Orient.* Pp. 498. Boston and New York, 1903.

FUENTES, HILDEBRANDO. *La inmigración en el Perú; Proyectos de ley y colecciones de artículos publicados en "El Comercio" de Lima.* Pp. 70. Lima, 1892, Admission of Chinese opposed; critical of their qualities.

GÁLVEZ, PEDRO. *Proyecto de Inmigración al Perú.* Pp. 88. Lima, 1871. Proposes subsidy by government for bringing Europeans.

HUTCHINSON, THOMAS J. *Two years in Peru with Explorations of Its Antiquities.* 2 vols. London, 1873.

Inmigración Asiática. Pp. 19. Lima, c. 1871.

LARRABURE Y CORREA, CARLOS. *Colonización de la Costa Peruana por medio de la Inmigración Europea.* Pp. 94. Lima, 1900. Thesis, Greater University of San Marcos. Indicates relation of latifundia to the immigration problem.

LINDLEY, AUGUSTUS. *Ti-Ping Tien-Kwoh: The History of the Ti-Ping Revolution.* Pp. 424. London, 1866.

MACNAIR, HARLEY FARNSWORTH. *The Chinese Abroad: Their Position and Protection; a Study in International Law and Relations.* Pp. 340. Shanghai, 1924.

———. *Modern Chinese History: Selected Readings.* Pp. 910. Shanghai, 1923.

MIDDENDORF, E. W. *Peru: Beobachten und Studien über das Land und Seiner Bewohner während eines 25 Jährigen Aufenthalts.* I Band Lima. (Mit 21 Textbilderen und 32 Tafeln.) Pp. 638. Berlin, 1893.

MORSE, HOSEA BALLOU. *The International Relations of the Chinese Empire.* 3 vols. London and New York, 1910, 1918.

PARDO, MANUEL. *Estudios sobre la Provincia de Jauja.* Pp. 65. Lima, 1862.

PAZOS VARELA, J. F. *La inmigración en el Perú.* Pp. 46. Lima, 1891. Thesis, Greater University of San Marcos. Explains failure of European immigration.

PUENTE ARNAO, JUAN ANGULO. *Inmigración y Medios de Adquirirla.* Pp. 49. Lima, 1907. Thesis, Greater University of San Marcos.

Railroads of Peru, The. Pp. 71. Lima, 1873.

RÍO, MARIO E. DEL. *La inmigración y su desarrollo en el Perú.* Pp. 315. Lima, 1929. Thesis, Greater University of San Marcos.

SÁNCHEZ, LUIS ALBERTO. *La Literatura Peruana; derrotero para una historia espiritual del Perú.* Pp. xvii, 253. Lima, 1946.

SQUIER, EPHRAIM GEORGE. *Incidents of Travel and Exploration in the Land of the Incas.* Pp. 599. New York, 1877.

STEWART, WATT. *Henry Meiggs: Yankee Pizarro.* Pp. 370. Durham, N. C., 1946.

UGARTE, CÉSAR ANTONIO. *Bosquejo de la Historia Económica del Perú.* Pp. 214. Lima, 1946.

ULLOA SOTOMAYOR, ALBERTO. *La organización social y legal del trabajo en el Perú.* Pp. 242. Lima, 1916.

WILLIAMS, FREDERICK WELLS. *The Life and Letters of Samuel Wells Williams, LL.D., Missionary, Diplomatist, Sinologue.* Pp. 490. New York, 1899.

WILLIAMS, S. WELLS. *Chinese Immigration.* Pp. 48. New York, 1879.

———. *The Middle Kingdom: A Survey of the Geography, Government, Education, Social Life, Arts, Religion, etc., of the Chinese Empire and Its Inhabitants.* 2 vols. New York and London, 1848.

XAMMAR, LUIS FABIO. *Juan de Arona, Romántico del Perú.* Pp. 24. Lima, 1943.

ZEGARRA, FÉLIX CIPRIANO C. *La condición jurídica de los estranjeros en el Perú.* Pp. 715. Santiago de Chile, 1872. Very critical of treatment of Chinese; of much value to this study.

INDEX